THE EXAMINER

and Other Pieces Written in 1710-11

JONATHAN SWIFT

Jonathan Swift
from the portrait by Charles Jervas in the National Portrait Gallery

Frontispiece to Vol. III

JONATHAN SWIFT

The EXAMINER

and Other Pieces Written in

1710 - 11

Edited by Herbert Davis

Oxford: Basil Blackwell: 1957

Printed in Great Britain
at the Shakespeare Head Press
Saint Aldates, Oxford.

Reprinted by photolithography 1957 by
The Compton Printing Works (London) Ltd.
and bound by
The Kemp Hall Bindery, Oxford.

The CONTENTS

ILLUSTRATIONS

FACSIMILES *of* TITLE PAGES, *&c.*

The INTRODUCTION

THE works contained in this volume were written during the first year of Swift's political activity in the service of the new ministry, which followed the Queen's dismissal of Godolphin in August, 1710, and the success of the Tories in the subsequent elections. The change had been brought about partly as a result of the natural antagonism between the Queen and the Whig ministers she had never liked, and her estrangement from the Duke and the Duchess of Marlborough, and partly as a result of the popular feeling which had been aroused against the Dissenters by the Sacheverell trial. But in spite of the overwhelming Tory majority in the House of Commons, the Ministry for the next two years was a coalition composed of the more moderate elements of both sides, supported by the Church of England party, in accord with the wish of the Queen for a 'moderate or comprehensive scheme' and with Harley's own instinct for a national government. Already in 1708 St John had suggested this scheme to Harley: 'there is no hope I am fully convinced but in the Church of England party, nor in that on the foot it now stands, and without more confidence than is yet re-established between them and us.' And again: 'The fiery trial of affliction has made the gentlemen of the Church of England more prepared to form such a party than from their former conduct it might have been expected.'[1]

Before the end of 1710 Swift was on terms of intimate and cordial friendship with Harley, and had devoted himself with enthusiasm to the support of the new government. His own account of what had happened was written later in his *Memoirs relating to that Change in the Queen's Ministry in 1710*.

A much fuller and more exciting day to day record is to be found in the *Journal to Stella*, and in his letters to Archbishop King during these months. He had at first been concerned at the

---

[1] St John to Harley, Oct. 11 and Nov. 6, 1708 (*H.M.C. Bath*, i, 191, 194), quoted by Keith Feiling, *History of the Tory Party, 1640–1714*, Clarendon Press, 1924, p. 415.

disappearance of the Whigs from office: 'I never remember such bold steps taken by a Court: I am almost shocked at it, though I did not care if they were all hanged.'[1] And he looked forward to a winter of party struggles, of which he would be an indifferent spectator. But that mood did not last long. He occupied himself in sending a long paper[2] to the *Tatler*, concerned with current fashions in writing which he disapproved of, and in writing a lampoon on Godolphin, entitled *The Virtues of Sid Hamet the Magician's Rod.*[3] On September 30 he reported that he was to be introduced to Harley, in connection with the business of the First-Fruits for the Church of Ireland, and by that time he was clearly aware of the possibility of the new situation. 'Tis good to see what a lamentable confession the Whigs all make me of my ill usage; but I mind them not. I am already represented to Harley as a discontented person, that was used ill for not being Whig enough; and I hope for good usage from him. The Tories dryly tell me, I may make my fortune, if I please; but I do not understand them, or rather, I do understand them.'

A fortnight later he was confident that the business of the First-Fruits would certainly be done; and he was on good terms with his new friends whom he had delighted by his verses on Godolphin: 'Lord Peterborough would let nobody read them but himself; so he did; and Mr Harley bobbed me at every line to take notice of the beauties.'[4] Before the end of October he had been set to work at an arduous and important work, to carry on the weekly *Examiner*, which had been started by St John at the beginning of the previous August.

Swift's own account of this arrangement was given in the *Memoirs* as follows:

> When the affair of the First-Fruits was fully dispatched, I returned my humble thanks to Mr Harley, in the name of the clergy of Ireland, and of my own; and offered to take my leave, as intending immediately to return to that Kingdom. Mr Har-

[1] *Journal to Stella*, Sept. 20, 1710.
[2] No. 230. See Vol. II of this edition, p. 173.
[3] *Poems*, ed. H. Williams (Clarendon Press) 1937. Pp. 131–5.
[4] *Journal to Stella*, Oct. 15, 1710.

ley told me he and his Friends knew very well what useful Things I had written against the Principles of the late discarded Faction; and that my personal Esteem for several among them would not make me a favourer of their Cause: That there was now an entirely new Scene, that the Queen was resolved to employ None but those who were Friends to the Constitution of Church and State: that their great Difficulty lay in the Want of some good Pen, to keep up the Spirit raised in the People, to assert the Principles, and justify the Proceedings of the new Ministers. . . .

Upon the Rise of this Ministry, the principal Persons in Power thought it necessary that some weekly Paper should be published, with just Reflections upon former Proceedings, and defending the present Measures of Her Majesty. This was begun about the Time of Godolphin's Removal, under the Name of the *Examiner*. About a dozen of these Papers, written with much Spirit and Sharpness, some by Mr Secretary St John, since Lord Bolingbroke; others by Dr Atterbury, since Bishop of Rochester; and others again by Mr Prior, Dr Freind, &c.; were published with great Applause; but, these Gentlemen, grown weary of the Work, or otherways employed, the determination was, that I should continue it; which I did accordingly for about eight Months. But, my style being soon discovered, and having contracted a great Number of Enemies, I let it fall into other Hands, who held it up in some manner till Her Majesty's Death.

The purpose of the *Examiner* had been stated in *A Letter to the Examiner*,[1] written by St John in August, and afterwards printed as an Introduction to the collected volume of *Examiners*, 1712. In its criticism of the Junto and in its attitude towards the war, it provided an outline of the policy which it was Swift's business to reiterate and develop. It was answered by *A Letter to Isaac Bickerstaff*,[2] where it is pointed out that the writer appears by the whole tenor of the book to be 'conversant at Court, and with the

[1] See Appendix A.

[2] *Letter to Isaac Bickerstaff, Esq: Occasion'd by the Letter to the Examiner*. London, 1710, p. 4.

Principles of his Party'; 'so that, in short, it seems to be the Sum and Quintessence of what can be said for them.'

Swift first acknowledges the *Letter to the Examiner* in his *Examiner* for February 15, and then complains of the difficulties he had encountered in trying to carry out his task. 'I have been very careful,' he says, 'in obeying some of your Commands; and am going on as fast as I can with the rest. . . . But, Sir, I labour under a much greater Difficulty upon which I should be glad to hear your Advice. I am worried on the one Side by the *Whigs* for being too *severe*; and by the *Tories* on the other for being too *gentle*.'[1]

In this way he would support his claim that he had remained as he was from the beginning neither Whig nor Tory, but simply a Church-of-England man; though he had deserted his friends Lord Somers and Lord Halifax, and gone over to the side of Harley and St John. It was not hypocrisy or deceit that the very first words of the new *Examiner* had been these:

> It is a Practice I have generally followed, to converse in equal Freedom with the deserving Men of both Parties; and it was never without some Contempt, that I have observed Persons wholly out of Employment, affect to do otherwise.[2]

He continued to emphasize the evils of the two extremes of party:

> The Evils we must fence against are, on the one side, Fanaticism and Infidelity in Religion; and Anarchy, under the Name of a Commonwealth, in Government: On the other Side, Popery, Slavery, and the Pretender from *France*.[3]

He professed as Examiner to occupy an impartial position, which exposed him to the constant attacks of fanatics responsible for papers like the *Review* and the *Observator*, as well as from the Non-juror, Charles Leslie in his even more 'pernicious', if less 'stupid', *Rehearsal*. As for the distinction between Whig and Tory, that seemed to him to have no longer any meaning: 'I would be glad to ask a Question about *two Great Men* of the late Ministry [i.e. Marlborough and Godolphin] how they came to

---

[1] See below, pp. 85, 88.

[2] See below, p. 3.

[3] See below, p. 13.

be *Whigs*? And by what figure of Speech, half a Dozen others, lately put into great Employments, can be called *Tories*?'[1]

This contempt for party was not an affectation, nor was it merely strategy. Swift, like Harley, refused to believe that it was inevitable that the Government should be either Whig or Tory. They still hoped that it might be possible for the ministers of the Crown to rely upon the support of conservative and moderate opinion, without delivering themselves up to a dual party system, which had actually been in existence only since the Revolution. If it is true to say that 'Harley desired neither a government wholly Tory, nor the dismissal of Marlborough, but he wished to destroy the increasing influence of the Whig Lords over the Cabinet, and to continue a moderate ministry, relying as heretofore not on either party but on the favour of the Queen and the support of the nation',[2] it is clear why Swift joined him; for that was exactly Swift's own view in 1710, and remained his conviction so long as he continued to write the *Examiner*.

When he first took up his task, he accepted it as his main function to justify the changes in the ministry that the Queen was making. He pointed out that power was getting too much into the hands of the moneyed men, the new war-profiteers, whose interest it was to continue the war; and that by the change in her ministers the Queen had saved the country from the knavery of these stock-jobbers, who had been responsible for many scandalous abuses in all sorts of public management since the Revolution. His next argument was to stress the revolutionary plans of the former men in power, and to show what would be likely to happen if they came back, particularly in endangering the Church and the Monarchy. He admitted that one or two among the former ministers possessed very valuable qualities; but they had proceeded by a system of politics which the constitution could not suffer; for the moneyed men were obliged to enlarge the circle of their supporters, by taking in 'a whole Herd of Presbyterians, Independants, Atheists, Anabaptists, Deists, Quakers and

[1] See below, p. 15.

[2] G. M. Trevelyan, *England under Queen Anne*, London, 1930–4, ii, 317.

Socinians.' [1]Again and again he returned with the same answer to the question '*Why was the late Ministry changed?*'

> It was become necessary by the Insolence and Avarice of some about the Queen, who, in order to perpetuate their Tyranny, had made a monstrous Alliance with those who profess Principles destructive to our Religion and Government: ... [it] was changed for the same Reason that Religion was reformed; because a thousand Corruptions had crept into the *Discipline* and *Doctrine* of the *State*, by the Pride, the Avarice, the Fraud, and the Ambition of those *who administered to us in Secular Affairs*.[2]

But the full powers of the *Examiner* were shown when he proceeded to more particular enquiries, and laid bare the evidences of corruption in the Army, the Church and the Ministry, as particular incidents occurred to bring them to notice. The new ministers were naturally not popular among Marlborough's friends in the army; and certain incidents took place in December, 1710, which caused the government to take vigorous action. The details are given in the *Journal to Stella* for December 13:

> Meredyth, Macartney, and Colonel Honeywood are obliged to sell their commands at half value, and leave the army, for drinking destruction to the present ministry, and dressing up a hat on a stick, and calling it Harley; then drinking a glass with one hand, and discharging a pistol with the other at the maukin, wishing it were Harley himself; and a hundred other such pretty tricks, as enflaming their soldiers and foreign ministers against the late changes at Court. Cadogan has had a little paring; his mother told me yesterday he had lost the place of envoy....

The *Examiner* for the following week, December 21, made use of this incident to discuss the place of the army in the state, and the danger of allowing the officers of the army any political influence while on active service, or of putting too much power into the hands of army leaders by granting commissions for life. 'A General and his Army are *Servants*, *hired* by the Civil Power to act as they are directed from thence.' They must not 'concern

[1] See below, p. 92.

[2] See below, p. 95.

themselves in Matters of the Cabinet, which are always either far above, or much beside their Capacities . . . especially in what relates to the *Choice of Ministers*, who are never so likely to be ill chosen as when approved by them.'[1]

In the Church, the opposition came only from the Whig bishops, whom Swift took occasion to attack over the differences between the upper and lower Houses of Convocation, and the unwillingness of the Bishops to take proper notice of the Queen's address—'an unhappy Circumstance when the Majority of the Bishops draws one way, and that of the Lower Clergy another.' Unfortunately, this opposition was not easy to deal with, as Swift pleasantly admits in this neat sentence. 'Time and *Mortality* can only remedy these Inconveniences in the Church, which are not to be cured, like those in the State, by a *Change of Ministry*.'[2] This paper was followed by an ironical account of all that the late ministry had done for the Church, and in particular their attempts to remove the Test Act.

But the weight of the Examiner's attack was reserved for the political leaders; it was necessary to discredit the late ministry and to convict them of the many great abuses which had been visibly committed, but which owing to the defectiveness of the laws and the weakness of the Prerogative could not be legally punished. It was his business to supply such defects as these by the use of satire:

> whereby those whom neither Religion, nor natural Virtue, nor fear of Punishment were able to keep within the Bounds

---

[1] See below, p. 43.

[2] See below, pp. 50, 51. To this *Examiner*, Dec. 25, 1710, attacking the Upper House of Convocation, Swift's old antagonist, the Rev William Wotton, replied in a pamphlet entitled *The Case of the Present Convocation considered etc.*, in which he explains the full propriety of Convocation's proceedings and defends 'this See of Bishops', as the chief defenders of Christianity against these impious writers and freethinkers still left unpunished by the new government. He compliments the *Examiner* on his style—'he wants not that Life and Spirit which are necessary to make his Papers be read'—but promises to watch him closely whenever he comes to deal with Church matters.

> of their Duty, might be with-held by the Shame of having their Crimes exposed to open View in the strongest Colours, and themselves rendered odious to Mankind. Perhaps all this may be little regarded by such hardened and abandoned Natures as I have to deal with; but, next to taming or binding a savage Animal, the best Service you can do the Neighbourhood, is to give them warning, either to arm themselves, or not come in its Way.[1]

Godolphin had been dealt with already in those scornful verses, *Sid Hamet's Rod*, which had celebrated his downfall; but it was a more serious and more urgent matter to begin to undermine the reputation of the Duke of Marlborough at the height of his power and success, and to rouse feeling against the most successful party manager among the Whigs, lavish of money and promises, the Earl of Wharton, who had just returned to resign his post as Lord Lieutenant of Ireland.

The relations of the new men in power with Marlborough were bound to be difficult. The Duchess had succeeded in completely alienating the Queen, but the public reputation of the General had not suffered. And there is reason to believe that both Harley and St John were anxious not to break with Marlborough; and also that it would not have been wholly impossible for him to have remained on good terms with them.[2] Swift's *Examiner* of November 23, 1710 was not so much an attack on Marlborough, as a reply to the violent 'clamour of Tongues and Pens' for some time past 'against the Baseness, the Inconstancy and Ingratitude of the whole Kingdom to the Duke of *Marlborough*, in return of the most eminent Services that ever were performed by a Subject to his Country.'[3] The comparison between the recognition given to Marlborough and the Triumph granted to a Roman General was intended to show the generosity with which he had been treated, and to convey a discreet warning against the danger of ambition and avarice. The *Medley* for December 4, 1710 replied by putting forward a very different account, in which the

[1] See below, p. 141.
[2] See *Diary of Mary, Countess Cowper*, London, 1864, p. 112.
[3] See *The Medley*, VI and VII.

estimated cash value of towns taken by Marlborough was most satisfactorily balanced against all the benefits that he had received.

Swift gives his own view of Marlborough very honestly in the *Journal* for December 31, 1710

> [St John] told me he had been with the duke of Marlborough, who was lamenting his former wrong steps in joining with the Whigs, and said he was worn out with age, fatigues and misfortunes. I swear it pityed me; and I really think they will not do well in too much mortifying that man, although indeed it is his own fault. He is covetous as Hell, and ambitious as the Prince of it: he would fain have been general for life, and has broken all endeavours for Peace, to keep his greatness and get money. He told the queen, he was neither covetous nor ambitious. She said, if she could have conveniently turned about, she would have laughed, and could hardly forbear it in his face. He fell in with all the abominable measures of the late ministry, because they gratified him for their own designs. Yet he has been a successful general, and I hope he will continue his command.

In February, 1710, Swift attacked Marlborough again, with intent to discredit the man who was covetous as hell, and ambitious as the prince of it; but was careful not to touch the successful general. The *Letter to Crassus* is the perfection of what Swift aimed at in his role of Examiner. The quiet intensity and restraint give his words a quality of aloofness, as if beyond bias and passion. Not the slightest intonation is allowed to disturb this effect of judicial calm. 'I am an *Examiner* only,' he says, 'not a *Reformer*.'[1] And when he reads what he has written, he finds it good. 'Yes,' he remarks in the *Journal* for March 7, 1710–11, 'I do read the *Examiners*, and they are written very finely as you judge. I do not think they are too severe on the duke; they only tax him of avarice, and his avarice has ruined us. You may count upon all things in them to be true.' Some felt that they were not severe enough; Lord Rivers in conversation with Swift had cursed the *Examiner* for speaking civilly of the Duke. On the

[1] See below, p. 82.

other hand the *Medley* retorted with violence that it had been said '*he was to maul the Whigs,*' and it was evident that he had 'a conscience exactly suited to such an undertaking, and a complexion to carry him through with it; for he would stick at nothing.'[1]

Thus again Swift could boast that he had maintained his position between the two extremes of party. But when he comes to deal with the Earl of Wharton, it must be admitted that he moves from examination to invective. The violence of his attack has roused the suspicion that he must have been moved by feelings of strong personal dislike, owing to Wharton's coldness towards him in Ireland. Swift may have been piqued by the fact that Wharton not only did not trust him and was unwilling to make use of him, but also seemed unaware of the danger of making Swift his enemy.[2] But to account for the violence of Swift's disapproval, it is not necessary to look beyond the fact that Wharton represented all that Swift most disliked and feared among the Whig leaders. He was the most dangerous opponent of all that Swift stood for. His zeal in using his immense wealth at elections against the Church party, and the 'success with which it was attended, the choice of sometimes twenty, sometimes thirty Members of Parliament chosen by his Procurement, made him the Butt of the *Tories* Hatred and Scandal.' He claimed to be a Churchman by choice, though by education a Dissenter; nevertheless he always declared himself to be a 'Friend to the Dissenters, not taking them in a religious but a civil Capacity, because they were always Friends to the Constitution; and for this Reason he was against everything which tended to put any Hardship upon them.' He gave the most sincere evidence of this in the case of the *Occasional Bill*. He had been very active in bringing about the union with Scotland. When rewarded by being made Lord Lieutenant of Ireland, his main aim there was 'to reconcile the Church of England and the Dissenting Protestants as the surest means to weaken the Popish interest.'[3]

[1] See *The Medley*, Feb. 12, 1711 (p. 235).

[2] Cf. *Journal to Stella*, Sept. 12, 1710: 'I never expected anything from Lord Wharton, and Lord Wharton knew that I understood it so.'

[3] See *Memoirs of the Life of Thomas late Marquess of Wharton*, London, 1715, pp. 27–35, 37–8, 61.

He was therefore suspected of wishing to tamper with the Test Act, as a means of gaining the support of the Dissenters. The new ministry would gladly have left Wharton in Ireland; but after hearing the news of Godolphin's removal in August 1710, he made hurried preparations to return, and told Swift that he did not expect to continue in the government;[1] on his return to England he immediately became active again in the elections in opposition to the new ministers.

One of Swift's first tasks, therefore, as Examiner was to attack Wharton; and in his fourth paper, on November 30, 1710, taking his cue from Addison's speech of Alcibiades in the *Whig Examiner* of September 28, he imitated Cicero's speech against Verres to expose Wharton's government of Ireland.

What elements of truth were in the charges Swift brought against him can be easily recognized by comparing them with the account of his manner of life by an admirer in the *Memoirs of the Life of that most noble Thomas late Marquess of Wharton*, from which extracts have been given above. It is there, for example, clearly stated that he obtained the Lord Lieutenancy as a means of reimbursing himself for the vast expenses he had incurred in his lavish bribery of electors: 'he had expended such immense sums for the good of the Publick . . . that the Government were obliged to advance him to a Post of equal Honour and Advantage.' His way of living is described as agreeable to the humour of the Inhabitants of Ireland. 'The Day was for Council, the Night for Balls, Gaming Tables, and other Diversions, wherein his Lordship did not so much study Profusion as *Elegance*: and as he was a Man of Sense, he never quitted that Character to be thought Generous and Liberal, fine Names for Prodigality.' As to some other charges that Swift brings against him, this biographer also cheerfully admits that although his wife 'was a Woman of Wit and Virtue, yet her Person was not so agreeable to him as was necessary to secure his Constancy.'[2]

Probably about the same time Swift occupied himself with a much fuller examination of the character and activities of Wharton. This first appeared as a libellous pamphlet, which was dis-

---

[1] *Corr.* i, 190.

[2] *Memoirs of Wharton*, p. 18.

tributed by dozens to several gentlemen's lodgings; 'then some bold cur ventured to do it publickly, and sold two thousand in two days.'[1] It was dated August 30, 1710; but this date was probably chosen by Swift simply because Wharton's activities in Ireland came to an end at that time. It was certainly not printed before December 1710. 'The character,' says Swift, 'is here reckoned admirable, but most of the facts are trifles.'[2] This is a formula that he frequently used to distinguish between his own writings and those of his understrappers. In this edition therefore, the *Short Character of Wharton* is included among Swift's authentic work, but the *Relation of several Facts etc.* is printed separately in the Appendix. There can be no doubt that he was responsible for the appearance of the whole; but the detailed information was supplied from Ireland, and there is no evidence that Swift had bothered to rewrite it. To the *Short Character* he had given all his attention; not merely as a piece of party journalism, but as a 'character', the study of a man whose easy insolence and complete unconsciousness of ordinary standards of behaviour must have made him the object of Swift's careful observation. Swift writes as one fascinated by the object before him; he had had the honour of much conversation with his Lordship, while he was in Dublin; he had even returned to England with him, whether in some sort of official attendance or not. He had been on the closest terms of intimacy with Addison, Wharton's secretary in Dublin. He had thus probably had the opportunity of studying his subject very carefully at a number of sittings.[3] He had been able to work at it with thoroughness but without partiality and without passion, which would anyhow be wasted upon a man as indifferent to applause as he is insensible of reproach;[4] a creature of a dangerous species, whose behaviour

[1] *Journal to Stella*, Dec. 8, 1710.

[2] *Journal to Stella*, Jan. 1, 1711.

[3] For instance, on one occasion Swift had discussed with Wharton and Middleton, the Lord Chancellor, such subjects as 'the meaning of that word Liberty with Relation to Ireland.' Cf. *Drapier's Letters*, Clarendon Press, 1925, pp. 124–5.

[4] A year later they met at White's Chocolate house, and Wharton behaved exactly as Swift here prophesies, coming through the

must be thoroughly investigated in the interests of the public safety.

Nevertheless Swift does not attempt to hide the fact that he had been urged to this important work—'it is thought expedient, for some reasons, that the world should be informed of his Excellency's merits as soon as possible.'[1] The *Post-Boy* was also called in to give assistance, with a crude acrostic, printed on December 12; and the following month the *Examiner* attacked again, singling out Wharton as one of the chief enemies of the Church.[2]

Swift's next function was to calm the fears of those who thought that any change of ministry at that time would be bad for credit, and that a ministry depending largely upon the support of the Tories would be sure to lead to the restoration of Popery, arbitrary power and the Pretender. He was committed to a defence of the new leaders against the criticism of the party newspapers.

At the beginning of February, 1710–11, he turns from invective to panegyric.

> Why should not the present Ministry find a Pen to praise them as well as the last? This is what I shall now undertake, and it may be more impartial in me, from whom they have deserved so little. I have, *without being called*, served them half a Year in Quality of *Champion*; and by the help of the Queen, and a Majority of nine in ten of the Kingdom, have been able to protect them against a routed Cabal of hated Politicians, with a dozen of Scribblers at their Head: Yet so far have they been from rewarding me suitable to my Deserts, that to this Day they never so much as sent to the Printer to enquire who I was; . . . Therefore, my Resentments shall so far prevail, that in praising those who are now at the Head of Affairs, I shall at the same Time take Notice of their Defects.[3]

crowd, calling after him, and asking how he did. But Swift adds with some pleasure: 'This was pretty; and I believe he wished every word he spoke was a halter to hang me.' *Journal to Stella*, Dec. 1, 1711.

[1] See below, p. 184.
[2] See below, p. 57.
[3] See below, p. 78.

Even in panegyric, he will preserve still his character of Examiner. Even when he praises, he prefers if possible to use a kind of irony, by borrowing the standards which he assumes his opponents must be willing to accept. Thus he is ready to grant that the new Lord Keeper is wholly ignorant in the speculative as well as practical part of polygamy, and that he is no freethinker, nor has the courage to be the patron of an atheistical book while he is the keeper of the Queen's conscience. The greatest admirers of Mr Harley must also confess that his skill at cards and dice is very low and superficial: in horse-racing he is utterly ignorant, and to save a few millions to the public, he never regards how many worthy citizens he hinders from making their plumb. And Mr St John has still not procured himself a busy, important countenance, nor learned that profound part of wisdom, to be difficult of access.[1]

On March 8, 1710–11, an event occurred which gave Swift a splendid opportunity to exalt the character of Harley, and to turn upon all his detractors with violent denunciation. I quote from the account which appeared in the *Daily Courant*, under the date March 9:

> Yesterday in the Afternoon, the Marquis de Guiscard was seiz'd, and carried before a Committee of Council at White-hall. While he was under Examination, he moved towards the Right Honourable Mr Harley, and with a penknife suddenly stabb'd him in the Breast. In the first surprize at so detestable an Action, a Gentleman drew his Sword and wounded the Marquis; who was afterwards committed to Newgate. 'Tis believed Mr Harley is in no Danger from his Wound.

The *Examiner* for March 15 is taken up with a very detailed account of the scene, in which Harley's quiet courage and magnanimity is effectively contrasted with the savagery of the vicious assailant. 'I think,' says Swift, 'there are few greater Instances of [magnanimity] to be found in Story.... He shewed no Sort of Resentment, or spoke one violent Word against *Guiscard*; but appeared all the while the least concerned of any in the Company. A State of Mind, which in such an Exigency, nothing but

[1] See below, pp. 78–80.

Innocence can give; and is truly worthy of a Christian Philosopher.'[1]

Swift's own private concern may be seen in the perturbed comments which appear in his *Journal* for that week. On March 8, he wrote: 'O dear M D, my heart is almost broken.... I am in mortal pain for him.... I now think of all his kindness to me.... pity me; I want it.' It is sometimes suggested that Swift's anxiety was largely due to the hope of advancement which he had placed entirely upon Harley's influence. But Swift's position cannot be fairly understood at this time without recognizing that his loyalty to Harley arose from a complete acceptance of his policy and methods as well as from a strong personal liking for the man. He may have been flattered by Harley's friendship, but he never admitted that he had been mistaken in valuing him so highly. Fifteen years later, in his *Letter to Lord Chancellor Middleton* he still maintained that Harley was 'the greatest, the wisest, and the most uncorrupt Minister, I ever conversed with.'[2]

Guiscard's attack also gave him a chance to turn upon Harley's political enemies, and to accuse them of being just as guilty as this wretch in their attempts to ruin him, 'both agreeing in the great End of taking away Mr Harley's Life, although differing in their Methods: The first proceeding by Subornation, the other by Violence; wherein *Guiscard* seems to have the Advantage, as aiming no further than his Life; while the others designed to destroy at once both That and his Reputation.'[3]

This attempt to incriminate some of the late ministry in connection with their examination of William Gregg, a clerk in Harley's office, who had been found guilty of selling secrets to the French, started a controversy which Swift kept alive during the rest of the summer and even after he had given up the *Examiner*. On March 22, he replied to the *Medley* and the *Observator*, who had accused him of lies and blunders, and provoked them further by taunting them with a desire to clear Guiscard from a design against Mr Harley's life, though they cannot 'clear their other Friends, who in the business of *Gregg*, were equally guilty

[1] See below, p. 109.
[2] *Drapier's Letters*, p. 127.
[3] See below, p. 108.

of the *same Design* against the *same Person; whose Tongues were very Swords*, and whose *Penknives* were *Axes*.'[1]

Many of Swift's *Examiners* were concerned with such particular occurrences. Even those which seem to deal with more general considerations will also be found to be answers to particular charges against the new government. The *Medley* and the *Observator* reiterated their warnings against the designs of the Tories to bring in Popery, Arbitrary Power, and the Pretender.[2] To meet their attacks, Swift undertook to examine the real principles of the so-called Whigs and Tories. As a moderate man, scornful of party strife, he exposed the Whigs as a dangerous, republican, anti-Christian faction, defended the supporters of the new ministry as upholders of the Constitution and the Church and the Landed Interest, and dismissed the other faction of extremists as Jacobites, Non-jurors and sympathisers with Popery. But he is never content with defence; he always recognized the advantages of aggression. He moves forward with such confidence and vigour that he is sometimes carried beyond a tenable position. He can even attempt to prove, for example, that not the Tories but the Whigs are more likely to bring in the Pretender:

> What could be more consistent with the *Whiggish* Notion of a *Revolution-Principle*, than to bring in the *Pretender*? . . . the Whigs have a natural Faculty of bringing in *Pretenders*, and will therefore probably endeavour to bring in the great One at last: How many *Pretenders* to Wit, Honour, Nobility, Politicks, have they brought in these last twenty Years? In short, they have been sometimes able to procure a Majority of *Pretenders* in Parliament; and wanted nothing to render the Work compleat, except a *Pretender* at their Head.[3]

Or he will even appeal to the Dissenters against the Whigs, with whom he suggests they can have nothing in common except the 'Antimonarchical Principle and a few false Notions about Liberty,' and therefore as they have no hope of getting power they ought to be careful to secure the indulgence of the new govern-

[1] See below, p. 116.

[2] See *Medley* XXV, March 19, and XXVII, April 2, 1711; *Observators* for March, 1711.

[3] See below, p. 147.

ment, and forsake the exhausted Whig cause.[1] So exhausted indeed, that by April 1711 the new government was beginning to be accepted inevitably; in the eyes of this impartial Examiner nothing could be found to justify any further objection against their management.

In his paper for April 26 he raised the question of a Peace without the entire restitution of Spain; such conditions were set up by the former faction 'to pin down the War upon us; consequently to increase their own Power and Wealth, and multiply Difficulties on the Queen and Kingdom, until they had fixed their Party too firmly to be shaken.'[2]

To this the *Observator* immediately replied:

> 'Tis very necessary, according to the Schemes of the Faction, to sink the Trading and Moneyed Interest, so as they mayn't be able to cope with the Landed Interest; therefore I don't wonder at the Examiner's being for leaving *Spain* and the *West Indies* in the hands of the French.[3]

This was followed by a much fuller reply in a pamphlet, entitled *A Few Words upon the Examiner's Scandalous Peace*, in which the attitude of the Queen and the Ministry towards Spain is shown as it appeared in the Addresses of 1701, the Declaration of War in 1702, and the speeches and addresses of Parliament down to November 1709. The tenour of them all was that 'no Peace can be safe or honourable, unless the whole Spanish Monarchy be restor'd. And the Queen is pleased to declare, more than once, that she is of the same Opinion.' And finally the *Examiner* is challenged to explain why the Allies must dwindle in their terms of peace, when all goes so well.[4]

Swift did not reply directly to these arguments, but continued in his latest papers to try and prepare the public for a peace. Even in referring to the Queen's encouragement for building new Churches in London he is mainly concerned to show that all such designs must be checked by the necessities of a long and

[1] See below, p. 129.

[2] See below, p. 140.

[3] *Observator*, April 25–28, 1711.

[4] *A Few Words upon the Examiner's Scandalous Peace*, London, 1711, pp. 17, 21.

ruinous war, though, he adds maliciously, the cost of the whole project at an estimate of six thousand pounds for a church, is somewhat *under* the price of a *Subject's Palace*.

At the end of his campaign, he returned once more to deal with the question with which he had begun—why was the last ministry changed? Not because they were Whigs with a certain set of principles, but because they were a certain set of persons, supported by those who hated the monarchy and the church, 'as Unbelievers and *Dissenters* of all Sizes: Or Men in Office, who had been guilty of much Corruption, and dreaded a Change; which would not only put a Stop to further Abuses for the Future, but might perhaps, introduce Examinations of what was past: Or those who had been too highly obliged, to quit their Supporters with any common Decency. Or, lastly, the *Money-Traders*, who could never hope to make their Markets so well of *Præmiums* and Exorbitant Interest, and high Remittances, by any other Administration.'[1]

He insisted that party divisions had become meaningless, and that the only real difference left between Whigs and Tories was that the one side apprehended greater danger from the Pretender and his party, and the other from the violence and cunning of other Enemies to the constitution; and it was clear that, since the Revolution of 1688, there had been less reason to fear Popery than the other faction.

He further justified the change that had been made by rendering an account of what the new Parliament had done during its first long session to enquire into abuses, to raise a fund for the national debt, establish credit, encourage trade and strengthen by the Qualification Bill and by Acts for the benefit of the church in England and Ireland both the landed and the church interest.

This *Examiner* appeared on June 7, 1711; and in the *Journal* for that date Swift says plainly enough: 'As for the *Examiner*, I have heard a whisper, that after that of this day, which tells what this Parliament has done, you will hardly find them so good. I prophecy they will be trash for the future; and methinks in this day's *Examiner* the author talks doubtfully, as if he would write no

[1] See below, p. 165.

more.' Swift left London the next day, and stayed in the country at Wycombe with Lord Shelburn until June 20. On June 22 he comments again in the *Journal*: 'Yesterday's was a sad *Examiner*, and last week was very indifferent, though some little scraps of the old spirit, as if he had given some hints; but yesterday's is all trash. It is plain the hand is changed.' And again on July 17: 'No, I don't like anything in the *Examiner* after the 45th, except the first part of the 46th; all the rest is trash; and if you like them, especially the 47th, your judgment is spoiled by ill company and want of reading.'

The first part of the *Examiner* for June 14 really continues the last paragraph of the paper of the week before, and completes the attack on the Whig party-writers. It is unlikely that Swift had anything else to do with the last six *Examiners*, that completed the year from June 14 until July 26. A later statement in the *Journal* for November 3 is very definite: 'the first thirteen were written by several hands, some good, some bad; the next three and thirty were all by one hand, that makes forty-six: then that author, whoever he was, laid it down on purpose to confound guessers; and the last six were written by a woman.'

He does not admit that he gave hints to Mrs Manley, or was responsible in any way for providing her with information. It is strange therefore that they were allowed to be included in the fifth volume of the collected works, printed by Faulkner in 1738. Swift was careful however to have a note prefixed to them, which gives a little more information about those who were originally responsible for the *Examiner*. 'It was esteemed to be the Work of several eminent Hands, among which were reckoned my Lord Bolingbroke, Dr Atterbury, Bishop of Rochester, Mr Prior and some others.' His own work is stated here to consist of numbers 13 to 44. Those were the numbers of the *Examiners* for the dates November 2, 1710 until June 7, 1711, according to the reprint in a small volume which was printed for John Morphew and A. Dodd in 1712. The original numbering was 14 to 45; but in the reprint the *Examiner* for October 26, which was the original number 13, was omitted. It was an able exposition of the doctrine of Non-Resistance, almost certainly written by Atterbury. After insisting that he was against the

Pretender, and zealously affected to her Majesty and the most illustrious House of Hanover, the writer undertakes to make it appear that 'the doctrine of *Non-Resistance* is entirely consistent with the *Liberty* of a free People; nay, that it tends to the *Security* of it, much more than the *contrary Principle*; that it is neither a DAMNABLE, nor a SLAVISH Doctrine; that it is *true* in *it self*, and *beneficial* in its *Consequences*; that it is the greatest support of our present happy Establishment; and so far from being likely to *bring in the Pretender*, that it is the best Means in the World to *keep him out*.' A year later when the collected edition was printed it evidently seemed safer quietly to drop this paper, and to change the numbers of the following papers. Faulkner printed from the collected edition, and therefore used the same numbering.

I do not wish to suggest that Swift took much interest in the preparation of this fifth volume; but it may be worth pointing out one or two omissions in the Faulkner text, which must have been deliberately made, and are not likely to have been made by anyone except the author, with whose known sentiments they agree. During the reign of Queen Anne Swift had urged that the Royal Prerogative should be upheld and increased. On January 25, 1711, he had included in his list[1] of the wilder projects to be feared from the Whigs 'a Bill for further limiting the Prerogative;' and on March 22, he had referred to the many laws of late years made to limit the Prerogative, and had added that 'according to the judgment of those who know our constitution best, Things rather seem to lean to the other Extreme, which is equally to be avoided.' These passages against limiting the

[1] See below, pp. 71f. A further deliberate change was made in the list. Among the Tory leaders whom the Whigs would have liked to charge with High Treason the first place had originally been given to Charles, Duke of Shrewsbury, who afterwards changed sides. In Faulkner's text his name is omitted and James, Duke of Ormonde, put in its place. It should be noted also that the name of the Earl of Oxford, i.e. Robert de Vere, the favourite of Richard II, was omitted in the *Examiner* for Feb. 22, to avoid any possible misunderstanding for those readers to whom the name would inevitably be associated with Harley.

prerogative may well have seemed to Swift a dangerous doctrine in the reign of George II. They were both omitted.[1]

Though Swift had handed on the *Examiner* to be completed by Mrs Manley, there was one controversy he had started which continued to produce a whole crop of pamphlets, and drew from him a reply in August, 1711.

One of the worst charges he had brought against the former ministry was that, when Gregg, a clerk in Harley's office, had been condemned for treasonable correspondence with France, 'they would have enticed the condemned criminal with Promise of a Pardon, to write and sign an accusation against Harley.'[2] The *Medley* immediately replied that the House of Lords and not the ministry was concerned, and quoted from the Lords' address a passage reflecting on the efficiency of Harley's office.[3] In April, 1711, there had thereupon appeared a reprint of the *Paper left by William Gregg &c.*, in which he had solemnly declared that Harley had no knowledge of his writing to France. Later, after Harley had been made Earl of Oxford, another pamphlet appeared giving a full account of the *Secret Transactions During the Hundred Days Mr. William Gregg lay in Newgate under Sentence of Death for High Treason from the day of his Sentence to the day of his Execution.* The author, Francis Hoffman, quotes the account given by Mr Lorrain, the ordinary of Newgate, who had had the best opportunity 'to know the very bottom of Gregg's heart', and who was convinced of Harley's innocence and of the endeavours that had been made to corrupt Gregg's conscience by offers of great preferments and advantages. He repeats the accusation of the *Examiner* that 'some Persons stabbed as directly and villainously at Mr. Harley's life then, as Guiscard did since.' The committee had consisted of the Dukes of Devonshire, Somerset and Bolton, the Earl of Wharton, Lord Townsend, Lord Somers and Lord Halifax; and their frequent examination of Gregg, even after he had been tried and condemned, provided some grounds for the suspicion that they hoped to implicate Harley.[4]

[1] See Textual Notes, pp. 273, 279.

[2] See below, p. 108.

[3] *Medley* XXVI, March 26, 1711.

[4] G. M. Trevelyan, *op. cit.*, ii, 332 & 439.

In July, a reply to these charges appeared, entitled *A Letter to the Seven Lords of the Committee appointed to examine Gregg.*[1] This was answered by *More Secret Transactions &c.* in which Hoffman repeats his charges against the Committee, and adds a postscript, dated July 22, giving a further confirmation of the dying speech of Gregg. Finally in August Swift wrote *Some Remarks upon a Letter to the Seven Lords*. He refers to the publication of this paper in the *Journal* on August 24, and states that 'it is by the real author of the *Examiner*, as I believe, for it is very well written.'

It is much more than a paper dealing with the business of Gregg. That is adequately done; but, in addition, Swift takes the opportunity to sum up the work of the *Examiner*, and to repeat his justification of the new ministry. First, as the author of the *Examiner*, he replies with superb arrogance to the taunt that he wished the world to believe that he had been set to work by great people:

> If I durst tell him my Name which he is so desirous to know, he would be convinced that I am of a Temper to think no Man great enough to set me on Work;...what I have published...is nothing more than the common Observations of a private Man deducing Consequences and Effects from very natural and visible Causes.[2]

Then, on behalf of his order, the clergy of the church of England, whom this 'son of obscurity' regards as 'the tools of their cunning managers', Swift speaks with the power and dignity of his priestly office, though he will not go so far as to defend the Whig bishops, who may, he admits, have been made their tools although 'even those few they were able to seduce, would not be their Tools at a lower Rate.' But, he continues:

> because this Author, and Others of his Standard, affect to make use of that Word *Tool*, when they have a mind to be Shrewd and Satyrical; I desire once for all to set them right. A *Tool* and an *Instrument*, in the metaphorical Sense, differ thus: the Former, is an Engine in the Hands of *Knaves*, the latter in those of wise and honest Men. The greatest Ministers are *Instruments* in the Hands of Princes, and so are Princes themselves in the Hands of God; and in this Sense the Clergy are

[1] See Appendix C.

[2] See below, pp. 194-5.

ready to be *Instruments* of any Good to the Prince or People.[1]
Even on behalf of the ministry he writes in the same tone of exultant pride and confidence, when, after referring to the excellent measures already taken and the abuses in good part redressed, he adds

> Besides, there are some Circumstances known by the Names of Honour, Probity, good Sense, great Capacity for Business; as likewise, certain Principles of Religion and Loyalty, the Want or Possession of all which, will make a mighty Difference even in the Pursuit of the same Measures.[2]

These *Remarks* are written in the manner of one who, after a period of hard and constant training, occupied with his weekly examination, has taken his ease for awhile, and now again delights in using his strength.

Shortly afterwards Swift had an opportunity of indulging himself in a 'bite' at the town's expense. Towards the end of August things seemed to him to 'stand very ticklish'; and whispers were heard that the ministry had begun to differ among themselves. Then rumours leaked out that Prior had been in France, presumably concerned with some sort of preliminary negotiations for peace. On August 31, he writes in the *Journal*:

> I am apt to think we shall soon have a Peace, by the little words I hear thrown out by the ministry. I have just thought of a project to bite the town. I have told you, that it is now known that Mr Prior has been lately in France. I will make a printer of my own sit by me one day, and I will dictate to him a formal relation of Prior's journey, with several particulars, all pure invention; and I doubt not but it will take.

A New Journey to Paris was written on September 4; it appeared on September 11, and a thousand were sold the first day. Swift dined with Prior that evening:

> when I came in Prior showed me the pamphlet, seemed to be angry, and said, Here is our English liberty: I read some of it, and said I liked it mightily, and envied the rogue the thought; for had it come into my head, I should have certainly done it myself.[3]

[1] See below, p. 190. [2] See below, pp. 188-9.
[3] *Journal to Stella*, Sept. 11, 1711.

He then explains that it was a formal grave lie, of which he had written all but about the last page, which he dictated to the printer. He discussed its real purpose at greater length in a letter to Archbishop King, written October 1, 1711, to inform him of the steps that were then being taken towards a peace. He had himself been for some time concerned about the difficulty of continuing the war, and the danger of an ill peace; and now to quiet the clamours of those who insisted on no peace without Spain, he had written this fiction 'by way of furnishing fools with something to talk of.'

> Meantime, your Grace may count that a peace is going forward very fast. Mr Prior was actually in France; and there are now two Ministers of that Court in London, which you may be pretty sure of, if you believe what I tell you, that I supped with them myself in the house where I am now writing, Saturday last; . . . Mr Prior was with us too, . . . All matters are agreed between France and us, and very much to the advantage and honour of England; but I believe no farther steps will be taken without giving notice to the allies.[1]

Two days before the *New Journey to Paris* appeared, a sermon had been preached before the Duke of Marlborough by his chaplain Dr Francis Hare, in celebration of the surrender of Bouchain.[2] It contained an urgent warning against the danger of making a premature peace. It was immediately published under the title *The Charge of God to Joshua*, with a modest Preface by the publisher explaining that the copy was obtained from a friend, as the author would by no means hear of printing what was drawn up in such haste. This cant particularly annoyed Swift, who remarks that it seems needless for one who had so often been complimented on his productions, though he had never

[1] *Corr.* i, 290.

[2] The same occasion produced another attack on the *Examiner* in a pamphlet entitled *Bouchain: In a Dialogue Between the Late Medley and Examiner* (London 1711). It provides a long account of the course of the action, and the Examiner is finally brought to admit that he has a great honour and esteem for Marlborough and to apologize for the attack he had made upon him in the *Letter to Crassus*. See p. 35.

wasted on them either art or care. Dr Hare had become well-known as an apologist of the war-party. He had preached 'a sermon before the House of Commons, on February 17, 1708–9, the day of Thanksgiving for the great success of her Majesty's Arms under. . . the Duke of Marlborough,' which had gone into a third enlarged edition in 1709. And in 1710, he had written four *Letters addressed to a Tory-Member on the management of the war*, the first two in November, the third in December, and the fourth in January 1711. In these he had attacked the *Letter to the Examiner*, written by St John, as 'a mere Declamation, a pretty smart Performance, with some fire and imagination, but no reasoning, judgment or experience, plain marks of a young writer, who may in time ripen into something considerable.' The *Examiner* is only dealt with in a postscript to the third Letter, in which Hare refuses to enter the lists with so prostitute a writer, a mercenary writer who has dared to treat the Duke of Marlborough and the victorious troops under his command with such insolence in his weekly libels.

This last attack, *The Charge of God to Joshua*, demanded an answer, particularly as negotiations were actually going on for preliminaries of peace, and a secret agreement was signed on September 27th. The answer was entitled *A Learned Comment upon Dr Hare's Excellent Sermon &c.*:[1] and Swift had some part in it. In the *Journal* on November 3, 1711, he says that it was written by Mrs Manley—'only hints sent to the printer from Presto, to give her.'

There is no reason to doubt Swift's account; the paper is therefore included here in the Appendix as a work prompted and partly written by him. He may well have sent to the printer a copy of the original sermon with his own comments in the margin; and this material would then have been used by Mrs Manley, whose hand may be detected easily enough in many parts of the paper. The passages from Hare's sermon which are quoted and answered were probably those marked by Swift; and it is not difficult to pick out certain phrases which sound as though they had been first written down by him as marginal

[1] See Appendix D.

comments. For instance, all that Swift probably wrote opposite the first passage he comments on, was 'is this sense or truth?' And opposite the words, 'if we be content to wait His Leisure' he may have written the query 'God's or Marlborough's?' Perhaps a sentence like this was suggested by Swift:

> But if he means the present Ministry, it is certain they could find their own Interest in continuing the War as well as other People; their Capacities are no less, nor their Fortunes so great, neither need they be at a loss how to follow in a path so well-beaten.[1]

Swift was not in a mood to bother much with such an antagonist as Dr Hare. He had just brought to a successful conclusion his first year in the service of the Ministry, and had attained a position among them of independence and dignity and power not often reached by a man without either title, office, or even an honourable preferment. He was still needed. He had still one task to do, and there was no one else who could do it. This was to reconcile the nation to a peace which the Ministry had already secretly arranged.

It must have been for him almost a jest, just at this moment in the middle of September, 1711, to receive from Archbishop King a letter of gracious condescension, full of warnings and good advice. He urges Swift first to make use of the favour and interest he at present possesses to obtain some preferment that may be called a settlement; and secondly charges him with his duty to make use of his knowledge of the world and his reading in order to deal with some subject in divinity upon which he could produce something new and surprising 'with such uncommon remarks, as will render it both profitable and agreeable, above most things that pass the press.'[2]

It is difficult to believe that so astute an Archbishop could write such a letter to a man like Swift; but it may be taken as a proof that outside a small circle of his friends, no one really knew what exactly he had written, and what power he now held in his hands. Swift replied from Windsor Castle, on October 1, 1711, in a letter which is a complete revelation of the mind of the

[1] See below, pp. 263-4, 266.

[2] *Corr.* i, 285-6.

Examiner; and for that reason it may be fitting to quote a few sentences from it here. At this moment he could say with justice and with satisfaction:

> I am as well received and known at Court, as perhaps any man ever was of my level; I have formerly been the like. I left it then, and will perhaps leave it now—when they please to let me—without any concern, but what a few months will remove. It is my maxim to leave great Ministers to do as they please; and if I cannot distinguish myself enough by being useful in such a way as becomes a man of conscience and honour, I can do no more; for I never will solicit for myself, although I often do for others.[1]

In this quiet pause before a period of great activity and success he examines his own position in this world of courtiers and great ministers, delighting in a sense of his power, but above all proud of his independence and his freedom. And this is what he claimed to be—one whom no man was great enough to set on work, though voluntarily and in friendship devoted to the service of the Ministry; one who would be no man's tool, though ready to be an instrument of good to the prince or people; no party politician, but a judicial Examiner of the state of public affairs, who valued his dignity and his integrity so highly that he refused to solicit a reward or to demand preferment.

---

[1] *Corr.* i, 291.

THE EXAMINERS FOR THE Year 1711.

To which is prefix'd,

A

Letter to the *Examiner*.

——————Si quis
Opprobriis dignum latraverit, integer ipse,
Solventur risu tabulæ: tu missus abibis.

LONDON:

Printed for *John Morphew*, near *Stationers-Hall*; and *A. Dodd*, at the *Peacock* without *Temple-Bar*. 1712.

111 b

In the Month of August, 1710, *a weekly Paper, called*, The EXAMINER, *began to be published. It was esteemed to be the Work of several eminent Hands, among which were reckoned my Lord* B——KE, *Dr.* ATTERBURY, B. *of* R. *Mr.* PRIOR, *and some Others. However it came about, the general Opinion is, That those Persons proceeded no further than to the first twelve Papers; after which, it seems to be agreed, that the Undertaking was carried on by the supposed Author of the four preceding Volumes, who began with Number* 13, *and ended at Number* 44. *For, although the Paper continued many Months after to be published, under the Title of*, The EXAMINER; *yet by the Inequality of the Performance, it was manifest to all judicious Persons, that the aforesaid supposed Author had not the least Share in them. Several of the supposed Author's Friends, who were assistant in correcting the foregoing Volumes, have done us the like Favour in revising these two Volumes.*

THE EXAMINER.

No. 13. *Thursday, November* 2, 1710.

. . . Longa est Injuria, longæ
Ambages, sed summa sequar fastigia rerum.

IT is a Practice I have generally followed, to converse in equal Freedom with the deserving Men of both Parties; and it was never without some Contempt, that I have observed Persons wholly out of Employment, affect to do otherwise: I doubted whether any Man could owe so much to the side he was of, altho' he were retained by it; but without some great point of Interest, either in Possession or Prospect, I thought it was the Mark of a low and narrow Spirit.

It is hard, that for some Weeks past, I have been forced, in my own Defence, to follow a Proceeding that I have so much condemned in others. But several of my Acquaintance, among the declining Party, are grown so insufferably Peevish and Splenatick, profess such violent Apprehensions for the Publick, and represent the State of Things in such formidable Ideas, that I find myself disposed to share in their Afflictions, although I know them to be groundless and imaginary; or, which is worse, purely affected. To offer them Comfort one by one, would be not only an endless, but a disobliging Task. Some of them, I am convinced, would be less melancholy, if there were more Occasion. I shall therefore, instead of hearkning to further Complaints, employ some Part of this Paper for the future, in letting such Men see, that their natural or acquired Fears are ill-grounded, and their artificial ones as ill-intended. That all our present Inconveniences are the Consequence of the very Counsels they so much admire, which would still have encreased, if those had continued: And that neither our Constitution in

Church or State, could probably have been long preserved, without such Methods as have been already taken.

THE late Revolutions at Court, have given room to some specious Objections, which I have heard repeated by well-meaning Men, just as they had taken them up on the Credit of others, who have worse Designs. They wonder the QUEEN would chuse to change her Ministry at this Juncture, and thereby give Uneasiness to a General who hath been so long successful Abroad; and might think himself injured, if the entire Ministry were not of his own Nomination. That there were few Complaints of any Consequence against the late Men in Power, and none at all in Parliament; which on the contrary, passed Votes in favour of the Chief Minister. That if her Majesty had a mind to introduce the other Party, it would have been more seasonable after a Peace, which now we have made desperate, by spiriting the *French*, who rejoice at these Changes, and by the Fall of our Credit, which unqualifies us for continuing the War. That the Parliament, so untimely dissolved, had been diligent in their Supplies, and dutiful in their Behaviour. That, one Consequence of these Changes appears already in the Fall of the Stocks: That, we may soon expect more and worse: And lastly, That, all this naturally tends to break the Settlement of the Crown, and call over the *Pretender*.

THESE and the like Notions are plentifully scattered abroad, by the Malice of a ruined Party, to render the QUEEN and her Administration odious, and to inflame the Nation. And these are what, upon Occasion, I shall endeavour to overthrow, by discovering the Falshood and Absurdity of them.

IT is a great Unhappiness, when in a Government constituted like ours, it should be so brought about, that the Continuance of a War must be for the Interest of vast Numbers (Civil as well as Military) who otherwise would have been as unknown as their Original. I think our present Condition of Affairs, is admirably described by two Verses in *Lucan*.

Hinc usura Vorax, avidumque in tempore fœnus,
Hinc concussa fides, & multis utile bellum.

Which, without any great Force upon the Words, may be thus translated.

Hence are derived those exorbitant Interests and Annuities; hence those large Discounts for Advances and prompt Payment; hence publick Credit is shaken, and hence great Numbers find their Profit in prolonging the War.

It is odd, that among a free Trading People, as we call ourselves, there should so many be found to close in with those Counsels, who have been ever averse from all Overtures towards a Peace. But yet there is no great Mystery in the Matter. Let any Man observe the Equipages in this Town; he shall find the greater Number of those who make a Figure, to be a Species of Men quite different from any that were ever known before the Revolution; consisting either of Generals and Colonels, or of such whose whole Fortunes lie in Funds and Stocks: So that *Power*, which, according to the old Maxim, was used to follow *Land*, is now gone over to *Money*; and the Country Gentleman is in the Condition of a young Heir, out of whose Estate a Scrivener receives half the Rents for Interest, and hath a Mortgage on the Whole; and is therefore always ready to feed his Vices and Extravagancies while there is any Thing left. So that if the War continue some Years longer, a Landed Man will be little better than a Farmer at a rack Rent, to the Army, and to the publick Funds.

It may perhaps be worth inquiring from what Beginnings, and by what Steps we have been brought into this desperate Condition: And in search of this we must run up as high as the Revolution.

Most of the Nobility and Gentry who invited over the Prince of *Orange*, or attended him in his Expedition, were true Lovers of their Country and its Constitution, in Church and State; and were brought to yield to those Breaches in the Succession of the Crown, out of a Regard to the Necessity of the Kingdom, and the Safety of the People, which did, and could only, make them lawful; but without Intention of drawing such a Practice into Precedent, or making it a standing Measure by which to proceed in all Times to come; and therefore we find their Counsels ever tended to keep Things as much as possible in the old Course. But soon after, an under Sett of Men, who had nothing to lose, and had neither born the Burthen nor Heat of the Day, found means to whisper in the King's Ear, that the Principles of Loyalty in the Church of *England*, were wholly inconsistent with the *Revolution*. Hence began the early Practice of caressing the Dissenters, reviling the Universities, as Maintainers of Arbitrary Power, and reproaching the Clergy with the Doctrines of Divine-Right, Passive-Obedience, and Non-resistance. At the same time, in order to fasten wealthy People to the New Government, they proposed those pernicious Expedients of borrowing Money by vast *Premiums*, and at exorbitant Interest: A Practice as old as *Eumenes*, one of *Alexander*'s Captains, who setting up for himself after the Death of his Master, persuaded his principal Officers to lend him great Sums, after which they were forced to follow him for their own Security.

THIS introduced a Number of new dextrous Men into Business and Credit: It was argued, that the War could not last above two or three Campaigns; and that it was easier for the Subject to raise a Fund for paying Interest, than to tax them annually to the full Expence of the War. Several Persons who had small or encumbred Estates, sold them, and turned their Money into those Funds to great Advantage: Merchants, as well as other monied Men, finding Trade was dangerous, pursued the same Method: But the War continuing, and growing more expensive, Taxes were encreased, and Funds multiplied every Year, 'till they have arrived at the monstrous Height we now behold them. And that which was at first a Corruption, is at last grown necessary, and what every good Subject must now fall in with, although he may be allowed to wish it might soon have an End; because it is with a Kingdom, as with a private Fortune, where every new Incumbrance adds a double Weight. By this means the Wealth of the Nation, that used to be reckoned by the Value of Land, is now computed by the Rise and Fall of Stocks: And although the Foundation of Credit be still the same, and upon a Bottom that can never be shaken; and although all Interest be duly paid by the Publick, yet through the Contrivance and

Cunning of *Stock-Jobbers*, there hath been brought in such a Complication of Knavery and Couzenage, such a Mystery of Iniquity, and such an unintelligible *Jargon* of Terms to involve it in, as were never known in any other Age or Country of the World. I have heard it affirmed by Persons skilled in these Calculations, that if the Funds appropriated to the Payment of Interest and Annuities, were added to the Yearly Taxes, and the Four-Shilling Aid strictly exacted in all Counties of the Kingdom, it would very near, if not fully, supply the Occasions of the War, at least such a Part, as in the Opinion of very able Persons, had been at that Time prudent not to exceed. For I make it a Question, whether any wise Prince or State, in the Continuance of a War, which was not purely defensive, or immediately at his own Door, did ever propose that his Expence should perpetually exceed what he was able to impose annually upon his Subjects? Neither if the War last many Years longer, do I see how the next Generation will be able to begin another; which in the Course of Human Affairs, and according to the various Interests and Ambition of Princes, may be as necessary for them as it hath been for us. And if our Fathers had left us as deeply involved as we are like to leave our Children, I appeal to any Man what sort of Figure we should have been able to make these twenty Years past. Besides, neither our Enemies, nor Allies, are upon the same Foot with us in this Particular. *France* and *Holland*, our nearest Neighbours, and the farthest engaged, will much sooner recover themselves after a War. The first, by the absolute Power of the Prince, who being Master of the Lives and Fortunes of his Subjects, will quickly find Expedients to pay his Debts: And so will the other, by their prudent Administration, the Greatness of their Trade, their wonderful Parsimony, the Willingness of their People to undergo all kind of Taxes, and their Justice in applotting as well as collecting them. But above all, we are to consider, that *France* and *Holland* fight in the Continent, either upon, or near their own Territories; and the greatest Part of the Money circulates among themselves; whereas ours crosses the Sea, either to *Flanders*, *Spain*, or *Portugal*; and every Penny of it, whether in Specie or Returns, is so much lost to the Nation for ever.

UPON these Considerations alone, it was the most prudent Course imaginable in the QUEEN, to lay hold of the Disposition of the People for changing the Parliament and Ministry at this Juncture; and extricating her self, as soon as possible out of the Pupilage of those who found their Accounts only in perpetuating the War. Neither have we the least Reason to doubt, but the ensuing Parliament will assist her MAJESTY with the utmost Vigour, until her Enemies *again* be brought to sue for Peace, and *again* offer such Terms as will make it both honourable and lasting; only with this Difference, that the Ministry perhaps will not *again* refuse them.

Audiet pugnas vitio parentum
Rara Juventus.

No. 14. *Thursday, November* 9, 1710.

E quibus hi vacuas implent Sermonibus aures,
Hi narrata ferunt alio: mensuraque ficti
Crescit, & auditis aliquid novus adjicit autor,
Illic Credulitas, illic temerarius Error,
Vanaque Lætitia est, consternatique Timores,
Seditioque recens, dubioque autore susurri.

I AM prevailed on, through the Importunity of Friends, to interrupt the Scheme I had begun in my last Paper, by an Essay upon the Art of *Political Lying*. We are told, *The Devil is the Father of Lyes*, and *was a Lyar from the beginning*; so that, beyond Contradiction, the Invention is old: And, which is more, his first Essay of it was purely *Political*, employed in undermining the Authority of his Prince, and seducing a third Part of the Subjects from their Obedience. For which he was driven down from Heaven, where (as *Milton* expresseth it) he had been VICEROY of a great *Western Province*; and forced to exercise his Talent in inferior Regions among *other fallen Spirits*, or *poor deluded Men*, whom he still daily tempts to *his own Sin*, and will ever do so till he be *chained in the bottomless Pit*.

BUT although the Devil be the Father of *Lyes*, he seems, like other great Inventors, to have lost much of his Reputation, by the continual Improvements that have been made upon him.

WHO first reduced *Lying* into an Art, and adapted it to *Politicks*, is not so clear from History; although I have made some diligent Enquiries: I shall therefore consider it only according to the modern System, as it hath been cultivated these twenty Years past in the Southern Part of our own Island.

THE Poets tell us, That after the Giants were overthrown by the Gods, the *Earth* in revenge produced her last Offspring, which was *Fame*. And the Fable is thus interpreted; That when Tumults and Seditions are quieted, Rumours and false Reports are plentifully spread through a Nation. So that by this Account, *Lying* is the last Relief of a *routed, earth-born, rebellious Party* in a State. But here, the Moderns have made great Additions, applying this Art to the gaining of Power, and preserving it, as well as revenging themselves after they have lost it: As the same Instruments are made use of by Animals to feed themselves when they are hungry, and bite those that tread upon them.

BUT the same Genealogy cannot always be admitted for *Political Lying*; I shall therefore desire to refine upon it, by adding some Circumstances of its Birth and Parents. A *Political Lye* is sometimes born out of a discarded Statesman's Head, and thence delivered to be nursed and dandled by the *Rabble*. Sometimes it is produced a Monster, and *licked* into Shape; at other Times it comes into the World compleatly formed, and is spoiled in the *licking*. It is often born an Infant in the regular Way, and requires Time to mature it: And often it sees the Light in its full Growth, but dwindles away by Degrees. Sometimes it is of noble Birth; and sometimes the Spawn of a *Stock-jobber*. *Here*, it screams aloud at opening the Womb; and *there*, it is delivered with a *Whisper*. I know a *Lye* that now disturbs half the Kingdom with its Noise, which although too proud and great at present to own its Parents, I can remember in its *Whisper-hood*. To conclude the Nativity of this Monster; when it comes into the World without a *Sting*, it is still-born; and whenever it loses its *Sting*, it dies.

No Wonder, if an Infant so miraculous in its Birth, should be destined for great Adventures: And accordingly we see it hath been the *Guardian Spirit* of a *prevailing Party* for almost twenty Years. It can conquer Kingdoms without Fighting, and sometimes with the Loss of a Battle: It gives and resumes Employments; can sink a Mountain to a Mole-hill, and raise a Mole-hill to a Mountain; hath presided for many Years at Committees of Elections; can wash a *Black-a-moor* white; make a Saint of an Atheist, and a Patriot of a Profligate; can furnish *Foreign Ministers* with Intelligence; and raise or let fall the Credit of the Nation. This Goddess flies with a huge *Looking-glass* in her Hands to dazzle the Crowd, and make them see, according as she turns it, their Ruin in their Interest, and their Interest in their Ruin. In this Glass you will behold your best Friends clad in Coats powdered with *Flower-de-Luce's* and *Triple Crowns*; their Girdles hung round with *Chains*, and *Beads*, and *Wooden Shoes*: And your worst Enemies adorned with the Ensigns of *Liberty*, *Property*, *Indulgence*, *Moderation*, and a *Cornucopia* in their Hands. Her large Wings, like those of a flying Fish, are of no Use but while they are moist; she therefore dips them in *Mud*, and soaring aloft scatters it in the Eyes of the Multitude, flying with great Swiftness; but at every Turn is forced to stoop in *dirty Ways* for new Supplies.

I HAVE been sometimes thinking, if a Man had the Art of the *Second Sight* for seeing *Lyes*, as they have in *Scotland* for seeing Spirits; how admirably he might entertain himself in this Town; to observe the different Shapes, Sizes and Colours, of those Swarms of *Lyes* which buz about the Heads of *some People*, like Flies about a Horse's Ears in Summer: Or those Legions hovering every Afternoon in *Exchange-Alley*, enough to darken the Air; or over a Club of discontented Grandees, and thence sent down in Cargoes to be scattered at Elections.

THERE is one essential Point wherein a *Political Lyar* differs from others of the Faculty; That he ought to have but a short Memory, which is necessary according to the various Occasions he meets with every Hour, of differing from himself, and swearing to both Sides of a Contradiction, as he finds the Persons disposed, with whom he hath to deal. In describing the Virtues and Vices of Mankind, it is convenient, upon every Article, to have some eminent Person in our Eye, from whence we copy our Description. I have strictly observed this Rule; and my Imagination this Minute represents before me a certain * *Great Man* famous for this Talent, to the constant Practice of which he owes his twenty Years Reputation of the most skilful Head in *England*, for the Management of nice Affairs. The Superiority of his Genius consists in nothing else but an inexhaustible Fund of *Political Lyes*, which he plentifully distributes every Minute he speaks, and by an unparallelled Generosity forgets, and consequently contradicts the next half Hour. He never yet considered whether any Proposition were True or False, but whether it were convenient for the present Minute or Company to affirm or deny it; so that if you think to refine upon him, by interpreting every Thing he says, as we do Dreams by the contrary, you are still to seek, and will find your self equally deceived, whether you believe or no: The only Remedy is to suppose that you have heard some inarticulate Sounds, without any Meaning at all. And besides, that will take off the Horror you might be apt to conceive at the Oaths wherewith he perpetually Tags both ends of every *Proposition*: Although at the same Time, I think, he cannot with any Justice be taxed for Perjury, when he invokes *God* and *Christ*; because he hath often fairly given publick Notice to the World, that he believes in neither.

Some People may think that such an Accomplishment as this, can be of no great Use to the Owner or his Party, after it hath been often practised, and is become notorious; but they are widely mistaken: Few *Lyes* carry the Inventor's Mark; and the most prostitute Enemy to Truth may spread a thousand without being known for the Author. Besides, as the vilest Writer hath his Readers, so the greatest *Lyar* hath his Believers; and it often happens, that if a *Lye* be believed only for an Hour, it hath done its Work, and there is no farther Occasion for it. *Falshood flies*, and *Truth* comes *limping* after it; so that when Men come to be undeceived, it is too late, the Jest is over, and the Tale has had its Effect: Like a Man who has thought of a good Repartee, when the Discourse is changed, or the Company

* *The late Earl of* Wharton.

parted: Or, like a Physician who hath found out an infallible Medicine after the Patient is dead.

CONSIDERING that natural Disposition in many Men to *Lye*, and in Multitudes to *Believe*; I have been perplexed what to do with that Maxim, so frequent in every Bodies Mouth, That *Truth will at last prevail*. Here, has this Island of ours, for the greatest Part of twenty Years lain under the Influence of such Counsels and Persons, whose Principle and Interest it was to corrupt our Manners, blind our Understandings, drain our Wealth, and in Time destroy our Constitution both in Church and State; and we at last were brought to the very Brink of Ruin; yet by the Means of perpetual Misrepresentations, have never been able to distinguish between our Enemies and Friends. We have seen a great Part of the Nation's Money got into the Hands of those, who by their Birth, Education and Merit, could pretend no higher than to wear our Liveries. While others, who by their Credit, Quality and Fortune, were only able to give Reputation and Success to the Revolution, were not only laid aside, as dangerous and useless; but loaden with the Scandal of *Jacobites*, Men of *Arbitrary Principles*, and *Pensioners* to *France*; while Truth, who is said to *lie in a Well*, seemed now to be buried there under a heap of Stones. But I remember it was a usual Complaint among the *Whigs*, that the Bulk of Landed-Men was not in their Interests, which some of the Wisest looked on as an ill Omen; and we saw it was with the utmost Difficulty that they could preserve a Majority, while the Court and Ministry were on their Side; till they had learned those admirable Expedients for deciding Elections, and influencing distant Boroughs, by *powerful Motives* from the City. But all this was meer Force and Constraint, however upheld by most dextrous Artifice and Management; until the People began to apprehend their *Properties*, their *Religion*, and the *Monarchy* itself in Danger; then we saw them greedily laying hold on the first Occasion to interpose. But of this mighty Change in the Dispositions of the People, I shall discourse more at large in some following Paper; wherein I shall endeavour to undeceive or discover those deluded or deluding Persons, who hope or pretend, it is only a short Madness in the Vulgar, from which they may soon recover. Whereas, I believe, it will appear to be very different in its Causes, its Symptoms, and its Consequences; and prove a great Example to illustrate the Maxim I lately mentioned, That *Truth* (however sometimes late) *will at last prevail.*

No. 15. *Thursday, November* 16, 1710.

... Medioq; ut limite curras,
Icare, ait, moneo: ne si demissior ibis,
Unda gravet pennas, si celsior, ignis adurat.

IT must be avowed, that for some Years past, there have been few Things more wanted in *England*, than such a Paper as this ought to be; and such as I will endeavour to make it, as long as it shall be found of any Use, without entring into the Violences of either Party. Considering the many grievous Misrepresentations of Persons and Things, it is highly requisite, at this Juncture, that the People throughout the Kingdom, should, if possible, be set right in their Opinions by some impartial Hand; which hath never been yet attempted: Those who have hitherto undertaken it, being upon every Account the least qualified of all Human-kind for such a Work.

WE live here under a limited Monarchy, and under the Doctrine and Discipline of an excellent Church: We are unhappily divided into two Parties, both which pretend a mighty Zeal for our Religion and Government, only they disagree about the Means. The Evils we must fence against are, on one side Fanaticism and Infidelity in Religion; and Anarchy, under the Name of a Commonwealth, in Government: On the other Side, Popery, Slavery, and the Pretender from *France*. Now to inform and direct us in our Sentiments, upon these weighty Points; here are on one Side two stupid illiterate Scribblers, both of them *Fanaticks* by Profession; I mean the *Review* and *Observator*. On the other Side we have an open *Nonjuror*, whose Character and Person, as well as good Learning and Sense, discovered upon other Subjects, do indeed deserve Respect and Esteem; but his *Rehearsal*, and the rest of his Political Papers, are yet more pernicious than those of the former two. If the Generality of the People know not how to *Talk* or *Think*, until they have read their *Lesson* in the Papers of the Week; what a Misfortune is it that their Duty should be conveyed to them through such *Vehicles* as those? For let some Gentlemen think what they please; I cannot but suspect, that the two *Worthies* I first mentioned, have in a Degree done Mischief among us; the mock authoritative Manner of the one, and the insipid Mirth of the other, however insupportable to reasonable Ears, being of a Level with great Numbers among the lowest Part of Mankind. Neither was the Author of the *Rehearsal*, while he continued that Paper, less infectious to many Persons of better Figure, who perhaps were as well qualified, and much less prejudiced, to judge for themselves.

It was this Reason, that moved me to take the Matter out of those *rough*, as well as those *dirty* Hands; to let the remote and uninstructed Part of the Nation see, that they have been misled on both Sides, by mad, ridiculous Extreams, at a wide Distance on each Side from the Truth; while the right Path is so broad and plain, as to be easily kept, if they were once put into it.

Further: I had lately entered on a Resolution to take very little Notice of other Papers, unless it were such, where the Malice and Falshood had so great a Mixture of Wit and Spirit, as would make them dangerous; which in the present Circle of Scribblers, from twelve Pence to a Half-penny, I could easily foresee would not very frequently occur. But here again, I am forced to dispense with my Resolution, although it be only to tell my Reader, what Measures I am like to take on such Occasions for the Future. I was told that the Paper called the *Observator*, was twice filled last Week with Remarks upon a late *Examiner*. These I read with the first Opportunity, and to speak in the News-Writers Phrase, they gave me *Occasion for many Speculations*. I observed with singular Pleasure, the Nature of those *Things*, which the Owners of them, usually call *Answers*; and with what Dexterity this matchless Author had fallen into the whole Art and Cant of them. To transcribe here and there three or four detatched Lines of least Weight in a Discourse, and by a foolish Comment mistake every Syllable of the Meaning, is what I have known many of a superior Class, to this formidable Adversary, entitle an *Answer*. This is what he hath exactly done in about thrice as many Words as my whole Discourse; which is so mighty an Advantage over me, that I shall by no Means engage in so unequal a Combat; but as far as I can judge of my own Temper, entirely dismiss him for the Future; heartily wishing he had a Match exactly of his own Size to meddle with, who should only have the odds of Truth and Honesty; which as I take it, would be an effectual Way to silence him for ever. Upon this Occasion, I cannot forbear a short Story of a *Fanatick Farmer*, who lived in my Neighbourhood, and was so great a Disputant in Religion, that the Servants in all the Families thereabouts, reported, how he had confuted the Bishop and all his Clergy. I had then a Footman who was fond of reading the Bible; and I borrowed a Comment for him, which he studied so close, that in a Month or two I thought him a Match for the *Farmer*. They disputed at several Houses, with a Ring of Servants and other People always about them; where *Ned* explained his Texts so full and clear, to the Capacity of his Audience, and shewed the Insignificancy of his Adversary's Cant, to the meanest Understanding; that he got the whole Country of his Side, and the Farmer was cured of his Itch of Disputation for ever after.

THE worst of it is, That this Sort of outrageous Party-Writers I have above spoke of, are like a couple of Make-bates, who inflame small Quarrels by a thousand Stories, and by keeping Friends at Distance, hinder them from coming to a good Understanding, as they certainly would, if they were suffered to meet and debate between themselves. For, let any one examine a reasonable honest Man of either Side, upon those Opinions in Religion and Government, which both Parties daily buffet each other about; he shall hardly find one material Point in difference between them. I would be glad to ask a Question about *two Great Men* of the late Ministry, how they came to be *Whigs?* And by what figure of Speech, half a Dozen others, lately put into great Employments, can be called *Tories?* I doubt, whoever would suit the Definition to the Persons, must make it directly contrary to what we understood it at the Time of the Revolution.

In order to remove these Misapprehensions among us, I believe it will be necessary upon Occasion, to detect the Malice and Falshood of some popular Maxims, which those Idiots scatter from the Press twice a Week, and draw an hundred absurd Consequences from them.

For Example: I have heard it often objected as a great Piece of Insolence in the Clergy and others, to say or hint that the *Church was in Danger*, when it was voted otherwise in Parliament some Years ago: And the Queen her self in her last Speech, did openly condemn all such Insinuations. Notwithstanding which, I did then, and do still believe, the Church hath, since that Vote, been in very imminent Danger; and I think I might then have said so, without the least Offence to her Majesty, or either of the two Houses. The Queen's Words, as near as I can remember, mentioned the Church being in Danger from *her Administration*; and whoever says or thinks That, deserves, in my Opinion, to be hanged for a Traitor. But, that the Church and State may be both in Danger under the best Princes that ever reigned, and without the least Guilt of theirs, is such a Truth, as a Man must be a great Stranger to History or common Sense, to doubt. The wisest Prince on Earth may be forced, by the Necessity of his Affairs, and the present Power of an unruly Faction, or deceived by the Craft of ill designing Men: One or two Ministers, most in his Confidence, may *at first* have good Intentions, but grow corrupted by Time, by Avarice, by Love, by Ambition, and have fairer Terms offered them, to gratify their Passions or Interests, from *one Set of Men* than another, until they are too far involved for a Retreat; and so be forced to take *seven Spirits more wicked than themselves*. This is a very possible Case; and will not *the last State of such Men be worse than the first?* That is to say, will not the Publick, which was safe at first, grow in Danger by such Proceedings as these? And shall a faithful Subject, who foresees and trembles at the Consequences, be called *Disaffected*, because he delivers his Opinion, although the Prince declares, as he justly may, that the Danger is not owing to his Administration? Or, shall the Prince himself be blamed, when in such a Juncture he puts his Affairs into other Hands, *with the universal Applause of his People?* As to the Vote against those who should affirm the Church was in Danger, I think it likewise referred to Danger from or under the Queen's Administration, (for I neither have it by me, nor can suddenly have recourse to it;) but if it were otherwise, I know not how it can refer to any Dangers but what were past, or at that Time present; or how it could affect the Future, unless the Senators were all *inspired*, or at least that Majority which voted it. Neither do I see any Crime further than ill Manners, to differ in Opinion from a Majority of either or both Houses; and that ill Manners, I must confess I have been often guilty of for some Years past, although I hope I never shall again.

ANOTHER Topick of great Use to these weekly Inflamers, is the young *Pretender* in *France*, to whom their whole Party is in a high Measure indebted for all their Greatness; and whenever it lies in their Power, they may perhaps return their Acknowledgments, as out of their Zeal for frequent *Revolutions*, they were ready to do to his supposed Father: Which is a Piece of *Secret History*, that I hope will one Day see the Light; and I am sure it shall, if ever I am Master of it, without regarding *whose Ears may tingle*. But at present, the Word *Pretender* is a Term of Art in *their* Possession: A Secretary of State cannot *desire leave to resign*, but the *Pretender* is at bottom: The Queen cannot dissolve a Parliament, but it is a Plot to dethrone herself, and bring in the *Pretender*. Half a Score Stock-Jobbers are playing the Knave in *Exchange-Alley*, and there goes the *Pretender* with a *Sponge*. One would be apt to think they bawl out the *Pretender* so often, to take off the Terror; or tell so many Lies about him, to slacken our Caution, that when he is really coming, *by their Connivance*, we may not believe them; as the Boy served the Shepherds about the *coming of the Wolf*. Or perhaps they scare us with the *Pretender*, because they think he may be like some Diseases, that *come with a Fright*. Do they not believe, that the Queen's present Ministry love her Majesty, at least as well as *some others* loved the *Church?* And why is it not as great a Mark of *Disaffection* now to say the *Queen is in Danger*, as it was some Months ago to affirm the same of the *Church?* Suppose it be a false Opinion, that the Queen's Right is *hereditary* and *indefeasible*; yet how is it possible that those who hold and believe such a Doctrine, can be in the

Pretender's Interest? His Title is weakened by every Argument that strengthens Hers. It is as plain as the Words of an Act of Parliament can make it, That her present Majesty is Heir to the Survivor of the late King and Queen her Sister. Is not that an *Hereditary Right?* What need we explain it any further? I have known an *Article of Faith* expounded in much looser and more general Terms; and that, by an Author whose Opinions are very much followed by a certain Party. Suppose we go further, and examine the Word *Indefeasible*, with which some writers of late have made themselves so merry: I confess it is hard to conceive, how any Law which the supream Power makes, may not by the same Power be repealed: So that I shall not determine, whether the Queen's Right be *indefeasible* or no. But this I will maintain; that whoever affirms it so, is not guilty of a Crime. For in that Settlement of the Crown after the Revolution, where her present Majesty is named in Remainder, there are (as near as I can remember) these remarkable Words, *To which we bind ourselves, and our Posterity for ever*. Lawyers may explain this, or call them Words of Form, as they please: And Reasoners may argue, that such an Obligation is against the very Nature of Government: But a plain Reader, who takes the Words in their natural Meaning, may be excused, in thinking a Right so confirmed, is *indefeasible*; and if there be an Absurdity in such an Opinion, he is not to answer for it.

P. S. When this Paper was going to the Press, the Printer brought me two more *Observators*, wholly taken up in my *Examiner* upon Lying, which I was at the Pains to read; and they are just such an Answer, as the two others I have mentioned. This is all I have to say on that Matter.

No. 16. *Thursday, November* 23.

Qui sunt boni cives? qui belli, qui domi de patriâ bene merentes, nisi qui patriæ beneficia meminerunt?

I WILL employ this present Paper upon a Subject which of late hath very much affected me, which I have considered with a good deal of Application, and made several Enquiries about, among those Persons who I thought were best able to inform me; and if I deliver my Sentiments with some Freedom, I hope it will be forgiven, while I accompany it with that Tenderness which so nice a Point requires.

I SAID in a former Paper (Numb. 13.) that one specious Objection to the late Removals at Court, was the Fear of giving Uneasiness to a General, who hath been long successful abroad: And accordingly, the common Clamour of Tongues and Pens for some Months past, hath run against the Baseness, the Inconstancy and Ingratitude of the whole Kingdom to the Duke of *Marlborough*, in return of the most eminent Services that ever were performed by a Subject to his Country; not to be equalled in History. And then to be sure some bitter Stroak of Detraction against *Alexander* and *Cæsar*, who never did us the least Injury. Besides, the People who read *Plutarch* come upon us with Parallels drawn from the *Greeks* and *Romans*, who ungratefully dealt with I know not how many of their most deserving Generals: While the profounder Politicians, have seen Pamphlets, where *Tacitus* and *Machiavel* have been quoted to shew the Danger of too resplendent a Merit. If a Stranger should hear these furious Out-cries of Ingratitude against our General, without knowing the Particulars, he would be apt to enquire where was his Tomb, or whether he were allowed Christian Burial? Not doubting but we had put him to some ignominious Death. Or, hath he been tried for his Life, and very narrowly escaped? Hath he been accused of high Crimes and Misdemeanours? Has the Prince seized on his Estate, and left him to starve? Hath he been hooted at as he passed the Streets, by an ungrateful Rabble? Have neither Honours, Offices nor Grants, been conferred on him or his Family? Have not he and they been barbarously stript of them all? Have not he and his Forces been ill payed abroad?

And doth not the Prince, by a scanty, limited Commission, hinder him from pursuing his own Methods in the Conduct of the War? Hath he no Power at all of disposing Commissions as he pleaseth? Is he not severely used by the Ministry or Parliament, who yearly call him to a strict Account? Has the Senate ever thanked him for good Success; and have they not always publickly censured him for the least Miscarriage? Will the Accusers of the Nation join Issue upon any of these Particulars; or, tell us in what Point our damnable Sin of Ingratitude lies? Why, it is plain and clear; for while he is commanding abroad, the Queen dissolveth her Parliament, and changeth her Ministry at home: In which *universal Calamity*, no less than *two Persons* allied by Marriage to the General, have lost their Places. Whence came this wonderful Sympathy between the Civil and Military Powers? Will the Troops in *Flanders* refuse to fight, unless they can have *their own* Lord Keeper; *their own* Lord President of the Council; *their own* chief Governor of *Ireland*; and *their own* Parliament? In a Kingdom where the People are free, how came they to be so fond of having their Counsels under the Influence of their Army, or those that lead it? Who in all well-instituted States, had no Commerce with the Civil Power; further than to receive their Orders, and obey them without Reserve.

WHEN a General is not so Popular, either in his Army, or at home, as one might expect from a long Course of Success; it may perhaps be ascribed to his *Wisdom*, or perhaps to his Complection. The Possession of some one *Quality*, or a Defect in *some other*, will extremely damp the Peoples Favour, as well as the Love of the Soldiers. Besides, this is not an Age to produce Favourites of the People, while we live under a Queen who engrosseth all our Love, and all our Veneration; and where, the only Way for a great General or Minister, to acquire any Degree of subordinate Affection from the Publick, must be by all Marks of the most *entire Submission and Respect* to her sacred Person and Commands; otherwise, no pretence of great Services, either in the Field or the Cabinet, will be able to skreen them from universal Hatred.

BUT the late Ministry was closely joined to the General, by

Friendship, Interest, Alliance, Inclination and Opinion; which cannot be affirmed of the present; and the Ingratitude of the Nation lieth in the People's *joining as one Man*, to wish, that such a Ministry should be changed. Is it not at the same Time notorious to the whole Kingdom, that nothing but a tender Regard to the General, was able to preserve that Ministry so long, until neither God nor Man could suffer their Continuance? Yet in the highest Ferment of Things, we heard few or no Reflections upon this great Commander; but all seemed Unanimous in wishing he might still be at the Head of the Confederate Forces; only at the same Time, in Case he were resolved to resign, they chose rather to turn their Thoughts somewhere else, than throw up all in Despair. And this I cannot but add, in Defence of the People, with Regard to the Person we are speaking of; that in the high Station he hath been for many Years past, his *real Defects* (as nothing Human is without them) have in a detracting Age been very sparingly mentioned, either in Libels or Conversation; and all his *Successes* very freely and universally applauded.

THERE is an active and a passive Ingratitude: Applying both to this Occasion; We may say, the first is, when a Prince or People returns good Services with Cruelty or ill Usage: The other is, when good Services are not at all, or very meanly rewarded. We have already spoke of the former; let us therefore in the second Place, examine how the Services of our General have been rewarded; and whether upon that Article, either Prince or People have been guilty of Ingratitude?

THOSE are the most valuable Rewards which are given to us from the certain Knowledge of the Donor, that they *fit our Temper best*: I shall therefore say nothing of the Title of *Duke*, or the *Garter*, which the Queen bestowed the General in the beginning of her Reign: But I shall come to *more substantial* Instances, and mention nothing which hath not been given in the Face of the World. The Lands of *Woodstock*, may, I believe, be reckoned worth 40,000 *l*. On the building of *Blenheim* Castle 200,000*l*. have been already expended, although it be not yet near finished. The Grant of 5000 *l*. *per Annum*, on the Post Office, is richly worth 100,000 *l*. His Principality in *Germany* may be computed at

30,000 *l.* Pictures, Jewels, and other Gifts from Foreign Princes, 60,000 *l.* The Grant at the *Pall-Mall*, the Rangership, *&c.* for want of more certain Knowledge, may be called 10,000 *l.* His own, and his Dutchess's Employments at five Years Value, reckoning only the known and avowed Salaries, are very low rated at 100,000 *l.* Here is a good deal above half a Million of Money; and I dare say, those who are loudest with the Clamour of Ingratitude, will readily own, that all this is but a Trifle, in Comparison of what is *untold*.

THE Reason of my stating this Account is only to convince the World, that we are not quite so ungrateful either as the *Greeks* or the *Romans*. And in order to adjust this Matter with all Fairness, I shall confine myself to the latter, who were much the more generous of the two. A Victorious General of *Rome* in the Height of that Empire, having *entirely subdued his Enemies*, was rewarded with the larger Triumph; and perhaps a Statue in the *Forum*; a Bull for a Sacrifice; an embroidered Garment to appear in; a Crown of Laurel; a Monumental Trophy with Inscriptions; sometimes five hundred or a thousand Copper Coins were struck on Occasion of the Victory; which, doing Honour to the General, we will place to his Account: And lastly, sometimes, although not very frequently, a Triumphal Arch. These are all the Rewards that I can call to Mind, which a victorious General received after his return from the most glorious Expedition; conquered some great Kingdom; brought the King himself, his Family and Nobles to adorn the Triumph in Chains; and made the Kingdom either a *Roman* Province, or at best, a poor depending State, in humble Alliance to that Empire. Now, of all these Rewards, I find but two which were of real Profit to the General: The *Laurel Crown*, made and sent him at the Charge of the Publick; and the *embroidered Garment*; but I cannot find whether this last were paid for by the Senate or the General: However, we will take the more favourable Opinion; and in all the rest, admit the whole Expence, as if it were ready Money in the General's Pocket. Now according to these Computations on both Sides, we will draw up two fair Accounts; the one of *Roman* Gratitude, and the other of *British* Ingratitude; and set them together in Ballance.

A Bill of ROMAN *Gratitude.*

Imprim.	*l*	*s.*	*d.*
For Frankincense and Earthen Pots to burn it in	4	10	0
A Bull for Sacrifice	8	0	0
An embroidered Garment	50	0	0
A Crown of Laurel	0	0	2
A Statue	100	0	0
A Trophy	80	0	0
A thousand Copper Medals, Value half-pence a Piece	2	1	8
A Triumphal Arch	500	0	0
A Triumphal Carr, valued as a Modern Coach	100	0	0
Casual Charges at the Triumph.	150	0	0
	994	11	10

A Bill of BRITISH *Ingratitude.*

Imprim.	*l*	*s.*	*d.*
Woodstock.	40000	0	0
Blenheim.	200000	0	0
Post-Office Grant.	100000	0	0
Mildenheim.	30000	0	0
Pictures, Jewels, *&c.*	60000	0	0
Pall Mall Grant, &c.	10000	0	0
Employments.	100000	0	0
	540000	0	0

THIS is an Account of the visible Profits on both Sides; and if the *Roman* General had any *private Perquisites*, they may be easily discounted, and by more probable Computations; and differ yet more upon the Ballance; if we consider, that all the Gold and Silver for *Safeguards* and *Contributions*; and all *valuable Prizes* taken in the War, were openly exposed in the Triumph; and then lodged in the Capital for the Publick Service.

So that upon the Whole, we are not yet quite so bad at *worst*, as the *Romans* were at *best*. And I doubt, those who raise this hideous Cry of Ingratitude, may be mightily mistaken in the Consequences they propose from such Complaints. I remember a Saying of *Seneca*, *Multos ingratos invenimus*, *plures facimus*: We find many ungrateful Persons in the World, but we *make* more, by setting too high a Rate upon our Pretensions, and undervaluing the Rewards we receive. When unreasonable Bills are brought in, they ought to be taxed, or cut off in the Middle. Where there have been long Accounts between two Persons, I have known one of them perpetually making large Demands, and pressing for Payments; who when the Accounts were cast up on both Sides, was found to be Debtor for some Hundreds. I am thinking, if a Proclamation were issued out for every Man to send in his *Bill of Merits*, and the lowest Price he set them at, what a pretty Sum it would amount to, and how many such Islands as this must be Sold to pay them. I form my Judgment from the Practice of those who sometimes happen to *pay themselves*; and I dare affirm, would not be so unjust to take a Farthing more than they think is due to their Deserts. I will Instance only in one Article. A * Lady of my Acquaintance, appropriated twenty six Pounds a Year out of her own Allowance, for certain Uses, which her † Woman received, and was to pay to the Lady or her Order, as it was called for. But after eight Years, it appeared upon the strictest Calculation, that the Woman had paid but four Pounds a Year, and sunk two and twenty for her own Pocket: It is but supposing instead of twenty six Pounds, twenty six thousand; and by that you may judge what the Pretensions of *Modern Merit* are, where it happens to be its own Paymaster.

No. 17. *Thursday*, *November* 30, 1710.

Quas res luxuries in flagitiis, avaritia in rapinis, superbia in contumeliis efficere potuisset; eas omnes sese hoc uno Prætore per triennium pertulisse, aiebant.

WHEN I first undertook this Paper, I was resolved to concern my self only with *Things*, and not with *Persons*. Whether I have kept or broken this Resolution, I can-

* *Supposed to be her late Majesty Queen* Anne.
† *The Duchess of* Marlborough.

not recollect; and I will not be at the Pains to examine, but leave the Matter to those little Antagonists, who may want a Topick for Criticism. Thus much I have discovered; that it is in Writing, as in Building; where, after all our Schemes and Calculations, we are mightily deceived in our Accounts, and often forced to make Use of any Materials we can find, that the Work may be kept a going. Besides, to speak my Opinion, the *Things* I have Occasion to mention, are so closely linked to *Persons*, that nothing but *Time* (the Father of *Oblivion*) can separate them. Let me put a parallel Case: Suppose I should complain, that last Week my Coach was within an Inch of overturning, in a smooth, even Way, and drawn by very gentle Horses; to be sure, all my Friends would immediately lay the Fault upon *John*, because they knew, he then *Presided* in my Coach-Box. Again, Suppose I should discover some Uneasiness to find my self, I knew not how, over Head-and-Ears in Debt, although I were sure my Tenants paid their Rents very well, and that I never spent all my *Income*; they would certainly advise me to turn off Mr. * *Oldfox* my *Receiver*, and take another. If, as a Justice of Peace, I should tell a Friend that my *Warrants* and *Mittimus*'s were never drawn up as I would have them; that I had the Misfortune to send an honest Man to Goal, and dismiss a Knave; he would bid me no longer trust † *Charles* and *Harry*, my two *Clerks*, whom he knew to be ignorant, wilful, assuming and ill-inclined Fellows. If I should add, That my Tenants made me very uneasy with their Squabbles and Broils among themselves; he would counsel me to Cashier || *Will Bigamy*, the *Seneschal* of my Mannor. And lastly, if my Neighbour and I happened to have a Misunderstanding about the *Delivery of a Message*, what could I do less than strip and discard the *blundering* or *malicious* Rascal who carried it?

It is the same Thing in the Conduct of publick Affairs, where they have been managed with Rashness or Wilfulness, Corruption, Ignorance or Injustice; barely to relate the Facts, at least, while they are fresh in Memory, will as much reflect upon

* *L.* Godolphin.

† *E.* Sunderland, *and Harry* Boyle, *Secretaries of State.*

|| *L.* Chancellor Cowper.

the *Persons* concerned, as if we had told their Names at length.

I HAVE therefore since thought of another Expedient, frequently practised with great Safety and Success by satyrical Writers: Which is, That of looking into History for some Character bearing a Resemblance to the Person we would describe; and with the absolute Power of altering, adding or suppressing what Circumstances we please, I conceived we must have very bad Luck, or very little Skill to fail. However, some Days ago in a Coffee-House, looking into one of the politick weekly Papers; I found the Writer had fallen into this Scheme; and I happened to light on that Part where he was describing a Person, who from small Beginnings grew (as I remember) to be Constable of *France*, and had a very *haughty*, *imperious Wife*. I took the Author for a Friend to our *Faction*, (for so with great Propriety of Speech they call the Queen and Ministry, almost the whole Clergy, and nine Parts in ten of the Kingdom) and I said to a Gentleman near me, that although I knew well enough what Persons the Author meant, yet there were several Particulars in the *Husband*'s Character, which I could not reconcile. For that of the *Lady* was just and adequate enough; but it seems I mistook the whole Matter, and applied all I had read to a couple of Persons, who were not at that Time in the Writer's Thoughts.

NOW to avoid such a Misfortune as this, I have been for some Time consulting *Livy* and *Tacitus*, to find out the Character of a *Princeps Senatus*, a *Prætor Urbanus*, a *Quæstor Ærarius*, a *Cæsari ab Epistolis*, and a *Proconsul*: But among the worst of them, I cannot discover One from whence to draw a Parallel, without doing Injury to a *Roman* Memory: So that I am compelled to have Recourse to *Tully*. But this Author relating Facts only as an Orator, I thought it would be best to observe his Method, and make an Extract from six Harangues of his against *Verres*, only still preserving the Form of an Oration. I remember a younger Brother of mine, who deceased about two Months ago, presented the World with a Speech of *Alcibiades*, against an *Athenian* Brewer: Now, I am told for certain, that in those Days there was no Ale in *Athens*; and therefore that Speech, or at least, a great Part of it, must needs be spurious. The Difference between me and my Brother is this; he makes *Alcibiades* say a great deal more than he really did; and I make *Cicero* say a great deal less. This * *Verres*, had been the *Roman* Governor of *Sicily* for three Years; and on return from his Government, the *Sicilians* entreated *Cicero* to impeach him in the Senate; which, he accordingly did, in several Orations: From whence I have faithfully Translated and Abstracted that which follows.

My Lords,

'A PERNICIOUS Opinion hath for some Time prevailed, not only at *Rome*, but among our neighbouring 'Nations; that a Man who hath Money enough, although 'he be ever so guilty, cannot be condemned in this Place. But, 'however industriously this Opinion be spread, to cast an Odium 'on the Senate; we have brought before your Lordships *Caius* '*Verres*, a Person, for his Life and Actions, already condemned by 'all Men; but as he hopes, and gives out, by the Influence of his 'Wealth, to be here absolved. In condemning this Man, you have 'an Opportunity of belying that general Scandal; of redeeming 'the *Credit lost by former Judgments*; and recovering the Love of the '*Roman* People, as well as of our Neighbours. I have brought here 'a Man before you, my Lords, who is a Robber of the Publick 'Treasure; an Overturner of Law and Justice; and the Disgrace, 'as well as Destruction of the *Sicilian* Province: Of whom, if you 'shall determine with Equity and due Severity, your Authority 'will remain entire, and upon such an Establishment as it ought 'to be: But if his great Riches will be able to force their Way 'through that Religious Reverence and Truth, which become so 'awful an Assembly, I shall, however, obtain thus much, That the 'Defect will be laid where it ought; and that it shall not be objected, the Criminal was not produced, or that there wanted an 'Orator to accuse him. This Man, my Lords, hath publickly said, 'That those ought to be afraid of Accusations who have only 'robbed enough for their own Support and Maintenance; but 'that he hath plundered sufficient to bribe Numbers; and that 'nothing is so High or Holy which Money cannot corrupt. Take 'that Support from him, and he can have no other left. For, what

* *Earl of* Wharton, *Lord Lieutenant of* Ireland.

'Eloquence will be able to defend a Man, whose Life hath been 'tainted with so many scandalous Vices, and who hath been so 'long condemned by the universal Opinion of the World? To 'pass over the foul Stains and Ignominy of his Youth; his corrupt 'Management in all Employments he hath born; his Treachery 'and Irreligion; his Injustice and Oppression: He hath left of late 'such Monuments of his Villainies in *Sicily*; made such Havock 'and Confusion there, during his Government, that the Province 'cannot by any Means be restored to its former State, and hardly 'recover it self at all under many Years, and by a long Succession 'of good Governors. While this Man governed in that Island, the '*Sicilians* had neither the Benefit of our Laws, nor their own, nor 'even of common Right. In *Sicily*, no Man now possesseth more 'than what the Governor's Lust and Avarice have overlooked; or 'what he was forced to neglect out of meer Weariness and Satiety 'of Oppression. Every thing where he presided, was determined 'by his arbitrary Will; and the best Subjects he treated as Enemies. 'To recount his abominable Debaucheries, would offend any 'modest Ear, since so many could not preserve their Daughters 'and Wives from his Lust. I believe, there is no Man who ever 'heard his Name, that cannot relate his Enormities. We bring 'before you in Judgment, my Lords, a publick Robber, an Adul-'terer, * a DEFILER OF ALTARS, an Enemy of Religion, and of 'all that is Sacred; in *Sicily* he sold all Employments of Judicature, 'Magistracy, and Trust, Places in the Council, and the *Priesthood* 'it self, to the highest Bidder; and hath plundered that Island of 'forty Millions of Sesterces. And here I cannot but observe to 'your Lordships, in what manner *Verres* passed the Day: The 'Morning was spent in taking Bribes, and selling Employments; 'the rest of it in Drunkenness and Lust. His Discourse at Table 'was scandalously unbecoming the Dignity of his Station; Noise, 'Brutality, and Obsceneness. One Particular I cannot omit, that 'in the high Character of Governor of *Sicily*, upon a solemn Day, 'a Day set a-part for Publick Prayer for the Safety of the Common-'wealth; he stole at Evening, in a Chair, to a married Woman of

* This Story of Lord *Wharton*, is true; who, with some other Wretches went into a Pulpit, and defiled it in the most filthy Manner.

'infamous Character, against all Decency and Prudence, as well 'as against all Laws both Human and Divine. Didst thou think, 'O *Verres*, the Government of *Sicily* was given thee with so large 'a Commission, only by the Power of That to break all the Barrs 'of Law, Modesty, and Duty, to suppose all Mens Fortunes thine, 'and leave no House free from thy Rapine, or Lust, *&c.*

THIS Extract, to deal ingenuously, hath cost me more Pains than I think it is worth, having only served to convince me, that modern Corruptions are not to be parallelled by ancient Examples, without having recourse to Poetry or Fable. For instance, I never read in Story of a Law enacted to take away the Force of all Laws whatsoever; by which a Man may safely commit upon the last of *June*, what he would infallibly be hanged for if he committed on the first of *July*; by which the greatest Criminals may escape, provided they continue long enough in Power to antiquate their Crimes; and by stifling them a while, can deceive the Legislature into an *Amnesty*, of which the Enacters do not at that Time foresee the Consequence. A cautious Merchant will be apt to suspect, when he finds a Man who has the Repute of a cunning Dealer, and with whom he hath old Accounts, urging for a general Release. When I reflect on this Proceeding, I am not surprised, that those who contrived a Parliamentary *Sponge* for their *Crimes*, are now afraid of a new Revolution *Sponge* for their *Money*: And if it were possible to contrive a *Sponge* that could only affect those who had need of the other, perhaps it would not be ill employed.

No. 18. *Thursday, December* 7.

Quippe ubi fas versum atq; nefas: tot bella per orbem:
Tam multæ Scelerum facies ——— ——— ———

I AM often violently tempted to let the World freely know who the Author of this Paper is; to tell them my Name and Titles at Length; which would prevent abundance of inconsistent Criticisms I daily hear upon it. Those who are Enemies to the Notions and Opinions I would advance, are sometimes apt to quarrel with the *Examiner* as defective in Point of Wit, and sometimes of Truth. At other Times they are so generous and candid, to allow, it is written by a Club; and, that very great *Hands* have *Fingers* in it. As for those who only appear its Adversaries in Print, they give me but very little Pain: The Paper I hold lies at my mercy, and I can govern it as I please; therefore, when I begin to find the Wit too bright, the Learning too deep, and the Satyr too keen for me to deal with, (a very frequent Case no doubt, where a Man is constantly attacked by such shrewd Adversaries) I peaceably fold it up, or fling it aside, and read no more. It would be happy for me to have the same Power over People's Tongues, and not be forced to hear my own Work railed at and commended fifty Times a Day; affecting all the while a Countenance wholly unconcerned; and joining out of Policy or good Manners with the Judgment of both Parties: This, I confess, is too great a Hardship for so bashful and unexperienced a Writer.

BUT, alas, I lye under another Discouragement of much more Weight: I was very unfortunate in the choice of my Party when I set up to be a Writer: Where is the Merit, or what Opportunity to discover our Wit, our Courage, or our Learning, in drawing our Pens for the Defence of a Cause, which the QUEEN and both Houses of Parliament, and nine Parts in ten of the Kingdom, have so unanimously embraced? I am cruelly afraid, we Politick Authors must begin to lessen our Expences, and lie for the Future at the Mercy of our Printers. All hopes now are gone of writing our Selves into Places or Pensions. A certain starveling Author who *worked* under the late Administration, told me with a heavy Heart, above a Month ago, That he and some others of his Brethren, had secretly offered their Service dog-cheap to the present Ministry; but were all refused, and are now maintained by Contribution, like *Jacobites* or *Fanaticks*. I have been of late employed out of perfect Commiseration, in doing them good Offices: For, whereas some were of Opinion that these hungry Zealots should not be suffered any longer in their malapert Way to snarl at the present Course of publick Proceedings; and whereas, others proposed, that they should be limited to a certain Number, and permitted to write for their *Masters*, in the same Manner as Counsel are assigned for other Criminals; that is, to say all they can in Defence of their Client, but not reflect upon the Court: I humbly gave my Advice, that they should be suffered to write on, as they used to do; which I did purely out of Regard to their Persons: For I hoped it would keep them out of Harms-way, and prevent them from falling into evil Courses, which although of little Consequence to the Publick, would certainly be *fatal to themselves*. If I have room at the Bottom of this Paper, I will transcribe a Petition to the present Ministry, sent me by one of these Authors, in Behalf of himself and fourscore of his Brethren.

FOR my own Part, notwithstanding the little Encouragement to be hoped for at this Time from the Men in Power, I shall continue my Paper 'till either the World or my self grow weary of it: The latter is easily determined; and for the former, I shall not leave it to the Partiality of either Party, but to the infallible Judgment of my Printer. One principal End I designed by it, was to undeceive those well-meaning People, who have been drawn unaware into a wrong Sense of Things, either by the common Prejudices of Education and Company, the great personal Qualities of some Party-leaders, or the foul Misrepresentations that were constantly made of all who durst differ from them in the smallest Article. I have known such Men struck with the Thoughts of some late Changes, which, as they pretend to think, were made without any Reason visible to the World. In Answer to this, it is not sufficient to alledge, that a good and wise Prince may be allowed to change his Ministers without giving a Reason to his Subjects; because it is probable, that he will not make such a Change without very important Reasons; and a good Subject ought to suppose, that in such a Case there are such Reasons, although he be not apprised of them; otherwise, he must inwardly tax his Prince of Capriciousness, Inconstancy, or ill Design. Such Reasons indeed, may not be obvious to Persons prejudiced, or at great Distance, or short Thinkers; and therefore if they be no Secrets of State, nor any ill Consequences to be apprehended from their Publication; it is no uncommendable Work in any private Hand to lay them open for the Satisfaction of all Men. And, if what I have already said, or shall hereafter say of this Kind, be thought to reflect upon *Persons*, although none have been named, I know not how it can possibly be avoided. The Queen in her Speech mentions *with great Concern*, that the *Navy and other Offices are burthened with heavy Debts*; and *desires that the like may be prevented for the Time to come*. And, if it be *now* possible to prevent the Continuance of an Evil that hath been so long growing upon us, and is arrived to such a Height; surely those Corruptions and Mismanagements must have been great which first introduced them, before our Taxes were eaten up by Annuities.

IF I were able to rip up, and discover in all their Colours only about eight or nine Thousand of the most scandalous Abuses, that have been committed in all Parts of publick Management for twenty Years past, by a certain Set of Men and their Instruments; I should reckon it some Service to my Country and to Posterity. But, to say the Truth, I should be glad the Authors Names were conveyed to future Times along with their Actions. For, although the present Age may understand well enough the little Hints we give, the Parallels we draw, and the Characters we describe; yet this will all be lost to the next. However, if these Papers, *reduced into a more durable Form*, should happen to live until our Grand-children be Men; I hope they may have Curiosity enough to consult Annals, and compare Dates, in order to find out what *Names* were then intrusted with the Conduct of Affairs, in the Consequence whereof, themselves will so deeply share; like a heavy Debt in a private Family, which often lies an Incumbrance upon an Estate for three Generations.

BUT leaving the Care of informing Posterity to better Pens, I shall with due Regard to Truth, Discretion, and the Safety of my Person from the Men of *the new-fangled Moderation*, continue to take all proper Opportunities of letting the misled Part of the People see how grosly they have been abused, and in what Particulars: I also shall endeavour to convince them, that the present Course we are in, is the most probable Means, with the Blessing of God, to extricate our selves out of all our Difficulties.

AMONG those who are pleased to write or talk against this Paper, I have observed a strange Manner of Reasoning, which

I should be glad to hear them explain themselves upon. They make no Ceremony of exclaiming upon all Occasions against a Change of Ministry, in so critical and dangerous a Conjuncture. What shall we, who heartily approve and join in those Proceedings, say in Defence of them? We own the Juncture of Affairs to be as they describe: We are pushed for an Answer, and are forced at last freely to confess, that the Corruptions and Abuses in every Branch of the Administration, were so numerous and intollerable, that all Things must have ended in Ruin, without some speedy Reformation. This I have already asserted in a former Paper; and the Replies I have read or heard, have been in plain Terms to affirm the direct Contrary; and not only to defend and celebrate the late Persons and Proceedings, but to threaten me with Law and Vengeance, for casting Reflections on so many great and honourable Men, whose *Birth, Virtues and Abilities; whose Morals and Religion, whose Love of their Country and its Constitution in Church and State*, were so universally allowed; and all this set off with odious Comparisons reflecting on the present Choice. Is not this in plain and direct Terms to tell all the World, that the Queen hath in a most dangerous Crisis turned out a whole Set of the best Ministers that ever served a Prince, without any Manner of Reason, but her Royal Pleasure; and brought in others of a Character directly contrary? And how so vile an Opinion as this can consist with the least Pretence to Loyalty or good Manners, let the World determine.

I CONFESS my self so little a Refiner in the Politicks, as not to be able to discover what other Motive, besides Obedience to the QUEEN, a Sense of publick Danger, and a true Love of their Country, joined with invincible Courage, could spirit up those great Men, who have now under Her Majesty's Authority undertaken the Direction of Affairs. What can they expect but the utmost Efforts of Malice from a Set of enraged domestick Adversaries, perpetually watching over their Conduct, crossing all their Designs, and using every Art to foment Divisions among them, in order to join with the Weakest upon any Rupture? The Difficulties they must encounter are nine Times more and greater than ever; and the Prospects of Interest, after the *Reapings* and *Gleanings* of so many Years, nine Times less. Every

Misfortune at Home or Abroad, although the necessary Consequence of former Counsels, will be imputed to them; and all the good Success given to the Merit of former Schemes. A Sharper hath held your Cards all the Evening, played Booty, and lost your Money; and when Things are almost desperate, you employ an honest Gentleman to retrieve your Losses.

I WOULD ask whether the QUEEN'S Speech doth not contain her Intentions, in every Particular relating to the Publick, that a good Subject, a *Briton* and a *Protestant*, can possibly have at Heart? *To carry on the War in all its Parts, particularly in* Spain, *with the utmost Vigour, in order to procure a safe and honourable Peace for Us and our Allies; to find some Ways of paying the Debts on the Navy; to support and encourage the Church of* England; *to preserve the* British *Constitution according to the* Union; *to maintain the Indulgence by Law allowed to scrupulous Consciences; and, to employ none but such as are for the Protestant Succession in the House of* Hanover. It is known enough, that Speeches on these Occasions are ever digested by the Advice of those who are in the chief Confidence; and consequently, that these are the Sentiments of her Majesty's Ministers, as well as her own; and we see, the two Houses have unanimously agreed with her in every Article. When the least Counterpaces are made to any of these Resolutions, it will then be Time enough for our Malecontents to bawl out *Popery*, *Persecution*, *Arbitrary Power*, and *the Pretender*. In the mean while, it is a little hard to think, that this Island can hold but six Men of Honesty and Ability enough to serve their Prince and Country; or that our Safety should depend upon their Credit, any more than it would upon the Breath in their Nostrils. Why should not a *Revolution* in the Ministry be sometimes necessary, as well as a *Revolution* in the Crown? It is to be presumed, the former is at least as lawful in it self; and perhaps the Experiment not quite so dangerous. The *Revolution* of the *Sun* about the *Earth* was formerly thought a necessary Expedient to solve Appearances, although it left many Difficulties unanswered; until Philosophers contrived a better, which is that of the *Earth's Revolution* about the *Sun*. This is found upon Experience to save much Time and Labour, to correct many irregular Motions, and is better suited to the Respect due from a *Planet* to a *fixed Star*.

No. 19. *Thursday, December* 14, 1710.

Sunt quibus in Satyra videar nimis acer, & ultra
Legem tendere opus: sine nervis altera, quicquid
Composui, pars esse putat —— ——

WHEN the Printer came last Week for his Copy, he brought along with him a Bundle of those Papers, which, in the Phrase of *Whig Coffee-Houses*, have *swinged off* the *Examiner*; most of which I had never seen or heard of before. I remember some Time ago in one of the *Tatlers*, to have read a Letter, wherein several Reasons are assigned for the present Corruption and Degeneracy of our Taste; but I think the Writer hath omitted the principal One, which I take to be the Prejudice of Parties. Neither can I excuse either Side of this Infirmity: I have heard the arrantest Drivellers *Pro* and *Con* commended for their *Shrewdness* even by Men of tolerable Judgment; and the best Performances exploded as Nonsense and Stupidity. This indeed may partly be imputed to Policy and Prudence; but it is chiefly owing to that Blindness, which Prejudice and Passion cast over the Understanding: I mention this, because I think it properly within my Province in quality of *Examiner*. And having granted more than is usual for an Enemy to do, I must now take Leave to say, that so weak a *Cause*, and so ruined a *Faction*, were never provided with Pens more resembling their Condition, or less suited to their Occasions.

Non tali auxilio, nec defensoribus istis
Tempus eget —— ——

THIS is the more to be wondered at, when we consider they have the full Liberty of the Press; that they have no other Way left to recover themselves; and that they want not Men of excellent Parts to set their Arguments in the best Light they will bear. Now, if two Men would argue on both Sides with Fairness, good Sense, and good Manners; it would be no ill Entertainment to the Town, and perhaps be the most effectual Means to reconcile us. But I am apt to think, that Men of a great Genius are hardly brought to prostitute their Pens in a very odious *Cause*; which, besides, is more properly undertaken by Noise and Impudence, by gross Railing and Scurrility, by Calumny and Lying, and by little trifling Cavils and Carpings in the wrong Place, which those *Whifflers* use for Arguments and Answers.

I WAS well enough pleased with a Story of one of these Answerers, who in a Paper last Week found many Faults with a late Calculation of mine. Being it seems more deep learned than his Fellows, he was resolved to begin his Answer with a *Latin* Verse, as well as other Folks: His Business was to look out for something against an *Examiner* that would pretend to *tax* Accounts; and turning over *Virgil*, he had the Luck to find these Words, *Fugiant Examina taxos*; so down they went, and out they would have come, if one of his unlucky *Prompters* had not hindered it.

I HERE declare once for all, that if these People will not be quiet, I shall take their Bread out of their Mouths, and answer the *Examiner* my self; which I protest I have never yet done, although I have been often charged with it; neither have those Answers been written or published with my Privity, as malicious People are pleased to give out; nor do I believe the common *Whiggish* Report, That the Authors are hired by the Ministry to give my Paper a Value.

BUT the Friends of this Paper have given me more Uneasiness with their Impatience, than its Enemies by their Answers. I heard my self censured last Week by some of the former, for promising to discover the Corruptions in the late Administration, but never performing any Thing. The latter, on the other Side, are thundering out their *Anathema's* against me for discovering so many. I am at a Loss how to decide between these Contraries, and therefore shall proceed after my own Way, as I have hitherto done; my Design being of more Importance than that of Writing only to gratify the Spleen of one Side, or provoke that of the Other, although it may occasionally have both Effects.

I SHALL therefore go on to relate some Facts, that, in my humble Opinion, were no Hindrance to the Change of the Ministry.

THE first I shall mention, was That of introducing certain new Phrases into the Court Style, which had been very seldom or never made Use of in former Times. They usually ran in the following Terms: *Madam, I cannot serve you while such a One is in Employment. I desire humbly to resign my Commission, if Mr. . . . continues Secretary of State. I cannot answer that the City will lend Money, unless my L---d . . . . . . be President of the Council. I must beg leave to surrender, except . . . . has the Staff. I must not accept the Seals, unless . . . . . . comes into the other Office.* This hath been the Language of late Years from Subjects to their Prince. Thus they stood upon Terms, and must have their own Conditions to ruin the Nation; nay, this dutiful Manner of Capitulating, had spread so far, that every under-strapper began at length to perk up and assume: He *expected a Regiment*; or, *his Son must be a Major*; or, *his Brother a Collector*; else he threatned to *Vote according to his Conscience.*

ANOTHER of their glorious Attempts, was the Clause intended in the Bill *for the Encouragement of Learning*; by taking off the Obligation upon Fellows of Colleges in both Universities to enter upon Holy Orders: The Design of which, as I have heard the Undertakers often confess, was to remove the Care of educating Youth out of the Hands of the Clergy, who are apt to infuse into their Pupils too great a Regard for the Church and the Monarchy. But there was a farther Secret in this Clause, which may best be discovered by the first Projectors, or at least the *Garblers* of it; and these are known to be *Collins* and *Tindall*, in Conjunction with a most *pious Lawyer* their Disciple.

WHAT shall we say to their prodigious Skill in *Arithmetick*, discovered so constantly in their Decision of Elections; where they were able to make out by the *Rule of False*, that *Three* were more than *Three and Twenty*, and *Fifteen* than *Fifty?* Nay, it was a Maxim which I never heard any of them dispute, that in determining Elections, they were not to consider where the Right lay, but which of the *Candidates* was likelier to be true to the *Cause*. This they used to illustrate by a very apt and decent Similitude, of gaming with a Sharper; if you cannot cheat as well as he, you are certainly undone.

ANOTHER Cast of their Politicks was that of endeavouring to

impeach an innocent * *Lady*, for no Reason imaginable, but her faithful and diligent Service to the Queen, and the Favour her Majesty bore to her upon that Account, when others had acted contrary in so shameful a Manner. What else was the Crime? Had she *treated her Royal Mistress with Insolence or Neglect?* Had she *enriched her self by a long Practice of Bribery, and obtaining exorbitant Grants?* Had she *engrossed her Majesty's Favours without admitting any Access but through her Means?* Had she *heaped Employments upon her self, her Family and Dependants?* Had she *an imperious, haughty Behaviour?* Or, after all, was it a perfect Blunder and Mistake of *one Person for another?* I have heard of a Man who lay all Night on a rough Pavement; and in the Morning, wondering what it could possibly be that made him rest so ill, happened to see a Feather under him, and imputed the Uneasiness of his Lodging to That. I remember likewise the Story of a Giant in *Rablais*, who used to feed upon *Wind-Mills*, but was unfortunately choaked with a small lump of *fresh Butter*, before a warm Oven.

AND here I cannot but observe how very refined some People are in their Generosity and Gratitude. There is a certain great Person (I shall not say of what Sex) who for many Years past was the constant Mark and Butt, against which our present Malecontents used to discharge their Resentment: Upon whom they bestowed all the Terms of Scurrility, that Malice, Envy and Indignation could invent; whom they publickly accused of every Vice that can possess a human Heart: Pride, Covetousness, Ingratitude, Oppression, Treachery, Dissimulation, Violence and Fury, all in the highest Extreams: But of late they have changed their Language on a sudden; that Person is now the most faithful and just that ever served a Prince; that Person, originally differing from them in Principles, as far as East and West; but united in Practice, and falling together, they are now reconciled, and find twenty Resemblances between each other, which they could never discover before. *Tanti est ut placeam tibi perire.*

BUT to return: How could it be longer suffered in a free Nation, that all Avenues to Preferment should be shut up, except a

* *The Lady* Masham.

very few, when one or two stood constant *Centry*, who docked all Favours they handed down; or spread a huge invisible Net between the Prince and Subject, through which nothing of Value could pass? And here I cannot but admire at one Consequence from this Management, which is of an extraordinary Nature: Generally speaking, Princes who have ill Ministers are apt to suffer in their Reputation, as well as in the Love of the People: But it was not so with the Queen. When the Sun is overcast by those Clouds he exhales from the Earth, we still acknowledge his Light and Influence, and at last find he can dispel and drive them down to the Horizon. The wisest Prince, by the Necessity of Affairs, the Misrepresentations of designing Men, or, the innocent Mistakes even of a good Predecessor; may find himself encompassed by a Crew of Courtiers, whom Time, Opportunity and Success, have miserably corrupted. And if he can save himself and his People from Ruin, under the *worst* Administration, what may not his Subjects hope for; when, with their universal Applause he changeth Hands, and maketh Use of the *best?*

ANOTHER great Objection with me against the late Party, was the cruel Tyranny they put upon *Conscience*, by a *barbarous Inquisition*, refusing to admit the least *Toleration* or *Indulgence*. They imposed a hundred *Tests*, but could never be prevailed with to *dispense* with, or *take off* the smallest, or even admit of *occasional Conformity*; but went on daily (as their Apostle *Tindall* expresseth it) *narrowing their Terms of Communion*; pronouncing nine Parts in ten of the Kingdom *Hereticks*, and shutting them out of the Pale of their Church. These very Men, who talk so much of a *Comprehension in Religion* among us, how came they to allow so little of it in *Politicks*, which is *their Sole Religion?* You shall hear them pretending to bewail the Animosities kept up between the Church of *England* and Dissenters, where the Differences in Opinion are so few and inconsiderable; yet these very Sons of *Moderation* were pleased to *excommunicate* every Man who disagreed with them in the smallest *Article* of their *Political Creed*; or, who refused to receive any new *Article*, how difficult soever to digest, which the Leaders imposed at Pleasure to serve their own Interest.

I WILL quit this Subject for the present, when I have told one Story.

'There was a great King in *Scythia*, whose Dominions were 'bounded to the North, by the poor, mountainous Territories 'of a petty Lord, who paid Homage as the King's Vassal. 'The *Scythian Prime Minister* being largely *Bribed*, indirectly ob-'tained his Master's Consent to suffer this Lord to build Forts, 'and provide himself with Arms, under Pretence of preventing 'the Inroads of the *Tartars*. This little depending Sovereign, 'finding he was now in a Condition to be troublesome, began to 'insist upon Terms, and threatned upon every Occasion to unite 'with the *Tartars*: Upon which the *Prime Minister*, who began to 'be in Pain about his *Head*, proposed a *Match* betwixt his Master 'and the only Daughter of this Tributary Lord, which he had the 'good Luck to bring to pass; and from that Time valued himself 'as Author of a most glorious *Union*, which indeed was grown of 'absolute Necessity by his Corruption.' This Passage, cited literally from an old History of *Sarmatia*, I thought fit to set down, on Purpose to perplex little smattering Remarkers, and put them upon the Hunt for an Application.

No. 20. *Thursday*, *December* 21, 1710.

——— *Pugnacem scirent sapiente minorem.*

I AM very much at a Loss how to proceed upon the Subject intended in this Paper, which a new Incident hath led me to engage in: The Subject I mean, is that of *Soldiers* and the *Army*; but being a Matter wholly out of my Trade, I shall handle it in as cautious a Manner as I am able.

IT is certain, that the Art of War hath suffered great Changes, almost in every Age and Country of the World; however, there are some Maxims relating to it, that will be eternal Truths, and which every reasonable Man must allow.

IN the early Times of *Greece* and *Rome*, the Armies of those States were composed of their Citizens, who took no Pay, because the Quarrel was their own; and therefore the War was usually decided in one Campaign; or, if it lasted longer, yet in Winter the Soldiers returned to their several Callings, and were not distinguished from the rest of the People. The *Gothick* Governments in *Europe*, although they were of Military Institution, yet observed almost the same Method. I shall Instance only in *England*. Those who held Lands in *Capite* of the King, were obliged to attend him in his Wars with a certain Number of Men, who all held Lands from them at easy Rents on that Condition. These fought without Pay; and when the Service was over, returned again to their Farms. It is recorded of *William Rufus*, that being absent in *Normandy*, and engaged in a War with his Brother, he ordered twenty thousand Men to be raised and sent over from hence to supply his Army; but having struck up a Peace before they were embarked, he gave them leave to disband, on Condition they would pay him ten Shillings a Man; which amounted to a mighty Sum in those Days.

CONSIDER a Kingdom as a great Family, whereof the Prince is the Father; and it will appear plainly, that Mercenary Troops are only *Servants armed*, either to awe the *Children* at home; or else to defend from Invaders, the Family who are otherwise employed, and chuse to contribute out of their Stock for paying their Defenders, rather than leave their Affairs to be neglected in their Absence. The Art of making Soldiery a Trade, and keeping Armies in Pay, seems in *Europe* to have had two Originals. The first was *Usurpation*, when popular Men destroyed the Liberties of their Country, and seized the Power into their own Hands; which they were forced to maintain by hiring Guards to bridle the People. Such were anciently the *Tyrants* in most of the small States of *Greece*; and such were those in several Parts of *Italy*, about three or four Centuries ago, as *Machiavel* informs us. The other Original of Mercenary Armies, seems to have risen from larger Kingdoms or Commonwealths, which had subdued Provinces at a Distance, and were forced to maintain Troops upon them, to prevent Insurrections from the Natives: Of this Sort were *Macedon*, *Carthage*, and *Rome* of old; *Venice* and *Holland* at this Day; as well as most Kingdoms of *Europe*. So that Mercenary Forces in a free State, whether *Monarchy* or *Commonwealth*, seem only necessary, either for preserving their Conquests (which in such Governments it is not prudent to extend too far) or else for maintaining a War at a Distance.

In this last, which at present is our most important Case, there are certain Maxims that all wise Governments have observed.

The first I shall mention is, That no *private* Man should have a Commission to be *General for Life*, let his Merit and Services be ever so great. Or, if a Prince be unadvisedly brought to offer such a Commission in one Hand, let him (to save Time and Blood) deliver up his *Crown* with the other. The *Romans*, in the Height and Perfection of their Government, usually sent out one of the new *Consuls* to be General against their most formidable Enemy, and recalled the old one, who often returned before the next Election; and according as he had Merit, was sent to command in some other Part; which, perhaps, was continued to him for a second, and sometimes a third Year. But if *Paulus Æmelius*, or *Scipio* himself, had presumed to move the *Senate* to continue their *Commissions for Life*, they certainly would have fallen a Sacrifice to the Jealousy of the People. *Cæsar* indeed (between whom and a *certain General*, some of late with much Discretion have made a *Parallel*) had his Command in *Gaul* continued to him for five Years, and was afterwards made perpetual *Dictator*; that is to say, *General for Life*, which gave him the Power and the Will of utterly destroying the *Roman* Liberty. But in his Time the *Romans* were very much degenerated; and great Corruptions had crept into their Morals and Discipline. However, we see there still were some Remains of a noble Spirit among them: For, when *Cæsar* sent to be chosen *Consul*, notwithstanding his Absence, they decreed he should come in Person, give up his Command, and *petere more majorum*.

It is not impossible but a *General* may desire such a Commission out of *Inadvertency*, at the *Instigation of his Friends*; or, perhaps of his *Enemies*; or, meerly for the *Benefit and Honour of it*, without intending any such *dreadful Consequences*; and in that Case, a wise Prince or State may barely refuse it without shewing any Marks of their Displeasure. But the Request in its own Nature is highly Criminal, and ought to be entered so upon Record, to terrify *Others* in Time to come from venturing to make it.

ANOTHER Maxim to be observed by a free State engaged in War, is to keep the Military Power in absolute Subjection to the Civil, nor ever suffer the former to influence or interfere with the latter. A General and his Army are *Servants*, *hired* by the Civil Power to act as they are directed from thence, and with a Commission large or limited as the Administration shall think fit; for which they are largely paid in Profit and Honour. The whole System by which Armies are governed, is quite *alien* from the peaceful Institutions of States at home; and if the Rewards be so inviting as to tempt a *Senator* to take a Post in the Army, whilst he is there on his Duty, he ought to consider himself in no other Capacity. I know not any Sort of Men so apt as Soldiers are, to reprimand those who presume to interfere in what relates to their Trade. When they hear any of us in a Coffee House, wondring that such a Victory was not pursued; complaining that such a Town cost more Men and Money than it was worth to take it; or that such an Opportunity was lost, of fighting the Enemy; they presently reprove us, and often with Justice enough, for meddling in Matters out of our Sphere; and clearly convince us of our Mistakes in Terms of Art that none of us understand. Nor do we escape so; for they reflect with the utmost Contempt on our Ignorance, that we who sit at home in Ease and Security, never stirring from our Fire-sides, should pretend from Books, and general Reason, to argue upon Military Affairs; which after all, if we may judge from the share of Intellectuals in some who are said to excel that Way, is not so very profound or difficult a Science. But, if there be any Weight in what they offer, as perhaps there may be a great deal; surely these Gentlemen have a much weaker Pretence to concern themselves in Matters of the Cabinet, which are always either far above, or much beside their Capacities. Soldiers may as well pretend to prescribe Rules for Trade; to determine Points in Philosophy; to be Moderators in an Assembly of Divines; or direct in a Court of Justice; as to misplace their Talent in examining Affairs of State, especially in what relates to the *Choice of Ministers*, who are never so likely to be ill chosen as when approved by them. It would be endless to shew how pernicious all Steps of this Nature have been in many Parts and Ages of the

World. I shall only produce two at present; one in *Rome*, and the other in *England*. The first is of *Cæsar*, when he came to the City with his Soldiers to *settle the Ministry*, there was an End of their Liberty for ever. The second was in the great Rebellion against King *Charles* the First. The King and both Houses were agreed upon the Terms of a Peace; but the Officers of the Army, (as *Ludlow* relates it) set a Guard upon the House of Commons, took a List of the Members, and kept all by Force out of the House, except those who were for bringing the King to a Tryal. Some Years after, when they erected a Military Government, and ruled the Island by *Major-Generals*, we received most admirable Instances of their Skill in Politicks. To say the Truth, such formidable Sticklers can have but two Reasons for desiring to interfere in the Administration; the first is that of *Cæsar* and *Cromwell*, of which, God forbid I should accuse or suspect any Body; since the second is pernicious enough, and that is, *To preserve those in Power who are for perpetuating a War, rather than see others advanced, who, they are sure, will use all proper Means to promote a safe and honourable Peace.*

THIRDLY, Since it is observed of Armies, that in the present Age they are brought to some Degree of Humanity, and a more regular Demeanour to each other, and to the World, than in former Times: It is certainly a good Maxim to endeavour preserving this Temper among them; without which, they would soon degenerate into *Savages*. To this End it would be prudent, among other Things, to forbid that detestable Custom of *drinking to the Damnation or Confusion* of any Person whatsoever.

SUCH desperate Acts, and the Opinions infused along with them, into Heads already inflamed by Youth and Wine, are enough to scatter Madness and Sedition through a whole Camp. So seldom *upon their Knees to Pray*, and so often to *Curse!* This is not properly Atheism, but a Sort of *Anti-Religion* prescribed by the Devil, and which an Atheist of common Sense would scorn as an Absurdity. I have heard it mentioned as a common Practice last Autumn, *somewhere or other*, to *drink Damnation and Confusion* (and this with Circumstances very aggravating and horrid) to the *New Ministry*, and to those who *had any Hand* in turning out the *Old*; that is to say, to those Persons whom her Majesty has thought fit to employ in her greatest Affairs; with something *more than a Glance against the Queen herself.* And if it be true, that these *Orgyes* were attended with certain *doubtful Words*, of *standing by their General*, who without Question abhorred them: Let any Man consider the Consequence of such Dispositions, if they should happen to spread. I could only wish, for the Honour of the Army, as well as of the Queen and Ministry, that a Remedy had been applied to the Disease, in the *Place* and *Time* where it grew. If Men of such Principles were able to propagate them in a Camp, and were sure of a *General for Life*, who had any Tincture of Ambition, we might soon bid farewel to Ministries and Parliaments, whether new or old.

I AM only sorry such an Accident hath happened towards the Close of a War, when it is chiefly the Interest of those Gentlemen who have Posts in the Army, to behave themselves in such a Manner as might encourage the Legislature to make some Provision for them, when there will be no further need of their Service. They are to consider themselves as Persons, by their Educations, unqualified for many other Stations of Life. Their Fortunes will not suffer them to retain to a Party after its *Fall*; nor have they Weight or Abilities to help towards its *Resurrection*. Their future Dependence is wholly upon the Prince and Parliament, to which they will never make their Way, by *solemn Execrations of the Ministry*; a Ministry of the Queen's own Election, and fully answering the Wishes of her People. This unhappy Step in some of *their Brethren*, may pass for an uncontroulable Argument, that Politicks are not their Business, or their Element. The Fortune of War hath raised several Persons up to swelling Titles, and great Commands over Numbers of Men, which they are too apt to transfer along with them into Civil Life, and appear in all Companies as if they were at the Head of their Regiments, with a Sort of Deportment that ought to have been dropt behind, in that short Passage to *Harwich*. It puts me in Mind of a Dialogue in *Lucian*, where *Charon* wafting one of their Predecessors over *Styx*, ordered him to strip off his Armour and fine Cloaths, yet still thought him too heavy; *but*, said he, *put off likewise that Pride and Presumption*; *those high swelling Words, and that vain Glory*; because they were of no Use on the other Side the

Water. Thus, if all that Array of Military Grandeur were confined to the proper Scene, it would be much more for the Interest of the Owners, and less offensive to their Fellow Subjects.

No. 21. *Thursday, December* 28, 1710.

Nam &, majorum instituta tueri sacris, cæremonisq; retinendis, sapientis est.

-------- *Ruituraq; semper*
Stat (mirum!) moles ------

WHOEVER is a true Lover of our Constitution, must needs be pleased to see what successful Endeavours are daily made to restore it in every Branch to its antient Form, from the languishing Condition it hath long lain in, and with such deadly Symptoms.

I HAVE already handled some Abuses during the *late Management*, and shall in convenient Time go on with the rest. Hitherto I have confined my self to those of the State; but with the good Leave of some who think it a Matter of small Moment, I shall now take Liberty to say something of the *Church*.

FOR several Years past, there hath not, I think, in *Europe*, been any Society of Men upon so unhappy a Foot, as the *Clergy* of *England*, or more hardly treated by those very Persons from whom they deserved much better Quarter, and in whose Power they chiefly had put it to use them so ill. I would not willingly misrepresent Facts; but I think it generally allowed by Enemies and Friends, that the bold and brave Defences made before the *Revolution* against those many Invasions of our Rights, proceeded principally from the Clergy; who are likewise known to have rejected all Advances made them to close with the Measures at that Time concerting; while the *Dissenters*, to gratify their Ambition and Revenge, fell into the basest Compliances with the Court; approved of all Proceedings by their numerous and fulsome Addresses; and took Employments and Commissions by Virtue of the dispensing Power, against the direct Laws of the Land. All this is so true, that if ever the *Pretender* come in, they will, next to those of his own Religion, have the fairest Claim and Pretensions to his Favour, from their Merit and eminent Services to his supposed Father, who without such Encouragement would probably never have been misled to go the Lengths he did. It should likewise be remembred to the everlasting Honour of the *London* Divines, that in those dangerous Times they Writ and Published the best Collection of Arguments against *Popery*, that ever appeared in the World. At the Revolution, the Body of the *Clergy* joined heartily in the common Cause (except a few, whose Sufferings perhaps have attoned for their Mistakes) like Men who are content to go about, for avoiding a Gulph or a Precipice, but come into the old strait Road again as soon as they can. But another Temper had now began to prevail. For, as in the Reign of King *Charles* the First, several well-meaning People were ready to join in reforming some Abuses; while others, who had deeper Designs, were still calling out for a *thorow Reformation*, which ended at last in the Ruin of the Kingdom; so, after the late King's coming to the Throne, there was a restless Cry from Men of *the same Principles*, for a *thorow Revolution*, which as *some* were carrying it on, must have ended in the Destruction of the Monarchy and Church.

WHAT a violent Humour hath run ever since against the Clergy, and from what Corner spread and fomented, is, I believe manifest to all Men. It looked like a set Quarrel against *Christianity*; and, if we call to mind several of the *Leaders*, it must in a great Measure have been actually so. Nothing was more common in Writing and Conversation, than to hear that Reverend Body charged in gross with what was utterly Inconsistent: Despised for their Poverty, hated for their Riches; reproached with Avarice, and taxed with Luxury; accused for promoting arbitrary Power, and resisting the Prerogative; censured for their Pride, and scorned for their Meanness of Spirit. The Representatives of the lower Clergy railed at for disputing the Power of the Bishops, by the known Abhorrers of Episcopacy; and abused for doing nothing in the Convocations, by those very Men who helped to bind up their Hands. The Vice, the Folly, the Ignorance of every single Man, were laid upon the Character. Their Jurisdiction, Censures and Discipline trampled under Foot, yet mighty Complaints against their excessive Power. The Men of Wit employed to turn the Priesthood it self into Ridicule. In short, groaning every where under the Weight of Poverty, Oppression, Contempt and Obloquy. A fair Return for the Time and Money spent in their Education to fit them for the Service of the Altar; and a fair Encouragement for worthy Men to come into the Church. However, it may be some Comfort for Persons of that Holy Function, that their Divine Founder, as well as His *Harbinger*, met with the like Reception. John *came neither eating nor drinking, and they say he hath a Devil; the Son of Man came eating and drinking, and they say, behold a Glutton and a Wine-bibber*, &c.

In this deplorable State of the Clergy, nothing but the Hand of Providence, working by its glorious Instrument, the QUEEN, could have been able to turn the Peoples Hearts so surprizingly in their Favour. This Princess, destined for the Safety of *Europe*, and a Blessing to her Subjects, began Her Reign with a noble Benefaction to the Church; and it was hoped, the Nation would have followed such an Example; which nothing could have prevented, but the false Politicks of a Set of Men, who form their Maxims upon those of every tottering Common-wealth, which is always struggling for Life, subsisting by Expedients, and often at the Mercy of every powerful Neighbour. These Men take it into their Imagination, that Trade can never flourish unless the Country becomes a common Receptacle for all Nations, Religions, and Languages; a System only proper for small popular States, but altogether unworthy; and below the Dignity of an Imperial Crown; which with us is best upheld by a Monarch in Possession of his just Prerogative, a Senate of Nobles and of Commons, and a Clergy established in its due Rights with a suitable Maintenance by Law. But these Men come with the Spirit of *Shop-keepers* to frame Rules for the Administration of Kingdoms; or, as if they thought the whole Art of Government consisted in the Importation of *Nutmegs*, and the Curing of *Herrings*. Such an Island as ours can afford enough to support the Majesty of a Crown, the Honour of a Nobility, and the Dignity of a Magistracy: We can encourage Arts and Sciences, maintain our Bishops and Clergy; and suffer our Gentry to live in a decent hospitable Manner; yet still there will remain Hands sufficient for Trade and Manufactures, which do always indeed deserve the best Encouragement, but not to a Degree of sending every living Soul into the *Warehouse* or the *Workhouse*.

THIS Pedantry of Republican Politicks hath done infinite Mischief among us: To this we owe those noble Schemes of treating Christianity as a System of *Speculative Opinions*, which no Man should be bound to believe; of making the *Being* and the Worship of God, a *Creature* of the State. In Consequence of these, that the Teachers of Religion ought to hold their Maintenance at Pleasure, or live by the Alms and charitable Collection of the People; and be equally encouraged of all Opinions: That, they should be *prescribed* what to teach, by those who are to learn from them; and upon Default, have a *Staff* and a *Pair of Shoes* left at their Door; with many other Projects of equal Piety, Wisdom, and Good Nature.

BUT, God be thanked, they and their Schemes are vanished, and *their Places shall know them no more*. When I think of that Inundation of Atheism, Infidelity, Prophaneness, and Licentiousness which were like to overwhelm us; from what Mouths and Hearts it first proceeded; and how the People joined with the QUEEN's Endeavours to divert this Flood; I cannot but reflect on that remarkable Passage in the *Revelations*, where *the Serpent with SEVEN Heads cast out of his Mouth Water after the Woman like a Flood, that he might cause Her to be carried away of the Flood: But the EARTH helped the Woman, and the Earth opened her Mouth, and swallowed up the Flood which the Dragon had cast out of his Mouth*. For, the QUEEN having changed her Ministry suitable to her own Wisdom, and the Wishes of her Subjects, and having called a Free Parliament; at the same Time summoned the Convocation, by Her Royal Writ, *as in all Times had been accustomed*: And soon after their Meeting, sent a most gracious Letter to the Archbishop of *Canterbury*, to be communicated to the Bishops and Clergy of his Province; taking Notice of *the loose and prophane Principles which had been openly scattered and propagated among her Subjects: That the Consultations of the Clergy were particularly requisite to repress and prevent such daring Attempts, for which her Subjects, from all Parts of the Kingdom have shewn their just*

Abhorrence. She *hopes, the Endeavours of the Clergy, in this Respect, will not be unsuccessful; and for Her Part, is ready to give them all fit Encouragement, to proceed in the Dispatch of such Business as properly belongs to them; and to grant them Powers requisite to carry on so good a Work*. In Conclusion, *earnestly recommending to them, to avoid Disputes; and determining to do all that in her lies to compose and extinguish them.*

It is to be hoped, that this last Part of Her Majesty's Letter, will be the first she will please to execute; for, it seems, this very Letter created the first Dispute. The Fact whereof was thus related: The Upper House having formed an Address to the QUEEN, before they received Her Majesty's Letter, sent both Address and Letter together, to the Lower House, with a Message, excusing their not mentioning the Letter in the Address, because *this* was formed before the *other* was received. The Lower House returned them, with a Desire, That an Address might be formed, with due Regard and Acknowledgments for the Letter. After some Difficulties, the same Address was sent down again with a Clause inserted, making some short mention of the said Letter. This the Lower House did not think sufficient, and sent it back again with the same Request: Whereupon the Archbishop, after a short Consultation with *some* of his Brethren, immediately adjourned the Convocation for a Month; and no Address at all was sent to the QUEEN.

I UNDERSTAND not Ecclesiastical Affairs well enough to comment upon this Matter; but it seems to me, that all Methods of doing Service to the Church and Kingdom, by Means of a *Convocation*, may be at any Time eluded, if there be no Remedy against such an Incident. And, if this Proceeding be agreeable to the Institution, *spiritual Assemblies* must needs be strangely contrived, very different from any *Lay Senate* yet known in the World. Surely from the Nature of such a *Synod*, it must be a very unhappy Circumstance, when the Majority of the Bishops draws one way, and that of the Lower Clergy another. The latter, I think, are not at this Time suspected for any Principles bordering upon those professed by Enemies to Episcopacy; and if they happen to differ from the greater Part of the *present Set* of Bishops, I doubt it will call *some Things* to mind, that may turn the Scale of general Favour on the inferior Clergies Side; who with a profound Duty to Her Majesty, are perfectly pleased with the *present Turn of Affairs*. Besides, *curious People* will be apt to enquire into the *Dates of some Promotions*; to call to mind what Designs were then upon the Anvil; and from thence make *malicious Deductions*. Perhaps they will observe the Manner of Voting on the Bishops Bench, and compare it with what shall pass in the Upper House of Convocation. There is, however, one Comfort, that under the present Dispositions of the Kingdom, a dislike to the Proceedings of any of their Lordships, even to the Number of a *Majority*, will be purely *Personal*, and not turned to the Disadvantage of the *Order*. And for my Part, as I am a true Lover of the Church, I had rather find the Inclinations of the People favourable to *Episcopacy* in general, than see a Majority of Prelates cryed up by those who are *known Enemies* to the Character. Nor, indeed, hath any Thing given me more Offence for several Years past, than to observe how *some* of that Bench have been caressed by *certain Persons*; and *others* of them openly celebrated by the infamous Pens of Atheists, Republicans, and Fanaticks.

TIME and *Mortality* can only remedy these Inconveniences in the Church, which are not to be cured, like those in the State, by a *Change of Ministry*. If we may guess the Temper of a *Convocation*, from the Choice of a *Prolocutor*, as it is usual to do that of a House of Commons by the *Speaker*; we may expect great Things from that Reverend Body, who have done themselves much Reputation, by pitching upon a *Gentleman* of so much Piety, Wit, and Learning, for that Office; and one who is so thoroughly versed in those Parts of Knowledge which are proper for it. I am sorry that the three *Latin* Speeches, delivered upon presenting the *Prolocutor*, were not made publick; they might perhaps have given us some Light into the Dispositions of each House: And besides, one of them is said to be so peculiar in the Style and Matter, as might have made up in *Entertainment*, what it wanted in *Instruction*.

No. 22. *Thursday, January* 4, 1710.

Nullæ sunt occultiores insidiæ, quam eæ quæ latent in simulatione officii, aut in aliquo necessitudinis nomine.

T*HE following Answer is written in the true Style, and with the usual Candour of such Pieces; which I have imitated to the best of my Skill; and doubt not but the Reader will be extreamly satisfied with it.*

The EXAMINER Cross-examined: *Or, A full Answer to the last* EXAMINER.

IF I durst be so bold with this Author, I would gladly ask him a familiar Question; *Pray, Sir, Who made you an Examiner?* He talks in one of his insipid Papers, of *eight or nine thousand Corruptions*, while *We* were at the Head of Affairs; yet, in all this Time he hath hardly produced fifty: *Parturiunt montes, &c.*——*Hor.* But I shall confine my self at present, to his last Paper. He tells us, *The Queen began her Reign with a noble Benefaction to the Church.* Here's *Priestcraft* with a Witness; this is the constant Language of your *High-Flyers*, to call those who are *hired* to teach *the Religion of the Magistrate*, by the Name of the *Church*. But this is not all; for in the very next Line he says, *It was hoped the Nation would have followed this Example.* You see the *Faction* begins already to speak out: This is an open Demand for the Abby-Lands; this furious Zealot would have us *Priest-ridden* again, like our Popish Ancestors: But, it is to be hoped the Government will take timely Care to suppress such audacious Attempts; else we have spent so much Blood and Treasure to very little Purpose, in maintaining *Religion* and *Revolution*. But what can we expect from a Man, who at one Blow endeavours to ruin our Trade? *A Country*, says he, *may flourish* (these are his own Words) *without being the common Receptacle for all Nations, Religions, and Languages.* What! We must immediately banish or murder the *Palatines*; forbid all Foreign Merchants, not only the *Exchange*, but the Kingdom; persecute the Dissenters with Fire and Faggot; and make it High Treason to speak any other Tongue but *English*. In another Place he talks of a *Serpent* with *seven Heads*, which is a manifest Corruption of the Text; for the Words *seven Heads* are not mentioned in that Verse. However, we know what *Serpent* he would mean; a *Serpent* with *fourteen Legs*; or, indeed, no *Serpent* at all, but seven great Men who were the *best Ministers*, the *truest Protestants*, and the most *disinterested Patriots* that ever served a Prince. But nothing is so inconsistent as this Writer; I know not whether to call him a Whig or a Tory, a Protestant or a Papist: He finds fault with Convocations; says, *they are Assemblies strangely contrived*; and yet lays the Fault upon Us, that we *bound their Hands*: I wish we could have bound their *Tongues* too; but as fast as their *Hands* were bound, they could make a Shift to hold their *Pens*, and have their Share in the Guilt of ruining the hopefullest Party and Ministry that ever *prescribed* to a Crown. This captious Gentleman is angry to *see a Majority of Prelates cried up by those who are Enemies to the Character*; now I always thought, that the Concessions of Enemies were more to a Man's Advantage than the Praise of his Friends. *Time and Mortality*, he says, *can only remedy these Inconveniencies in the Church*. That is, in other Words, When certain Bishops are dead, we shall have others of our own Stamp. Not so fast: You are not yet so sure of your Game. We have already got one *comfortable Loss* in *Spain*, although by a General of our own. For Joy of which, our Junta had a merry Meeting at the House of their great Proselyte, on the very Day we received the happy News. One or two more such *Blows* would, perhaps, set us right again; and then we can employ *Mortality* as well as others. He concludes with wishing, that *three Letters, spoke when the Prolocutor was presented, were made publick*. I suppose he would be content with *One*, and that is more than we shall humour him to grant. However, I hope he will allow it possible to have *Grace*, without either *Eloquence* or *Latin*; which is all I shall say to his malicious *Innuendo*.

HAVING thus, I hope, given a *full, satisfactory Answer* to the *Examiner*'s last Paper; I shall now go on to a more important Affair; which is, to prove, by several undeniable Instances, that the late Ministry, and their Abettors, were true Friends to the Church. It is yet, I confess, a Secret to the Clergy, wherein this

Friendship did consist. For Information therefore of that Reverend Body, that they may never forget their Benefactors, as well as of all others who may be equally ignorant; I have determined to display *our* Merits to the World upon that weighty Article. And I could wish, that what I am to say were to be written in Brass, for an eternal Memorial; the rather, because for the future, the Church must endeavour to stand unsupported by those Patrons, who expired in doing it their *last good Office*, and will never *rise* to preserve it any more.

LET us therefore produce the pious Endeavours of these Church-Defenders, who were its Patrons by their Power and Authority, as well as Ornaments of it by their Exemplary Lives.

First, ST. *Paul* tells us, *There must be Heresies in the Church, that the Truth may be manifest*; and therefore by due Course of reasoning, the more Heresies there are, the more *manifest* will the Truth be made. This being maturely considered by these Lovers of the Church, they endeavoured to propagate as many Heresies as they could, that the Light of Truth might shine the clearer.

Secondly, To shew their Zeal for the Church's Defence, they took the Care of it intirely out of the Hands of *God Almighty* (because that was a *foreign Jurisdiction*) and made it their own *Creature*, depending altogether upon them; and issued out their Orders to *Tindal*, and others, to give publick Notice of it.

Thirdly, BECAUSE *Charity* is the most celebrated of all Christian Virtues, therefore they extended theirs beyond all Bounds; and instead of shutting the Church against *Dissenters*, were ready to open it to all *Comers*, and *break down its Walls*, rather than that any should want room to enter. The Strength of a State, we know, consisteth in the Number of People, how different soever in their Callings; and why should not the Strength of a Church consist in the same, how different soever in their *Creeds?* For that Reason, they charitably attempted to abolish the Test, which tyed up so many Hands from getting Employments, in order to protect the Church.

I KNOW very well that this Attempt is objected to us as a Crime, by several *malignant Tories*; and denied as a Slander by many unthinking People among our selves. The latter are apt in their Defence to ask such Questions as these; *Was your Test re-*

pealed? Had we not a Majority? Might we not have done it if we pleased? To which the others answer, *You did what you could; you prepared the Way, but you found a fatal Impediment from that Quarter, whence the Sanction of the Law must come; and therefore to save your Credit, you condemned a Paper to be burnt which your selves had brought in.* But alas! The Miscarriage of that noble Project for the Safety of the Church, had another Original; the Knowledge whereof depends upon a Piece of secret History that I shall now lay open.

THESE Church Protectors had directed a *Presbyterian Preacher* to draw up a Bill for repealing the *Test*: It was accordingly done with great Art; and in the Preamble, several Expressions of Civility to the *established Church*; and when it came to the Qualifications of all those who were to enter on any Office, the Compiler had taken special Care to make them large enough for all *Christians* whatsoever, by transcribing the very Words (only formed into an *Oath*) which *Quakers* are obliged to profess by a former Act of Parliament; as I shall here set them down. *I* A. B. *profess Faith in God the Father, and in Jesus Christ his eternal Son, the true God; and in the Holy Spirit, one God blessed for ever more; and do acknowledge the holy Scriptures of the Old and New Testament to be given by divine Inspiration.* This Bill was carried to the chief Leaders for their Approbation, with these terrible Words turned into an Oath: What should they do? Those few among them who fancied they believed in *God*, were sure they did not believe in *Christ*, or the *Holy Spirit*, or one Syllable of the *Bible*; and they were as sure that every Body knew their Opinion in those Matters, which indeed they had been always too sincere to Disguise; how therefore could they take such an Oath as that, without ruining their Reputation with *Tindal*, *Toland*, *Coward*, *Collins*, *Clendon*, and all the Tribe of *Free-Thinkers*; and so *give a Scandal to weak Unbelievers*. Upon this nice Point of Honour and Conscience the Matter was hushed, the Project for repealing the *Test* let fall, and the *Sacrament* left as the smaller Evil of the two.

Fourthly, These Pillars of the Church, because *the Harvest was great, and the Labourers few*, and because they would ease the Bishops from that grievous Trouble of *laying on Hands*; were willing to allow that Power to all men whatsoever, to prevent that terrible Consequence of *unchurching* those, who thought a Hand from under a *Cloak*, as effectual as from *Lawn-Sleeves*. And indeed, what could more contribute to the Advancement of true Religion, than a Bill of General *Naturalization for Priesthood?*

Fifthly, IN order to fix Religion in the Minds of Men, because Truth never appears so fair as when confronted with Falshood; they directed Books to be Published, that denied the Being of a God, the Divinity of the *Second* and *Third Person*, the Truth of all Revelation, and the Immortality of the Soul. To this we owe that great Sense of Religion, that Respect and Kindness to the Clergy, and that true Love of Virtue so manifest of late Years among the Youth of our Nation. Nor could any Thing be more Discreet, than to leave the Merits of each Cause to such wise impartial Judges, who might otherwise fall under the Slavery of believing by *Education* and *Prejudice*.

Sixthly, BECAUSE nothing so much distracts the Thoughts, as too great Variety of Subjects; therefore they had kindly prepared a Bill, to prescribe the Clergy what Subjects they should Preach upon, and in what Manner, that they might be at no Loss; and this, no doubt, was a proper Work for such Hands, so thoroughly versed in the Theory and Practice of all Christian Duties.

Seventhly, TO save Trouble and Expence to the Clergy, they contrived that *Convocations* should meet as seldom as possible; and when they were suffered to assemble, would never allow them to meddle with any Business; because they said, the Office of a Clergyman was enough to take up the *whole Man*. For the same Reason they were very desirous to excuse the Bishops from sitting in Parliament, that they might be at more Leisure to stay at Home and look after the Clergy.

I SHALL mention at present but one more Instance of their pious Zeal for the Church. They had somewhere heard the Maxim, that *Sanguis Martyrum est Semen Ecclesiæ*; therefore, in order to *sow this Seed*, they began with *Impeaching a Clergyman*: And that it might be a true Martyrdom in every Circumstance, they proceeded as much as possible against common Law; which the *long-Robe Part* of the *Managers* knew was in a hundred Instances directly contrary to all their Positions, and *were sufficiently warned of it before-hand*; but their Love of the Church prevailed. Neither was this Impeachment an Affair taken up on a sudden. For, a certain great Person, (whose Character hath been lately Published by some stupid and lying Writer) who very much distinguished himself by his Zeal in forwarding this *Impeachment*, had several Years ago endeavoured to persuade the late King to give way to just such another Attempt. He told his Majesty, there was a certain Clergyman preached very dangerous Sermons, and that the only Way to put a Stop to such Insolence, was to Impeach him in Parliament. The King enquired the Character of the Man; *O Sir*, said my Lord, *the most violent, hot, positive Fellow in* England; *so extreamly wilful, that I believe he would be heartily glad to be a Martyr*. The King answered, *Is it so? Then I am resolved to disappoint him*; and would never hear more of the Matter; by which that hopeful Project unhappily miscarried.

I HAVE hitherto confined my self to those Endeavours for the good of the Church, which were common to all the Leaders and Principal Men of *Our* Party; but if my Paper were not drawing towards an End, I could produce several Instances of particular Persons, who by their exemplary Lives and Actions have confirmed the Character so justly due to the whole Body. I shall at present mention only two, and illustrate the Merits of each by a Matter of Fact.

THAT worthy Patriot and *true Lover* of the Church, whom a *late Examiner* is supposed to reflect on under the Name of *Verres*, felt a pious Impulse to be a Benefactor to the Cathedral of *Gloucester*; but how to do it in the most decent, generous Manner, was the Question. At last he thought of an Expedient: One Morning or Night he stole into the Church, mounted upon the Altar, and there did that which in cleanly Phrase is called *disburthening of Nature*: He was discovered, prosecuted, and condemned to pay a thousand *Pounds*; which Sum was all employed to *support the Church*, as no doubt, the *Benefactor* meant it.

THERE is another Person whom the same Writer is thought to point at under the Name of *Will Bigamy*. This Gentleman, knowing that Marriage Fees were a considerable Perquisite to the Clergy, found out a Way of improving them *Cent. per Cent.* for the *good of the Church*. His Invention was to marry a second Wife while the first was alive; convincing her of the Lawfulness by such Arguments, as he did not doubt would make others follow the same Example: These he had drawn up in Writing with Intention to publish for the *general Good*; and it is hoped he may *now* have Leisure to finish them.

No. 23. *Thursday, January* 11, 1710.

Bellum ita suscipiatur, ut nihil aliud nisi Pax quæsita videatur.

I AM satisfied, that no reasonable Man of either Party, can justly be offended at any Thing I said in one of my Papers relating to the Army: From the Maxims I there laid down, perhaps many Persons may conclude, that I had a mind the World should think, there had been Occasion given by some late Abuses among Men of that Calling; and they conclude right. For my Intention is, that my Hints may be understood, and my Quotations and Allegories applied; and I am in some Pain to think that in the *Orcades* on one Side, and the *Western* Coasts of *Ireland* on the other, the *Examiner* may want a *Key* in several Parts, which I wish I could furnish them with. As for the *French* King, I am under no concern at all; I hear he hath left off reading my Papers, and by what he hath found in them, dislikes our Proceedings more than ever; and intends either to make great Additions to his Armies, or propose new Terms for a Peace: So false is that which is commonly reported, of his mighty Satisfaction in our Change of Ministry: And I think it clear that his late Letter of Thanks to the *Tories* of *Great-Britain*, must either have been extorted from him against his Judgment; or was a Cast of his Politicks to set the People against the present Ministry; wherein it hath *wonderfully* succeeded.

BUT, although I have never heard, or never regarded any Objections made against that Paper, which mentions the Army; yet I intended this as a Sort of Apology for it. And first, I declare, (because we live in a mistaking World) that in hinting at some Proceedings, wherein a few Persons are said to be concerned, I did not intend to charge them upon the Body of the Army. I have too much detested that barbarous Injustice among the Writers of a late Party, to be ever guilty of it my self; I mean the accusing Societies for the Crimes of a few. On the other Side, I must take Leave to believe, that Armies are no more exempt from Corruptions than other Numbers of Men. The Maxims proposed were occasionally introduced by the Report of certain Facts, which I am bound to believe is true, because I am sure, considering what hath passed, it would be a Crime to think otherwise. All Posts in the Army; all Employments at Court, and many others, are (*or ought to be*) given and resumed at the meer Pleasure of the Prince; yet when I see a great Officer broke, a Change made in the Court, or the Ministry, and this under the most just and gracious Princess that ever reigned; I must naturally conclude it is done upon prudent Considerations, and for some great Demerit in the Sufferers. But then, is not the Punishment sufficient? Is it Generous or Charitable to trample on the Unfortunate, and expose their Faults to the World in the strongest Colours? And would it not suit better with Magnanimity as well as common good Nature, to leave them at quiet to their own Thoughts and Repentance? Yes, without Question, provided it could be so contrived, that their very Names, as well as Actions, might be forgotten for ever: *Such* an Act of Oblivion would be for the Honour of our Nation, and beget a better Opinion of us with Posterity; and then I might have spared the World and my self the Trouble of *Examining*. But, at present, there is a cruel *Dilemma* in the Case: The Friends and Abettors of the late Ministry are every Day publishing their Praises to the World, and casting Reflections upon the present Persons in Power. This is so barefaced an Aspersion upon the Queen, that I know not how any good Subject can with Patience endure it, although he were ever so indifferent with Regard to the Opinions in Dispute. Shall they who have lost all Power and Love of the People, be allowed to scatter their Poison; and shall not those, who are, at least, of the strongest Side, be suffered to bring an Antidote? And how can we undeceive the deluded Remainder, but by letting them see, that those discarded Statesmen were justly laid aside; and producing as many Instances to prove it as we can? Not from any personal Hatred to them, but in Justification to the best of Queens. The many Scurrilities I have heard and read against this poor Paper of mine, are in such a Strain, that considering the present State of Affairs, they look like a Jest. They usually run after the following Manner: *What? Shall this insolent Writer presume to censure the late Ministry, the ablest, the most faithful, and truest Lovers of their Country, and its Constitution, that ever served a Prince? Shall he reflect on the best House of Commons that ever sate within those Walls? Hath not the Queen changed both for a Ministry and Parliament of* Jacobites *and* High-flyers, *who are selling us to* France, *and bringing over the* Pretender? This is the very Sum and Force of all their Reasonings, and this their Method of complaining against the *Examiner*. In *Them* it is humble and loyal to reflect upon the Queen, and the Ministry, and Parliament she hath chosen with the universal Applause of her People: In *Us* it is insolent to defend her Majesty and her Choice; or to answer their Objections, by shewing the Reasons why those Changes were necessary.

THE same Style hath been used in the late Case concerning some Gentlemen in the Army: Such a Clamour was raised by a Set of Men, who had the Boldness to tax the Administration with Cruelty and Injustice, that I thought it necessary to interfere a little, by shewing the ill Consequences that might arise from some Proceedings, although without Application to particular Persons. And what do they offer in Answei? Nothing but a few poor Common-places against *Calumny* and *Informers*; which might have been full as just and seasonable in a Plot against the Sacred Person of the Queen.

BUT, by the Way; why are these idle People so indiscreet to name those *two Words*, which afford Occasion of laying open to the World such an infamous Scene of *Subornation* and *Perjury*, as well as *Calumny* and *Informing*, as I believe is without Example: When a whole *Cabal* attempted an *Action*, wherein a * *condemned Criminal* refused to join with them for the Reward of his Life? Not that I disapprove their Sagacity, who could foretel so long before, by what *Hand* they should one Day fall; and therefore thought any Means justifiable by which they might prevent it.

BUT waving this at present; it must be owned in Justice to the

* Greg.

Army, that those Violences did not proceed so far among them as some have believed; nor ought the Madness of a *Few* to be laid at their Doors. For the rest, I am so far from denying the due Praises to those victorious Troops, who did their Part in procuring so many Victories for the *Allies*; that I could wish every Officer and private Soldier had their full Share of Honour in proportion to their Deserts; being thus far of the *Athenian*'s Mind, who when it was proposed that the Statue of *Miltiades* should be set up *alone* in some publick Place of the City; said, they would agree to it, *whenever he conquered alone*, but not before. Neither do I at all blame the Officers of the Army, for preferring in their Hearts the late Ministry before the present; or, if wishing alone could be of any Use, to wish their Continuance; because then they might be secure of the Wars Continuance too: Whereas, since Affairs have been put into other Hands, they may perhaps lie under some Apprehensions of a Peace; which no Army, especially in a Course of Success, was ever inclined to; and which all wise States have in such a Juncture, chiefly endeavoured. This is a Point wherein the Civil and Military Politicks have always disagreed. And for that Reason, I affirmed it necessary in all free Governments, that the latter should be absolutely in Subjection to the former; otherwise, one of these two Inconveniencies must arise; either to be perpetually in War, or to turn the *Civil* Institution into a *Military*.

I AM ready to allow all that hath been said of the Valour and Experience of our Troops, who have fully contributed their Part to the great Successes abroad; nor is it their *Fault*, that those important Victories had no better Consequences at home, although it may be their *Advantage*. War is their Trade and Business: To improve and cultivate the Advantages of Success, is an Affair of the Cabinet; and the Neglect of this, whether proceeding from Weakness or Corruption, according to the usual Uncertainty of Wars, may be of the most fatal Consequence to a Nation. For, pray let me represent our Condition in such a Light, as I believe both Parties will allow, although perhaps not the Consequences I shall deduce from it. We have been for above nine Years blest with a QUEEN, who, besides all Virtues that can enter into the Composition of a private Person, possesseth every regal Quality that can contribute to make a People happy: Of great Wisdom, yet ready to receive the Advice of her Councellors: Of much Discernment in chusing proper Instruments, when she follows her own Judgment; and only capable of being deceived by that excess of Goodness, which makes her judge of others by herself. Frugal in her Management, in Order to contribute to the Publick, which in Proportion she doth, and that voluntarily, beyond any of her Subjects; but from her own Nature, generous and charitable to all who want or deserve; and in order to exercise those Virtues, denying herself all Entertainments of Expence, which many others enjoy. Then, if we look abroad, at least in *Flanders*, our Arms have been crowned with perpetual Success in Battles and Sieges; not to mention several fortunate Actions in *Spain*. These Facts being thus stated, which none can deny; it is natural to ask, how we have improved such Advantages, and to what Account they have turned? I shall Use no discouraging Terms. When a Patient grows daily worse by the tampering of Mountebanks, there is nothing left but to call in the best Physicians before the Case grows desperate: But I would ask whether *France*, or any other Kingdom, would have made so little Use of such prodigious Opportunities; the Fruits whereof could never have fallen to the Ground, without the extreamest Degree of Folly and Corruption; and where those have lain, let the World judge: Instead of aiming at Peace, while we had the Advantage of the War, which hath been the perpetual Maxim of all wise States; it hath been reckoned Factious and Malignant even to express our Wishes for it; and such a Condition imposed, as was never offered to any Prince who had an Inch of Ground to dispute; *Quæ enim est conditio pacis; in qua ei cum quo pacem facias, nihil concedi potest?*

It is not obvious to conceive what could move Men who sate at Home, and were called to consult upon the Good of the Kingdom, to be so utterly averse from putting an End to a long expensive War, which the victorious, as well as conquered Side, were heartily weary of. Few, or none of them were Men of the Sword; they had no Share in the Honour; they had made large Fortunes, and were at the Head of all Affairs. But, they well knew by what Tenure they held their Power; that the Queen saw through their Designs; that they had entirely lost the Hearts of the Clergy; that the Landed Men were against them; that they were detested by the Body of the People; and that nothing bore them up but their Credit with the Bank and other Stocks, which would be neither formidable nor necessary when the War was at an End. For these Reasons they resolved to disappoint all Overtures of a Peace, until they and their Party should be so deeply rooted as to make it impossible to shake them. To this End they began to precipitate Matters so fast, as in a little Time must have ruined the Constitution, if the Crown had not interposed, and rather ventured the accidental Effects of their Malice, than such dreadful Consequences of their Power. And indeed, if the former Danger had been greater than some hoped or feared, I see no Difficulty in the Choice; which was the same with his, who said, *he had rather be devoured by Wolves than by Rats*. I therefore still insist that we cannot wonder at, or find Fault with the Army, for concurring with a Ministry who was for prolonging the War. The Inclination is natural in them all; pardonable in those who have not yet made their Fortunes, and as lawful in the rest, as Love of Power or Love of Money can make it. But, as natural, as pardonable, and as lawful as this Inclination is, when it is not under Check of the Civil Power, or when a corrupt Ministry joins in giving it too great a Scope; the Consequence can be nothing less than infallible Ruin and Slavery to a State.

AFTER I had finished this Paper, the Printer sent me two small Pamphlets, called, *The Management of the War*, written with some Plausibility, much Artifice, and Abundance of Misrepresentation, as well as direct Falshoods in Point of Fact. These I have thought worth *Examining*, which I shall accordingly do when I find an Opportunity.

No. 24. *Thursday*, *January* 18, 1710.

Parva momenta in spem metumq; impellunt animos.

HOPES are natural to most Men, especially to sanguine Complexions; and, among the various Changes that happen in the Course of publick Affairs, they are seldom without some Grounds: Even in desperate Cases, where it is impossible they should have any Foundation, they are often affected to keep a Countenance, and make an Enemy think we have some Resource which they know nothing of. This appears to have been for several Months past the Condition of those People, whom I am forced for want of other Phrases, to call the *Ruined Party*. They have taken up since their Fall, some real and some pretended Hopes. When the Earl of *Sunderland* was discarded, they hoped Her Majesty would proceed no farther in the Change of Her Ministry; and had the Insolence to misrepresent Her Words to Foreign States. They *hoped* no Body durst advise the Dissolution of the Parliament: When this was done, and further Alterations made at Court, they *hoped* and endeavoured to ruin the Credit of the Nation. They likewise *hoped* that we should have some terrible Loss Abroad, which would force us to unravel all, and begin again upon their Bottom. But, of all their *Hopes*, whether real or assumed, there is none more extraordinary than that which they now would seem to place their whole Confidence in: That this great Turn of Affairs was only occasioned by a short Madness of the People, from which they will recover in a little Time, when their Eyes are open, and they grow cool and sober enough to consider the Truth of Things, and how much they have been deceived. It is not improbable, that some few of the deepest sighted among these Reasoners, are well enough convinced how vain all such *Hopes* must be: But for the rest, the wisest of them seem to have been very ill Judges of the People's Dispositions, the Want of which Knowledge was a principal Occasion to hasten their Ruin: For surely had they suspected which Way the popular Current inclined, they never would have run against it by that *Impeachment*. I therefore conclude, they generally are so blind, as to imagine some Comfort from this fantastical Opinion, that the People of *England* are at present distracted, but will shortly come to their Senses again.

FOR the Service therefore of our Adversaries, and Friends, I shall briefly *Examine* this Point, by shewing what are the Causes and Symptoms of a People's Madness; and how it differs from their natural Bent and Inclination.

IT is *Machiavel*'s Observation, that the People, when left to their own Judgment, do seldom mistake their true Interests; and indeed they naturally love the Constitution they are born under; never desiring to change but under great Oppressions. However, they are to be deceived by several Means. It hath often happened in *Greece*, and sometimes in *Rome*, that those very Men who have contributed to shake off a former Tyranny, have, instead of restoring the old Constitution, deluded the People into a worse and more ignominious Slavery. Besides, all great Changes have the same Effect upon Commonwealths that Thunder hath upon Liquors; making the *Dregs* fly up to the Top: The lowest *Plebeians* rise to the Head of Affairs, and there preserve themselves by representing the Nobles and other Friends to the old Government, as Enemies to the Publick. The encouraging of new Mysteries and new Deities, with the Pretences of further Purity in Religion, hath likewise been a frequent Topick to mislead the People. And, not to mention more, the promoting false Reports of Dangers from Abroad, hath often served to prevent them from fencing against real Dangers at Home. By these and the like Arts, in Conjunction with a great Depravity of Manners, and a weak or corrupt Administration, the Madness of the People hath risen to such a Height, as to break in Pieces the whole Frame of the best instituted Governments. But however, such great Frenzies being artificially raised, are a perfect Force and Constraint upon human Nature; and under a wise steddy Prince, will certainly decline of themselves; settling like the Sea after a Storm; and then the true Bent and Genius of the People will appear. Ancient and Modern Story are full of Instances to illustrate what I say. In our own Island we had a great Example of a long Madness in the People, kept up by a thousand Artifices like intoxicating Medicines, until the Constitution was destroyed; yet the Malignity being spent, and the Humour exhausted that served to foment it; before the Usurpers could fix upon a new Scheme, the People suddenly recovered, and peaceably restored the old Constitution.

FROM what I have offered, it will be easy to decide, whether this late Change in the Dispositions of the People were a new Madness, or a Recovery from an old One. Neither do I see how it can be proved that such a Change had in any Circumstance the least Symptoms of Madness, whether my Description of it be right or no. It is agreed, that the truest Way of judging the Dispositions of the People in the Choice of their Representatives, is by computing the County Elections; and in these it is manifest, that five in six are entirely for the present Measures; although the Court was so far from interposing its Credit, that there was no Change in the Admiralty, nor above one or two in the Lieutenancy; nor any other Methods used to influence Elections. The free unextorted Addresses sent some Time before from every Part of the Kingdom, plainly shewed what Sort of Bent the People had taken, and from what Motives. The Election of Members for this great City, carried contrary to all Conjecture against the united Interest of those two great Bodies, the *Bank* and *East-India Company*, was another convincing Argument. Besides, the *Whigs* themselves have always confessed, that the Bulk of Landed Men in *England* was generally of *Tories*. So that this Change must be allowed to be according to the natural Genius and Disposition of the People; whether it were just and reasonable in it self or no.

NOTWITHSTANDING all which, you shall frequently hear the Partisans of the late Men in Power, gravely and decisively pronounce, that the present Ministry cannot possibly stand. Now, they who affirm this, if they believe themselves, must ground their Opinion upon the Iniquity of the *last* being so far established, and deeply rooted, that no Endeavours of honest Men, will be able to restore Things to their former State. Or else these Reasoners have been so misled by twenty Years Mismanagement, that they have forgot our Constitution, and talk as if our Monarchy and Revolution began together. But, the Body of the People is wiser; and by the Choice they have made, shew they do understand our Constitution, and would bring it back to the old Form; which if the new Ministers take care to maintain, they will and ought to stand; otherwise they may fall like their Predecessors. But I think, we may easily foresee what a Parliament freely chosen, without Threatning or Corruption, is likely to do, when no Man shall be in any Danger to lose his *Place* by the Freedom of his *Voice*.

BUT, who are those Advancers of this Opinion, that the present Ministry cannot hold? It must be either such as are afraid to be called to an Account, in case it should hold; or those who keep Offices, from which others, better Qualified, were removed; and may reasonably apprehend to be turned out, for worthier Men to come into their Places; since perhaps it will be necessary to make some Changes, that the publick Business of the Nation may go on: Or lastly, *Stock-jobbers*, who industriously spread such Reports, that Actions may fall, and their Friends buy to Advantage.

YET these Hopes, thus freely expressed, as they are more sincere, so they are more supportable, than when they appear under the Disguise and Pretence of Fears. Some of these Gentlemen are employed to shake their Heads in proper Companies; to doubt where all This will end; to be in mighty Pain for the Nation; to shew how impossible it is, that the Publick Credit can be supported: To pray that all may do well in whatever Hands; but very much to doubt that the *Pretender* is at the Bottom. I know not any Thing so nearly resembling this Behaviour, as what I have often seen among the Friends of a Sick Man, whose Interest it is that he should die: The Physicians protest they sell no Danger; the Symptoms are good, the Medicines answer Expectation; yet still they are not to be Comforted; they whisper, he is a gone Man; it is not possible he should hold out; he hath perfect Death in his Face; they never liked this Doctor: At last the Patient recovers, and their Joy is as false as their Grief.

I BELIEVE there is no Man so Sanguine, who did not apprehend some ill Consequences from the late Change, although not in any Proportion to the good Ones: But it is manifest, the Former have proved much fewer and lighter than were expected, either at Home or Abroad, by the Fears of our Friends, or the Hopes of our Enemies. Those Remedies that stir the Humours in a diseased Body, are at first more painful than the Malady it self; yet certain Death is the Consequence of deferring them too long. Actions have fallen, and the Loans are said to come in slowly. But beside, that something of this must have been, whether there had been any Change or no; beside, that the Surprize of every Change, for the better as well as the worse, is apt to affect Credit for a while; there is a further Reason, which is plain and scandalous. When the late Party was at the Helm; those who were called the *Tories*, never put their Resentments in Ballance with the Safety of the Nation; but chearfully contributed to the Common Cause. Now the Scene is changed, the fallen Party seems to act from very different Motives: They have *given the Word about*; they will keep their Money and be passive; and in this Point stand upon the same Foot with *Papists* and *Nonjurors*. What would have become of the Publick, if the present great Majority had acted thus, during the late Administration? Had acted thus, before the others were Masters of that Wealth they have squeezed out of the Landed Men, and with the Strength of that, would now hold the Kingdom at Defiance.

THUS much I have thought fit to say, without pointing Reflections upon any particular Person; which I have hitherto but sparingly done, and that only towards those whose Characters are too profligate, that the Managing of them should be of any Consequence: Besides, as it is a Talent I am not naturally fond of, so, in the Subjects I treat, it is generally needless. If I display the Effects of Avarice and Ambition, of Bribery and Corruption, of gross Immorality and Irreligion; those who are the least conversant in Things, will easily know where to apply them. Not that I lay any Weight upon the Objections of such who charge me with this Proceeding: It is notorious enough that the Writers of the other Side were the first Aggressors. Not to mention their scurrilous Libels many Years ago, directly levelled at particular Persons; how many Papers do now come out every Week, full of rude Invectives against the present Ministry, with the first and last Letters of their Names to prevent Mistakes? It is good sometimes to let these People see, that we neither want Spirit nor Materials to retaliate; and therefore in this Point *alone* I shall follow their Example, whenever I find my self sufficiently provoked; only with one Addition, that whatever Charges I bring, either general or particular, shall be religiously true, either upon avowed Facts which none can deny, or such as I can prove from my own Knowledge.

BEING resolved publickly to confess any Mistakes I have been guilty of; I do here humbly desire the Readers Pardon for one of mighty Importance, about a Fact in one of my Papers, said to be done in the Cathedral of *Gloucester*. A whole *Hydra* of Errors in two Words: For as I am since informed, it was neither in the Cathedral, nor City, nor County of *Gloucester*, but some other Church of that Diocess. If I had ever met any other Objection of Equal Weight, although from the meanest Hands, I should certainly have answered it.

No. 25. *Thursday, January* 25, 1710.

Διαλεξάμενοι τινὰ ἡσυχῆ, τὸ μὲν συμπαν ἐπί τε τῆ δυναζεια καὶ καλὰ τῶν ἐχθρῶν συνώμοσαν.

Summissa quædam voce collocuti sunt; quorum summa erat de dominatione sibi confirmanda, ac inimicis delendis conjuratio.

NOT many Days ago I observed a Knot of discontented Gentlemen cursing the *Tories* to Hell for their Uncharitableness, in affirming, that if the late Ministry had continued to this Time, we should have had neither *Church* nor *Monarchy* left. They are usually so candid as to call that the Opinion of a Party, which they hear in a Coffee-house, or over a Bottle from some warm young People, whom it is odds but they have provoked to say more than they believed, by some Positions as absurd and ridiculous of their own. And so it proved in this very Instance: For, asking one of these Gentlemen, what it was that provoked those he had been disputing with, to advance such a Paradox? He assured me in a very calm Manner, it was nothing in the World, but that himself and some others of the Company had made it appear, that the Design of the present Parliament and Ministry, was to bring in *Popery, Arbitrary Power*, and the *Pretender*: Which I take to be an Opinion fifty Times more improbable, as well as more uncharitable, than what is charged upon the *Whigs*: Because I defy our Adversaries to produce one single Reason for suspecting such Designs in the Persons now at the Helm; whereas I can upon Demand produce twenty to shew, that some late Men had strong Views towards a *Commonwealth*, and the Alteration of the *Church*.

IT is natural indeed, when a Storm is over, that hath only untiled our Houses, and blown down some of our Chimnies; to consider what further Mischiefs might have ensued, if it had lasted longer. However, in the present Case, I am not of the Opinion above-mentioned; I believe the Church and State might have lasted *somewhat longer*, although the late Enemies to both had done their worst: I can hardly conceive how Things would have been so soon ripe for a new Revolution. I am convinced, that if they had offered to make such large and sudden Strides, it must have come to Blows; and, according to the Computation we have now Reason to think a right One, I can partly guess what would have been the Issue. Besides we are sure, the Queen would have interposed before they came to Extremities; and as little as they regarded the Regal Authority, would have been a Check in their Career.

BUT instead of this Question; What would have been the Consequence if the late Ministry had continued? I will propose another, which will be more useful for us to consider; and that is, *What we may reasonably expect They will do, if ever they come into Power again?* This, we know, is the Design and Endeavour of all those Scribbles which daily fly about in their Favour; of all the false, insolent, and scandalous Libels against the present Administration; and of all those Engines set at work to sink the *Actions*, and blow up the publick Credit. As for those who shew their Inclinations by writing, there is one Consideration, which I wonder doth not sometimes affect them: For, how can they forbear having a good Opinion of the Gentleness and Innocence of those, who permit them to employ their Pens as they do? It puts me in mind of an insolent pragmatical Orator somewhere in *Greece*, who railing with great Freedom at the chief Men in the State; was answered by one who had been very instrumental in recovering the Liberty of the City; That *he thanked the Gods, they had now arrived to the Condition he always wished them; when every Man in that City might securely say what he pleased.* I wish these Gentlemen would however compare the Liberty they take, with what their Masters used to give: How many Messengers and Warrants would have gone out against any who durst have opened their Lips, or drawn their Pens, against the Persons and

Proceedings of their *Junta*'s and *Cabals?* How would their weekly Writers have been calling out for *Prosecution* and *Punishment?* We remember when a poor Nick-name, borrowed from an old Play of *Ben. Johnson*, and mentioned in a Sermon without any particular Application; was made use of as a Motive to spur on an Impeachment. But after all, it must be confest, they had Reasons to be thus severe, which their Successors have not: Their Faults would never endure the Light; and to have exposed them sooner, would have raised the Kingdom against the Actors, before the proper Time.

BUT, to come to the Subject I have now undertaken; which is to Examine what the Consequences would be, upon Supposition that the *Whigs* were now restored to their Power. I already imagine the present free Parliament dissolved, and another of a different Epithet met, by the Force of Money and Management. I read immediately a Dozen or two stinging Votes against the Proceedings of the late Ministry. *The Bill now to be repealed would then be re-enacted, and the Birth-right of an *Englishman* reduced again to the Value of Twelve-pence. But, to give the Reader a stronger Imagination of such a Scene, let me represent the Designs of some Men, lately endeavoured and projected; in the Form of a Paper of Votes.

Ordered, *That a Bill be brought in for repealing the* Sacramental Test.

A Petition of Tindal, Collins, Clendon, Coward, Toland, *in Behalf of themselves and many Hundreds of their Disciples, some of which are Members of this Honourable House, desiring, that Leave be given to bring in a Bill for qualifying* Atheists, Deists *and* Socinians, *to serve their Country in any Employment, Ecclesiastical, Civil, or Military.*

Ordered, *That Leave be given to bring in a Bill according to the Prayer of the said Petition, and that Mr.* Lechmere *do prepare and bring it in.*

Ordered, *That a Bill be brought in for removing the Education of Youth out of the Hands of the Clergy.*

* *A Bill for a general Naturalization.*

Another, *To forbid the Clergy preaching certain Duties in* Religion, *especially* Obedience to Princes.

Another, *to take away the Jurisdiction of Bishops.*

Another, *for constituting a General* for Life; *with Instructions to the Committee, that Care may be taken to make the War last as long as the Life of the said General.*

A Bill *of Attainder against* James *Duke of* Ormonde; John *Duke of* Buckingham; Lawrence *Earl of* Rochester; *Sir* Simon Harcourt, *Knight*; Robert Harley, Henry St. John, *Esqrs.* Abigail Masham, *and others, for High Treason against the* Junta.

Resolved, *That* Sarah *Dutchess of* Marlborough, *hath been a most dutiful, just, and grateful Servant to her Majesty.*

Resolved, *That to advise the Dissolution of a* Whig *Parliament, or the Removal of a* Whig *Ministry, was in order to bring in* Popery *and the* Pretender; *and that the said Advice was High Treason.*

Resolved, *That by the* Original Contract *the Government of this Realm is by a* Junta, *and a* King *or* Queen; *but the* Administration *solely in the* Junta.

Ordered, *That it be a standing Order of this House, that the Merit of Elections be not determined by the Number of Voices, or Right of Electors; but by Weight; and that one* Whig *shall weigh down ten* Tories.

A Motion being made, and the Question being put, that when a Whig *is detected of manifest Bribery, and his Competitor being a* Tory, *hath Ten to One a Majority, there shall be a new Election; it passed in the Negative.*

Resolved, *That for a King or Queen of this Realm, to Read or Examine a Paper brought them to be signed by a* Junta *Minister, is Arbitrary and Illegal; and a Violation of the Liberties of the People.*

THESE and the like Reformations would, in all Probability, be the First-fruits of the *Whigs* Resurrection; and what Structures such able Artists might in a short Time build upon such Foundations, I leave others to conjecture. All Hopes of a *Peace* cut off; the Nation industriously involved in further Debts, to a Degree, that none would dare undertake the Management of Affairs, but those whose Interest lay in ruining the Constitution. I do not see how the wisest Prince, under such Necessities, could be able to extricate himself. Then, as to the *Church*; the Bishops would by Degrees be dismissed, first from the Parliament, next from their Revenues, and at last from their Office; and the Clergy, instead of their idle Claim of *Independancy* on the State, would be forced to depend for their daily Bread on every Individual. But, what System of future Government was designed; whether it were already digested, or would have been left for Time and Incidents to mature; I shall not now *Examine*. Only upon this Occasion, I cannot help reflecting on a Fact, which it is probable, the Reader knows as well as my self. There was a Picture drawn some Time ago, representing five Persons as large as the Life, sitting in Council together like a *Pentarchy*. A void Space was left for a Sixth, which was to have been the Queen, to whom they intended that Honour: But her Majesty having since fallen under their Displeasure, they have made a shift to crowd in *two better Friends* in Her Place, which makes it a compleat *Heptarchy*. This Piece is now in the Country, reserved until better Times; and hangs in a Hall, among the Pictures of *Cromwell*, *Bradshaw*, *Ireton*, and some other Predecessors.

I MUST now desire Leave to say something to a Gentleman, who hath been pleased to publish a Discourse against a Paper of mine relating to the Convocation. He promiseth to *set me right, without any undue Reflections or undecent Language*. I suppose he means in Comparison with others, who pretend to answer the *Examiner*: So far he is right; but if he thinks he hath behaved himself as becomes a candid Antagonist, I believe he is mistaken. He says, in his Title-Page, my *Representations are unfair, and my Reflections unjust*. And his Conclusion is yet more severe, where he *doubts I and my Friends are enraged against the* Dutch, *because they preserved us from Popery and Arbitrary Power at the Revolution; and since that Time, from being over-run by the exorbitant Power of* France, *and becoming a Prey to the* Pretender. Because this Author seems in general to write with an honest meaning, I would seriously put him the Question, whether he thinks, *I and my Friends* are for *Popery*, *Arbitrary Power*, *France* and the *Pretender?* I omit other Instances of smaller Moment, which however do not suit in my Opinion with *due Reflection or decent Language*. The Fact relating to the *Convocation*, came from a good Hand, and I do not find this Author differs from me in any material Circumstance about it. My Reflections were no more than what might be obvious to any other Gentleman, who had heard of their late Proceedings. If the Notion be right which this Author gives us of a Lower House of *Convocation*; it is a very Melancholy one, and to me seems utterly inconsistent with that of a Body of Men whom he owns to have a Negative; and therefore, since a great Majority of the Clergy differs from him in several Points, he advances, I shall rather chuse to be of their Opinion than his. I fancy, when the *whole Synod met in one House*, as this Writer affirms, they were upon a better Foot with their Bishops; and therefore, whether this Treatment so extreamly *de haut en bas*, since their Exclusion, be suitable to primitive Custom or Primitive Humility towards Brethren, is not my Business to enquire. One may allow the Divine or Apostolick Right of Episcopacy, and their great Superiority over Presbyters; and yet dispute the Methods of exercising the latter, which being of Human Institution, are subject to Encroachments and Usurpations. I know, every Clergyman in a Diocess hath a good Deal of Dependance upon his Bishop, and owes him Canonical Obedience: But, I was apt to think, that when the whole Representative of the Clergy met in a Synod, they were considered in another Light; at least since they were allowed to have a *Negative*. If I am mistaken, I desire to be excused, as talking out of my Trade: Only there is one Thing wherein I entirely differ from this Author: Since in the Disputes about Privileges *one Side must recede*; where so very few Privileges remain, it is a hundred to one odds, that the Encroachments are not on the Inferior Clergy's Side; and no Man can blame them for insisting on the small Number that is left. There is one Fact wherein I must take Occasion to set this Author right; that the * Person who first moved the QUEEN to remit the First-fruits and Tenths to the Clergy, was *an eminent Instrument in the late Turn of Affairs*; and as I am told, hath lately prevailed to have the same Favour granted for the Clergy of *Ireland* †.

BUT I must beg Leave to inform this *Author*, that my Paper

* *Earl of* Oxford, *Lord Treasurer.*

† *This was done by the Author's Sollicitation.*

is not intended for the Management of Controversy; which would be of very little Import to most Readers; and only mispend Time, that I would gladly employ to better Purposes. For, where it is a Man's Business to entertain a whole Room full; it is unmannerly to apply himself to a particular Person, and turn his Back upon the rest of the Company.

No. 26. *Thursday*, *February* 1, 1710.

Ea autem est gloria, laus recte factorum, magnorumq; in Rempublicam meritorum: Quæ cum optimi cujusque, tum etiam multitudinis testimonio comprobatur.

I AM thinking, what a mighty Advantage it is to be entertained as a Writer to a *ruined Cause*. I remember a *Fanatick* Preacher, who was inclined to come into the *Church*, and take Orders; but upon mature Thoughts was diverted from that Design, when he considered that the Collections of the *Godly* were a much heartier and readier Penny, than he could get by wrangling for Tythes. He certainly had Reason; and the two Cases are Parallel. If you write in Defence of a fallen Party, you are maintained by Contribution as a necessary Person; you have little more to do than to carp and cavil at those who hold the Pen on the other Side; you are sure to be celebrated and caressed by all your Party to a Man. You may affirm and deny what you please, without Truth or Probability, since it is but Loss of Time to contradict you. *Commiseration* is often on your Side; and you have a Pretence to be thought honest and disinterested, for adhering to Friends in Distress. After which, if your Friends ever happen to turn up again, you have a strong Fund of *Merit* towards making your Fortune. Then, you never fail to be well furnished with Materials; every one bringing in his *Quota*; and Falshood being naturally more plentiful than Truth. Not to mention the wonderful Delight of libelling Men in Power, and hugging yourself in a Corner with mighty Satisfaction for what you have done.

IT is quite otherwise with Us, who engage as Volunteers in the Service of a flourishing Ministry, in full Credit with the QUEEN, and beloved by the People; because they have no sinister Ends or dangerous Designs; but pursue with Steddiness and Resolution the true Interests of both. Upon which Account they little want or desire our Assistance; and we may write until the World is weary of reading, without having our Pretences allowed either to a *Place* or a *Pension*: Besides, we are refused the common *Benefit of the Party*, to have our Works cried up of Course; the Readers of our own Side being as ungentle and hard to please, as if we writ against them; and our Papers never make their Way in the World, but barely in Proportion to their Merit. The Design of *Their* Labours who write on the conquered Side, is likewise of greater Importance than *Ours*: They are like Cordials for dying Men, which must be repeated; whereas ours are, in the Scripture-Phrase, but *Meat for Babes*: At least, all I can pretend, is to undeceive the Ignorant, and those at Distance; but their Task is to keep up the sinking Spirits of a whole Party.

AFTER such Reflections, I cannot be angry with those Gentlemen for perpetually writing against me: It furnishes them largely with Topicks; and is besides, their proper Business: Neither is it Affectation, or altogether *Scorn*, that I do not Reply. But as Things are, we both act suitable to our several Provinces: Mine is, by laying open some Corruptions in the late Management, to set those who are ignorant, right in their Opinions of Persons and Things: It is theirs to cover with *Fig-Leaves* all the Faults of their Friends, as well as they can: When I have produced my Facts, and offered my Arguments, I have nothing farther to advance; it is their Office to deny and disprove; and then let the World decide. If *I* were as *They*, my chief Endeavour should certainly be to batter down the *Examiner*; therefore I cannot but approve their Design. Besides, they have indeed another Reason for barking incessantly at this Paper: They have in their Prints openly taxed a most ingenious Person as Author of it; one who is in great and very deserved Reputation with the World, both on Account of his Poetical Works, and his Talents for publick Business. They were wise enough to consider, what a Sanction it would give their Performances, to fall under the

Animadversion of such a Pen; and have therefore used all the Forms of Provocation commonly practised by little obscure Pedants, who are fond of distinguishing themselves by the Fame of an Adversary. So nice a Taste have these judicious Criticks, in pretending to discover an Author by his Style and Manner of Thinking: Not to mention the Justice and Candor of exhausting all the stale Topicks of Scurrility in reviling a Paper, and then flinging at a Venture the whole Load upon one who is entirely innocent; and whose greatest Fault, perhaps, is too much *Gentleness* towards a Party, from whose *Leaders* he hath received quite contrary Treatment.

THE Concern I have for the Ease and Reputation of so deserving a Gentleman, hath at length forced me, much against my Interest and Inclination, to let these angry People know who is *not* the Author of the *Examiner*. For, I observed, the Opinion began to spread; and I chose rather to sacrifice the Honour I received by it, than let injudicious People entitle him to a Performance, that perhaps he might have Reason to be ashamed of: Still faithfully promising, never to disturb those worthy Advocates; but suffer them in quiet to roar on at the *Examiner*, if they or their Party find any Ease in it; as Physicians say there is, to People in Torment, such as Men in the Gout, or Women in Labour.

HOWEVER, I must acknowledge my self indebted to them for one Hint, which I shall now pursue, although in a different Manner. Since the Fall of the late Ministry, I have seen many Papers filled with their Encomiums; I conceive, in Imitation of those who write the Lives of famous Men, where, after their Deaths, immediately follow their Characters. When I saw the poor *Virtues* thus dealt at Random, I thought the Disposers had flung their Names, like *Valentines* into a *Hat*, to be drawn as Fortune pleased, by the *Junta* and their Friends. There *Crassus* drew *Liberality* and *Gratitude; Fulvia*, *Humility* and *Gentleness; Clodius*, *Piety* and *Justice; Gracchus*, *Loyalty* to his Prince; *Cinna*, *Love of his Country and Constitution*; and so of the rest. Or, to quit this Allegory, I have often seen of late, the whole Set of discarded Statesmen, celebrated by their judicious Hirelings, for those very Qualities which their Admirers owned they chiefly wanted. Did these *Heroes* put off and lock up their *Virtues* when they came into Employment, and have they now resumed them since their Dismissions? If they wore them, I am sure it was *under* their *Greatness*, and without ever once convincing the World of their *Visibility* or *Influence*.

BUT, why should not the present Ministry find a Pen to praise them as well as the last? This is what I shall now undertake, and it may be more impartial in me, from whom they have deserved so little. I have, *without being called*, served them half a Year in Quality of *Champion*; and by help of the Queen, and a Majority of nine in ten of the Kingdom, have been able to protect them against a routed Cabal of hated Politicians, with a dozen of Scribblers at their Head: Yet so far have they been from rewarding me suitable to my Deserts, that to this Day they never so much as sent to the *Printer* to enquire who I was; although I have known a Time and Ministry, where a Person of half my Merit and Consideration would have had fifty *Promises*; and in the mean Time a *Pension* settled on him, whereof *the first Quarter should be honestly paid*. Therefore, my Resentments shall so far prevail, that in praising those who are now at the Head of Affairs, I shall at the same Time take Notice of their Defects.

WAS any Man more eminent in his Profession than the present *Lord Keeper*, or more distinguished by his Eloquence and great Abilities in the House of Commons? And, will not his Enemies allow him to be fully equal to the great Station he now adorns? But then it must be granted, that he is wholly ignorant in the Speculative as well as practical Part of *Poligamy*: He knows not how to metamorphose a sober Man into a *Lunatick*: He is no *Free-thinker* in Religion, nor hath Courage to be *Patron* of an Atheistical Book, while he is Guardian of the Queen's Conscience. Although, after all, to speak my private Opinion, I cannot think these such mighty Objections to his Character, as some would pretend.

THE Person who now * Presides at the Council, is descended from a Great and Honourable Father, not *from the Dregs of the People*; he was at the Head of the Treasury for some Years, and

* Lawrence Hyde, *Earl of* Rochester.

rather chose to enrich his Prince than himself. In the Height of Favour and Credit, he sacrificed the greatest Employment in the Kingdom to his *Conscience* and *Honour*: He hath been always firm in his Loyalty and Religion, zealous for supporting the Prerogative of the Crown, and preserving the Liberties of the People. But then, his best Friends must own that he is neither *Deist* nor *Socinian*: He hath never conversed with *Toland*, to open and enlarge his Thoughts, and dispel the Prejudices of Education; nor was he ever able to arrive at that Perfection of Gallantry, *to ruin and imprison the Husband, in order to keep the Wife without Disturbance.*

THE present *Lord Steward* hath been always distinguished for his Wit and Knowledge; is of consummate Wisdom and Experience in Affairs; hath continued constant to the true Interest of the Nation, which he espoused from the Beginning; and is every Way qualified to support the Dignity of his Office: But in Point of *Oratory*, must give Place to his Predecessor.

THE Duke of *Shrewsbury* was highly instrumental in bringing about the *Revolution*, in which Service he freely exposed his Life and Fortune. He hath ever been the Favourite of the Nation, being possessed of many amiable Qualities; but in the Agreeableness and Fragrancy of his Person, and the Profoundness of his Politicks, must be allowed to fall very short of ——

MR. *Harley* had the Honour of being chosen Speaker successively to three Parliaments; he was the first of late Years, who ventured to restore the forgotten Custom of treating his PRINCE with *Duty* and *Respect*. Easy and disengaged in private Conversation, with such a Weight of Affairs upon his Shoulders; of great Learning, and as great a Favourer and Protector of it; intrepid by Nature, as well as by the Consciousness of his own Integrity; and a Despiser of Money; pursuing the true Interest of his PRINCE and Country against all Obstacles. Sagacious to view into the remotest Consequences of Things, by which all Difficulties fly before him. A firm Friend, and a placable Enemy, sacrificing his justest Resentments, not only to publick Good, but to common Intercession and Acknowledgement. Yet with all these Virtues it must be granted, there is some Mixture of Human Infirmity: His greatest Admirers must confess his Skill at *Cards* and *Dice* to be very low and superficial: In *Horse-Racing* he is utterly ignorant: Then, to save a few Millions to the Publick, he never regards how many worthy *Citizens* he hinders from making up their Plumb. And surely there is one Thing never to be forgiven him; that he delights to have his Table filled with *Black-Coats*, whom he useth as if they were *Gentlemen*.

MY Lord *Dartmouth* is a Man of Letters, full of good Sense, good Nature and Honour, of strict Virtue and Regularity in his Life; but labours under one great Defect, that he treats his Clerks with more Civility and good Manners, than others in his Station, have done the QUEEN.

OMITTING some others, I will close this Character of the present *Ministry*, with that of Mr. *St. John*, who, from his Youth applying those admirable Talents of Nature, and Improvements of Art to publick Business, grew eminent in Court and Parliament, at an Age when the Generality of Mankind is employed in Trifles and Folly. It is to be lamented, that he hath not yet procured himself a *busy*, *important Countenance*, nor learned that profound Part of Wisdom, to be *difficult of Access*. Besides, he hath clearly mistaken the true Use of *Books*, which he has thumbed and spoiled with Reading, when he ought to have multiplied them on his Shelves: Not like a great Man of my Acquaintance, who knew a Book by the Back, better than a Friend by the Face, although he had never conversed with the former, and often with the latter.

No. 27. *Thursday, February* 8, 1710.

Caput est in omni procuratione negotii & muneris publici, ut avaritiæ pellatur etiam minima suspicio.

THERE is no Vice which Mankind carries to such wild Extreams as that of *Avarice*: Those two which seem to rival it in this Point, are Lust and Ambition: But, the former is checkt by Difficulties and Diseases; destroys itself by its own Pursuits, and usually declines with old Age: And the latter, requiring Courage, Conduct, and Fortune in a high Degree, and meeting with a thousand Dangers and Oppositions, succeeds too seldom in an Age to fall under common Observation. Or, is Avarice perhaps the same Passion with Ambition, only placed in more ignoble and dastardly Minds; by which the Object is changed from *Power* to *Money?* Or, it may be, that one Man pursues Power in order to Wealth; and another Wealth, in order to Power; which last is the safer Way, although longer about; and, suiting with every Period, as well as Condition of Life, is more generally followed.

HOWEVER it be, the Extreams of this Passion are certainly more frequent than of any other; and often to a Degree so absurd and ridiculous, that if it were not for their Frequency, they could hardly obtain Belief. The *Stage*, which carries other Follies and Vices beyond Nature and Probability, falls very short in the Representations of *Avarice*; nor are there any Extravagances in this Kind described by ancient or modern Comedies, which are not outdone by an hundred Instances, commonly told, among our selves.

I AM ready to conclude from hence, that a Vice which keeps so firm a Hold upon human Nature, and governs it with so unlimited a Tyranny; since it cannot be wholly eradicated, ought at least to be confined to particular Objects; to Thrift and Penury, to private Fraud and Extortion, and never suffered to prey upon the Publick; and should certainly be rejected as the most unqualifying Circumstance for any Employment, where Bribery and Corruption can possibly enter.

IF the Mischiefs of this Vice, in a publick Station, were confined to enriching only those particular Persons employed; the Evil would be more supportable: But it is usually quite otherwise. When a *Steward* defrauds his *Lord*, he must connive at the *rest of the Servants*, while they are following the same Practice in their several Spheres; so that in some Families you may observe a Subordination of Knaves in a Link downwards to the very *Helper* in the Stables, all cheating by Concert, and with Impunity. And, even if this were all, perhaps the Master could bear it without being undone; but it so happens, that for every Shilling the Servant gets by his Iniquity, the Master loseth twenty; the Perquisites of Servants being but small Compositions for suffering Shop-keepers to bring in what Bills they please. It is exactly the same Thing in a State: An avaricious Man in Office is in Confederacy with the whole *Clan* of his District or Dependance, which in modern Terms of Art is called, *To Live, and let Live*; and yet *their* Gains are the smallest Part of the Publick's Loss. Give a Guinea to a knavish *Land-Waiter*, and he shall connive at the Merchant for cheating the QUEEN of an Hundred. A *Brewer* gives a Bribe to have the Priviledge of selling Drink to the *Navy*; but the Fraud is a hundred Times greater than the Bribe; and the Publick is at the whole Loss.

MORALISTS make two kinds of Avarice; That of *Cataline*, *alieni appetens*, *sui profusus*; and the other more generally understood by that Name; which is, the endless Desire of Hoarding: But I take the former to be more dangerous in a State, because it mingles well with Ambition, which I think the latter cannot; for, although the same Breast may be capable of admitting both, it is not able to cultivate them; and where the Love of heaping Wealth prevails, there is not, in my Opinion, much to be apprehended from Ambition. The Disgrace of that sordid Vice is sooner apt to spread than any other; and is always attended with the Hatred and Scorn of the People: So that whenever those two Passions happen to meet in the same Subject; it is not unlikely, that Providence hath placed *Avarice* to be a Check upon *Ambition*; and I have Reason to think, *some great Ministers of State* have been of my Opinion.

THE Divine Authority of Holy Writ, the Precepts of Philosophers, the Lashes and Ridicule of Satyrical Poets, have been all employed in exploding this insatiable Thirst of Money; and all equally controlled by the daily Practice of Mankind. Nothing new remains to be said upon the Occasion; and if there did, I must remember my Character, that I am an *Examiner* only, and not a *Reformer*.

HOWEVER, in those Cases where the Frailties of particular Men do nearly affect the publick Welfare, such as a Prime Minister of State, or a great General of an Army; methinks there should be some Expedient contrived, to let them know impartially what is the World's Opinion in the Point: Encompassed with a Crowd of depending Flatterers, they are many Degrees blinder to their own Faults than the common Infirmities of Human Nature can plead in their Excuse; Advice dares not be offered, or is wholly lost, or returned with Hatred: And whatever appears in Publick against their prevailing Vice, goes for nothing; being either not applied, or passing only for Libel and Slander, proceeding from the Malice and Envy of a Party.

I HAVE sometimes thought, that if I had lived at *Rome* in the Time of the first *Triumvirate*, I should have been tempted to write a Letter, as from an unknown Hand, to those three great Men, who had then usurped the Sovereign Power; wherein I would freely and sincerely tell each of them that Fault which I conceived was most odious, and of worst Consequence to the Commonwealth: That, to *Crassus*, should have been sent to him after his Conquests in *Mesopotamia*, and in the following Terms.

To MARCUS CRASSUS, *Health:*

IF you apply as you ought, what I now write, you will be more obliged to me than to all the World, hardly excepting your Parents, or your Country. I intend to tell you, without Disguise or Prejudice, the Opinion which the World hath entertained of you. And, to let you see I write this without any Sort of ill Will, you shall first hear the Sentiments they have to your Advantage. No Man disputes the Gracefulness of your Person; you are allowed to have a good and clear Understanding, cultivated by the Knowledge of Men and Manners, although not by Literature. *You are no ill Orator in the Senate; you are said to excel in the Art of bridling and subduing your Anger, and stifling or concealing your Resentments; you have been a most successful General, of long Experience, great Conduct, and much Personal Courage; you have gained many important Victories for the Commonwealth, and forced the strongest Towns in* Mesopotamia *to surrender; for which, frequent* Supplications *have been decreed by the Senate. Yet with all these Qualities, and this Merit, give me Leave to say, you are neither beloved by the* Patricians *or* Plebeians *at home, nor by the Officers or private Soldiers of your own Army abroad. And, do you know* CRASSUS, *that this is owing to a Fault, of which you may cure yourself by one Minute's* Reflection*? What shall I say? You are the richest Person in the Commonwealth; you have no Male Child, your Daughters are all married to wealthy* Patricians; *you are far in the Decline of Life; and yet you are* *deeply stained with that odious and ignoble Vice of* Covetousness. *It is affirmed, that you descend even to the meanest and most scandalous Degrees of it; and while you possess so many Million; while you are acquiring so many more, you are sollicitous how to save a single* Sesterce, *of which a hundred ignominious Instances are produced, and in all Mens Mouths. I will only mention that Passage of the* * Buskins, *which after abundance of Persuasion, you would hardly suffer to be cut from your Legs, when they were so wet and cold, that to have kept them on, would have endangered your Life.*

Instead of using the common Arguments to dissuade you from this Weakness, I will endeavour to convince you, that you are really guilty of it; and leave the Cure to your own good Sense. For, perhaps, you are not yet perswaded that this is your Crime; you have probably never yet been reproached for it to your Face; and what you are now told, comes from one unknown, and it may be from an Enemy. You will allow your self indeed to be prudent in the Management of your Fortune; you are not a Prodigal, like Clodius *or* Cataline, *but surely that deserves not the Name of* Avarice. *I will inform you how to be convinced. Disguise your Person; go among the common People in* Rome; *introduce Discourses about your self; inquire your own Character; do the same in your Camp, walk about it in the Evening, hearken at every Tent; and, if you do not hear every Mouth Censuring, Lamenting, Cursing this Vice in you, and even you for this Vice; conclude your self innocent. If you be not yet persuaded; send for* Atticus, Servius Sulpicius, Cato, *or* Brutus; *they are all your Friends; conjure them to tell you ingenuously which is your great Fault, and which they would chiefly wish you to correct; if they do not agree in their Verdict*, in the Name of all the Gods, *you are acquitted.*

When your Adversaries reflect how far you are gone in this Vice, they are tempted to talk as if we owed our Successes, not to your Courage or Conduct, but to those Veteran *Troops you command; who are able to conquer under any* General, *with so many brave and experienced Officers to lead them. Besides, we know the Consequences your Avarice hath often occasioned. The Soldier hath been starving for Bread, surrounded with Plenty, and in an Enemies Country, but all under* Safeguards *and* Contributions; *which, if you had sometimes pleased to have exchanged for* Provisions, *might at the Expence of a few* Talents *in a Campaign,*

* Wet Stockings.

have so endeared you to the Army, that they would have desired you to lead them to the utmost Limits of Asia. *But you rather chose to confine your Conquests within the fruitful Country of* Mesopotamia, *where Plenty of Money might be raised. How far that fatal Greediness of Gold may have influenced you, in breaking off the Treaty with the old* Parthian *King* Orodes, *you best can tell; your Enemies charge you with it; your Friends offer nothing material in your Defence; and all agree, there is nothing so pernicious, which the Extreams of Avarice may not be able to inspire.*

The Moment you quit this Vice, you will be a truly Great Man; and still there will Imperfections enough remain to convince us, you are not a God. *Farewel.*

PERHAPS a Letter of this Nature sent to so reasonable a Man as *Crassus*, might have put him upon *Examining* into himself, and correcting that little sordid Appetite, so utterly inconsistent with all Pretences to a *Hero*. A Youth in the Heat of Blood may plead with some Show of Reason, that he is not able to subdue his Lusts: An ambitious Man may use the same Arguments for his love of Power, or perhaps other Arguments to justify it. But, Excess of Avarice hath neither of these Pleas to offer; it is not to be justified, and cannot pretend Temptation for Excuse: Whence can the Temptation come? Reason disclaims it altogether; and it cannot be said to lodge in the *Blood*, or the *Animal Spirits*. So that I conclude, *No Man of true Valour and true Understanding, upon whom this Vice hath stolen unawares, when he is convinced he is guilty, will suffer it to remain in his Breast an Hour.*

No. 28. *Thursday, February* 15, 1710.

Inultus ut tu riseris Cotyttia?

An Answer to the Letter *to the* EXAMINER.

SIR, *London, Feb.* 15, 1710–11.

ALTHOUGH I have wanted Leisure to acknowledge the Honour of a Letter you were pleased to write to me about six Months ago; yet I have been very careful in obeying some of your Commands; and am going on as fast as I can with the rest. I wish you had thought fit to have conveyed them to me by a more private Hand than that of the *Printing-House*: For, although I was pleased with a Pattern of Style and Spirit which I proposed to imitate; yet I was sorry the World should be a Witness how far I fell short in both.

I AM afraid you did not consider what an abundance of Work you have cut out for me; neither am I at all comforted by the Promise you are so kind to make, that when I *have performed my Task*, Dolben *shall blush in his Grave among the Dead*, Walpole *among the Living, and even* Volpone *shall feel some Remorse*. How the Gentleman in *his Grave*, may have kept his Countenance, I cannot inform you, having no Acquaintance at all with the Sexton: But for the *other two*, I take leave to assure you, there have not yet appeared the least Signs of *Blushing* or *Remorse* in either, although *some very good Opportunities* have offered, if they had thought fit to accept them: So that with your Permission, I had rather engage to continue this Work until *they* be *in their Graves* too; which I am sure, will happen much sooner than the other.

YOU desire I would collect *some of those Indignities offered last Year to her Majesty*. I am ready to oblige you; and have got a pretty tolerable Collection by me, which I am in doubt whether to publish by it self in a *large Volume in Folio*, or scatter them here and there occasionally in my Papers. Although indeed, I am sometimes thinking to stifle them altogether; because such a History will be apt to give Foreigners a monstrous Opinion of our Country. But, since it is your absolute Opinion, that the World should be informed; I will, with the first Occasion, pick out a few *choice Instances*, and let them take their Chance in the ensuing Papers. I have also in my Cabinet certain Quires of Paper filled with Facts of Corruption, Mismanagement, Cowardice, Treachery, Avarice, Ambition, and the like; with an Alphabetical Table, to save Trouble. And, perhaps, you will not wonder at the Care I take to be so well provided, when you consider the vast Expence I am at: I feed Weekly, two or three *Wit-starved* Writers, who have no other visible Support; besides several others, who live upon my Offals. In short, I am like a Nurse who suckles Twins at one Time, and hath besides, *one or two Whelps* constantly to draw her Breasts.

I MUST needs confess, (and it is with Grief I speak it) that I have been the innocent Cause of a great Circulation of Dulness: At the same Time, I have often wondered how it hath come to pass, that these industrious People, after poring so constantly upon the *Examiner*, a Paper writ with plain Sense, and in a tolerable Style; have made so little Improvement. I am sure it would have fallen out quite otherwise with me: For, by what I have seen of their Performances (and I am credibly informed they are all of a Piece) if I had perused them until now, I should have been fit for little but to make an Advocate in the same Cause.

YOU, Sir, perhaps will wonder, as most others do, what End these angry Folks propose, in writing perpetually against the *Examiner*: It is not to beget a better Opinion of the late Ministry, or with any Hope to convince the World that I am in the Wrong in any one Fact I relate; they know all that to be lost Labour; and yet their Design is important enough: They would fain provoke me by all Sort of Methods, within the Length of their Capacity, to answer their Papers; which would render mine wholly useless to the Publick: For, if it once came to Rejoinder and Reply, we should be all upon a Level; and then their Work would be done.

THERE is one * Gentleman indeed, who hath written three small Pamphlets upon the *Management of the War*, and *the Treaty of Peace*: These I had intended to have bestowed a Paper in *Examining*; and could easily have made it appear, that whatever he says of Truth, relates nothing at all to the Evils we complain of, or controuls one Syllable of what I have ever advanced. No Body, that I know of, did ever dispute the Duke of *Marlborough*'s Courage, Conduct, or Success; they have been always unquestionable, and will continue to be so, in spight of the Malice of his Enemies, or, which is yet more, the *Weakness of his Advocates*. The Nation only wished to see him taken out of ill Hands, and put into better. But, what is all this to the Conduct of the late Ministry, the shameful Mismanagements in *Spain*, or the wrong Steps in the Treaty of Peace; the Secret of which will not bear

* *Dr.* Hare, *now a Bishop.*

the Light, and is consequently by this Author very poorly defended? These, and many other Things, I would have shewn; but upon second Thoughts determined to have done it in a Discourse by it self, rather than take up room here, and break into the Design of this Paper, from whence I have resolved to banish Controversy as much as possible. But, the Postscript to his third Pamphlet was enough to disgust me from having any Dealings at all with such a Writer; unless that Part was left to some *Footman* he had picked up among the Boys who follow the Camp, whose Character it would suit much better than that of the supposed Author. At least, the foul Language, the idle impotent Menace, and the gross perverting of an innocent Expression in the fourth *Examiner*; joined to that Respect I shall ever have for the Function of a *Divine*, would incline me to believe so. But when he turns off his *Footman*, and disclaims that Postscript, I will tear it out, and see how far the rest deserves to be considered.

But, Sir, I labour under a much greater Difficulty, upon which I should be glad to hear your Advice. I am worried on one Side by the *Whigs* for being too *severe*; and by the *Tories* on the other for being too *gentle*. I have formerly hinted a Complaint of this; but having lately received two peculiar Letters, among many others; I thought nothing could better represent my Condition, or the Opinion which the warm Men of both Sides have of my Conduct, than to send you a Transcript of each. The former is exactly in these Words.

To the EXAMINER.

Mr. Examiner,

'BY your continual reflecting upon the Conduct of the late Ministry, and by your Encomiums on the present, it is *as clear as the Sun at Noon-Day*, that you are a *Jesuit* or *Non-*
'*juror*, employed by the Friends of the *Pretender*, to endeavour to
'introduce *Popery* and *Slavery*, and *Arbitrary Power*, and to in-
'fringe the *sacred* Act for *Toleration* of *Dissenters*. Now, Sir, since
'*the most ingenious Authors* who write Weekly against you, are

'not able to teach you better Manners, I would have you to 'know, that those Great and excellent Men, as low as you think 'them at present, do not want Friends that will take the first pro-'per Occasion to *cut your Throat*, as all such Enemies to *Modera-'tion* ought to be served. It is well you have cleared another Per-'son from being Author of your cursed Libels; although 'D-mme, perhaps after all, that may be a *Bamboozzle* too. How-'ever, I hope we shall soon Ferrit you out. Therefore, I advise 'you as a Friend, to let fall your Pen, and retire betimes; for our 'Patience is now at an End. It is enough to lose our Power and 'Employments, without setting the whole Nation against us. 'Consider three Years is the Life of a *Party*; and D--mme, *every 'Dog hath his Day*, and it will be our Turn next; therefore take 'Warning, and learn to *sleep in a whole Skin*, or whenever we are 'uppermost, by G-d you shall find no Mercy.

The other Letter was in the following Terms.

To the EXAMINER.

SIR,

'I AM a *Country Member*, and constantly send a Dozen of your Papers down to my *Electors*. I have read them all, but I confess, not with the Satisfaction I expected. It is plain you know 'a great deal more than you write; why will you not let us have it 'all out? We are told, that the QUEEN hath been a long Time 'treated with Insolence by those she hath most obliged; Pray, 'Sir, let us have a few good Stories upon that Head. We have 'been cheated of several Millions; why will not you set a Mark 'on the Knaves who are guilty, and shew us what Ways they 'took to rob the Publick at such a Rate? Inform us how we came 'to be disappointed of Peace about two Years ago: In short, turn 'the whole Mystery of Iniquity inside out, that every Body may 'have a View of it. But above all, explain to us, what was at the 'Bottom of that same *Impeachment*: I am sure I never liked it; for, 'at that very Time a *Dissenting* Preacher in our Neighbourhood, 'came often to see our Parson; it could be for no Good, for he 'would walk about the Barns and Stables, and desire to look 'into the Church, as *who should say*, *These will shortly be mine*; and 'we all believed he was then contriving some Alterations against 'he got into Possession: And I shall never forget, that a *Whig* '*Justice* offered me then very high for my *Bishop*'s Lease. I must 'be so bold to tell you, Sir, that you are too favourable: I am sure, 'there was no living in Quiet for us while they were in the *Saddle*. 'I was turned out of the Commission, and called a *Jacobite*, al-'though it cost me a thousand Pound in joining with the Prince 'of *Orange* at the *Revolution*. The Discoveries I would have you 'make, are of some Facts for which they ought to be hanged; 'not that I value their Heads, but I would see them *exposed*, 'which may be done upon the *Owners Shoulders*, as well as upon 'a *Pole*, &c.

THESE, Sir, are the Sentiments of a whole Party on one Side, and of considerable Numbers on the other: However, taking the Medium between these Extreams, I think to go on as I have hitherto done, although I am sensible my Paper would be more popular, if I did not lean too much to the favourable Side. For, nothing delights the People more than to see their Oppressors humbled, and all their Actions painted with proper Colours, set out in open View. *Exactos Tyrannos densum humeris bibit aure vulgus*.

BUT as for the *Whigs*, I am in some doubt, whether this mighty Concern they shew for the Honour of the late Ministry, may not be affected; at least whether their Masters will thank them for their Zeal in such a Cause. It is, I think, a known Story of a Gentleman who fought another for calling him *Son of a Whore*; but his Mother desired her Son to make no more Quarrels upon that Subject, *because it was true*. For pray, Sir, doth it not look like a Jest, that such a pernicious Crew, after draining our Wealth, and discovering the most destructive Designs against our Church and State; instead of thanking Fortune that they are got off safe in their Persons and Plunder, should hire these Bullies of the Pen to defend their Reputations? I remember, I thought it the hardest Case in the World, when a poor Acquaintance of mine, having fallen among Sharpers, where he lost all his Money, and then complaining he was cheated; got a good Beating into the Bargain, *for offering to affront Gentlemen*. I believe, the only Reason why these Purloiners of the Publick cause such a Clutter to be made about their Reputations, is to prevent Inquisitions that might tend towards making them refund: Like those Women they call *Shop-Lifters*, who when they are challenged for their Thefts, appear to be mighty angry and affronted, for Fear of being searched.

I WILL dismiss you, Sir, when I have taken notice of one Particular. Perhaps you may have observed in the tolerated factious Papers of the Week, that the Earl of *Rochester* is frequently reflected on for having been *Ecclesiastical Commissioner* and *Lord Treasurer* in the Reign of the late King *James*. The Fact is true; and it will not be denied to his immortal Honour, that because he could not comply with the Measures then taking, he resigned both those Employments; of which the latter was immediately supplied by a Commission, composed of two Popish Lords and the present Earl of *Godolphin*.

No. 29. *Thursday, February* 22, 1710.

Laus summa in fortunæ bonis, non extulisse se in Potestate, non fuisse insolentem in pecuniâ, non se prætulisse aliis propter abundantiam fortunæ.

I AM conscious to my self, that I write this Paper with no other Intention but that of doing good: I never received Injury from the late Ministry; nor Advantage from the present, farther than in common with every good Subject. There were among the former one or two, who must be allowed to have possessed very valuable Qualities; but proceeding by a System of Politicks, which our Constitution could not suffer; and discovering a Contempt of all Religion, especially of that which hath been so happily established among us ever since the Reformation; they seem to have been justly suspected of no very good Inclinations to either.

IT is possible, that a Man may speculatively prefer the Constitution of another Country, or an *Utopia* of his own, before that of the Nation where he is born and lives; yet from considering the Dangers of Innovation, the Corruptions of Mankind, and the frequent Impossibility of reducing Idea's to Practice, he may join heartily in preserving the present Order of Things, and be a true Friend to the Government already settled. So in Religion; a Man may perhaps have little or none of it at Heart; yet if he conceal his Opinions, if he endeavour to make no Proselytes, advance no impious Tenets in Writing or Discourse: If, according to the common Atheistical Notion, he believes Religion to be only a Contrivance of Politicians for keeping the Vulgar in Awe; and that the present Model is better adjusted than any other to so useful an End: Although the Condition of such a Man as to his own future State be very deplorable; yet Providence, which often works Good out of Evil, can make even such a Man an Instrument for contributing towards the Preservation of the Church.

ON the other side; I take a State to be truly in danger, both as to its Religion and Government, when a Set of Ambitious Politicians, bred up in a Hatred to the Constitution, and a Contempt for all Religion, are forced upon exerting these Qualities in order to keep or encrease their Power, by widening their Bottom, and taking in (like *Mahomet*) some Principles from every Party, that is any way discontented at the present Faith and Settlement; which was manifestly our Case. Upon this Occasion, I remember to have asked some considerable Whigs, whether it did not bring a Disreputation upon their Body, to have the whole Herd of Presbyterians, Independants, Atheists, Anabaptists, Deists, Quakers and Socinians, openly and universally Listed under their Banners? They answered, That all this was absolutely necessary, in order to make a Ballance against the *Tories*; and all little enough: For indeed, it was as much as they could possibly do, although assisted with the absolute Power of disposing every Employment; while the Bulk of *English* Gentry kept firm to their old Principles in Church and State.

BUT, notwithstanding whatever I have hitherto said, I am informed, several among the *Whigs* continue still so refractory, that they will hardly allow the Heads of their Party to have entertained any Designs of ruining the Constitution; or that they would have endeavoured it, if they had continued in Power. I beg their Pardon if I have discovered a Secret; but who could imagine they ever intended it should be One, after those *Overt-Acts* with which they thought fit to conclude their *Farce?* But perhaps they *now* find it convenient to deny vigorously; that the Question may remain; *Why was the old Ministry changed?* Which they urge *on* without ceasing, as if no Occasion in the least had been given; but that all were owing to the Insinuations of crafty Men, practising upon the Weakness of an easy Prince. I shall therefore offer, among a hundred, one Reason for this Change, which I think would justify any Monarch who ever reigned, for the like Proceeding.

It is notorious enough, how highly Princes have been blamed in the Histories of all Countries, particularly of our own, upon the Account of their *Minions*; who have been ever justly odious to the People, for their Insolence and Avarice, and engrossing the Favour of their Masters. Whoever hath been the least conversant in the *English* Story, cannot but have heard of *Gaveston*, the *Spencers*, and some others; who by the Excess and Abuse of their Power, cost the Princes they served, or rather governed, their Crowns and Lives. However, in the Case of *Minions*, it must at least be acknowledged, that the Prince is pleased and happy, although his Subjects be aggrieved; and he has the Plea of Friendship to excuse him; which is a Disposition of generous Minds. Besides, a wise *Minion*, altho' he be haughty to others, is humble and insinuating to his Master; and cultivates his Favour by Obedience and Respect. But, *Our* Misfortune hath been a great deal worse: We have suffered for some Years under the Oppression, the Avarice, and Insolence of those, for whom the QUEEN had neither Esteem nor Friendship; who rather seemed to snatch their own Dues, than receive the Favour of their Sovereign; and were so far from returning Respect, that they forgot common good Manners. They imposed on their Prince, by urging the Necessity of Affairs of their own creating: They first raised Difficulties, and then offered them as Arguments to keep themselves in Power. They united themselves against Nature and Principle, to a Party they had always abhorred, and which was now content to come in upon any Terms, leaving Them and their Creatures in full Possession of the Court. Then they urged the formidable Strength of that Party, and the Dangers which must follow by disobliging it. So that it seems, almost a Miracle, how a Prince, thus Besieged on all Sides, could *alone* have Courage and Prudence enough to extricate Herself.

AND indeed there is a Point of History relating to this Matter, which well deserveth to be considered. When Her Majesty came to the Crown, she took into Favour and Employment several Persons who were esteemed the best Friends of the old Constitution; among whom none were reckoned further gone in the *High Church* Principles (as they are usually called) than two or three, who had at that Time most Credit; and ever since, untill within these few Months, possessed all Power at Court. So that the first Umbrage given to the Whigs, and the Pretences for clamouring against *France* and the *Pretender*, were derived from Them. And I believe nothing appeared then more unlikely, than that such different Opinions should ever incorporate; that Party having upon former Occasions treated those very Persons with Enmity enough. But some Lords then about Court, and in the QUEEN's good Graces, not able to endure those growing Impositions upon the Prince and People, presumed to interpose; and were consequently soon removed and disgraced: However, when a most exorbitant Grant was proposed, antecedent to any visible Merit; it miscarried in Parliament, for want of being Seconded by those who had most Credit in the House; and, who having always opposed the like Excesses in a former Reign, thought it their Duty to do so still; to shew the World, that the Dislike was not against Persons but Things. But this was to cross the *Oligarchy* in the tenderest Point; a Point which outweighed all Considerations of Duty and Gratitude to their Prince, or Regard to the Constitution: And therefore, after having in several private Meetings concerted Measures with their old Enemies, and granted as well as received Conditions; they began to change their Style and their Countenance, and to put it as a Maxim in the Mouths of their Emissaries; That *England must be saved by* Whigs. This unnatural League was afterwards cultivated by another Incident; I mean the *Act of Security*, and the Consequences of it, which every Body knows; when (to use the Words of my Correspondent) *the Sovereign Authority was parcelled out among*

Letter to the Examiner.

the Faction, and made the Purchase of Indemnity for an offending Minister: Thus, the Union of the two Kingdoms improved That between the Ministry and the *Junta*, which was afterwards cemented by their mutual Danger in that Storm they so narrowly escaped about three Years ago; but however was not quite perfected till Prince *George*'s Death; and then they went lovingly on together, both satisfied with their several Shares, at full Liberty to gratifie their predominant Inclinations; the first, their Avarice and Ambition; the other, their Models of Innovation in Church and State.

THEREFORE, whoever thinks fit to revive that baffled Question, *Why was the late Ministry changed?* may receive the following Answer: That it was become necessary by the Insolence and Avarice of some about the QUEEN, who, in order to perpetuate their Tyranny, had made a monstrous Alliance with those who profess Principles destructive to our Religion and Government: If this will not suffice; let him make an Abstract of all the Abuses I have mentioned in my former Papers, and view them together; after which, if he still remain unsatisfied, let him suspend his Opinion a few Weeks longer. Although after all, I think the Question as trifling as that of the Papists, when they ask us, *Where was our Religion before* Luther? And indeed, the Ministry was changed for the same Reason that Religion was reformed; because a thousand Corruptions had crept into the *Discipline* and *Doctrine* of the *State*, by the Pride, the Avarice, the Fraud, and the Ambition of those *who administered to us in Secular Affairs*.

I HEARD my self censured the other Day in a Coffee-House, for seeming to glance in the Letter to *Crassus*, against a great Man, who is still in Employment, and likely to continue so. What if I had really intended that such an Application should be given it? I cannot perceive how I could be justly blamed for so gentle a Reproof. If I saw a handsome young Fellow going to a Ball at Court with a great *Smut* upon his Face; could he take it ill in me to point out the Place, and desire him with abundance of good Words to pull out his Handkerchief and wipe it off; or bring him to a Glass, where he might plainly see it with his own Eyes? Doth any Man think I shall suffer my Pen to inveigh against Vices, only because they are charged upon Persons who are no longer in Power? Every Body knows, that certain Vices are more or less pernicious, according to the Stations of those who possess them. For Example, Lewdness and Intemperance are not of so bad Consequences in a Town-Rake as in a Divine. Cowardice in a Lawyer is more supportable than in an Officer of the Army. If I should find Fault with an Admiral because he wanted *Politeness*; or an Alderman for not understanding *Greek*; That, indeed would be to go out of my way for an Occasion of Quarrelling: But excessive Avarice in a General, is, I think, the greatest Defect he can be liable to, next to those of Courage and Conduct, and may be attended with the most ruinous Consequences, as it was in *Crassus*; who to that Vice alone owed the Destruction of himself and his Army. It is the same Thing in praising Mens Excellencies; which are more or less valuable, as the Person you commend hath occasion to employ them. A Man may perhaps mean Honestly; yet if he be not able to Spell, he shall never have my Vote to be a Secretary: Another may have Wit and Learning in a Post where Honesty, with plain common Sense, are of much more Use: You may praise a Soldier for his Skill at *Chess*, because it is said to be a Military Game, and the Emblem of drawing up an Army; but this to a Treasurer would be no more a Compliment, than if you called him a *Gamester* or a *Jockey*.

P. S. I received a Letter relating to Mr. *Greenshields*, the Person who sent it may know, that I will say something to it in the next Paper.

No. 30. *Thursday, March* 1, 1710.

Quæ enim domus tam Stabilis, quæ tam firma civitas est, quæ non odiis atque discidiis funditus possit everti?

IF we examine what Societies of Men are in closest Union among themselves; we shall find them either to be those who are engaged in some evil Design, or who labour under one common Misfortune: Thus the Troops of *Banditti* in several

Countries abroad; the Knots of *Highwaymen* in our own Nation; the several Tribes of *Sharpers*, *Thieves* and *Pick-pockets*, with many others, are so firmly knit together, that nothing is more difficult than to break or dissolve their several *Gangs*. So likewise, those who are Fellow-Sufferers under any Misfortune, whether it be in Reality or Opinion, are usually contracted into a very strict Union; as we may observe in the *Papists* throughout this Kingdom, under those real Difficulties which are justly put on them; and in the several Schisms of *Presbyterians*, and other Sects, under that grievous Persecution of the modern kind, called *Want of Power*. And the Reason why such Confederacies are kept so sacred and inviolable, is very plain; because in each of those Cases I have mentioned, the whole Body is moved by one common Spirit, in pursuit of one general End, and the Interest of Individuals is not crossed by each other, or by the whole.

Now both these Motives are joined to unite the *High-flying Whigs* at present: They have been always engaged in an *evil Design*, and of late they are faster riveted by that terrible Calamity, the Loss of Power. So that whatever Designs a mischievous Crew of dark Confederates may possibly entertain, who will stop at no Means to compass them, may be justly apprehended from these.

On the other side, those who wish well to the Publick, and would gladly contribute to its Service, are apt to differ in their Opinions about the Methods of promoting it; and when their Party flourishes, are sometimes envious at those in Power; ready to over-value their own Merit, and be impatient untill it be rewarded by the Measure they have prescribed for themselves. There is a further Topick of Contention, which a Ruling Party is apt to fall into, in Relation to *Retrospections*, and Enquiry into past Miscarriages; wherein *some* are thought too warm and zealous; *others* too cool and remiss; while in the mean time these Divisions are industriously fomented by the discarded Faction; which, although it be an old Practice, hath been much improved in the Schools of the *Jesuits*; who when they despaired of perverting this Nation to *Popery*, by Arguments or Plots against the State, sent their Emissaries to subdivide us into Schisms. And this Expedient is now with great Propriety taken up by our Men of *incensed Moderation*; because they suppose themselves able to attack the strongest of our Subdivisions, and so subdue us one after another. Nothing better resembles this Proceeding, than that famous Combat between the *Horatii* and *Curiatii*; where two of the former being killed, the third who remained entire and untouched, was able to kill his three wounded Adversaries, after he had divided them by a Stratagem. I well know with how tender a Hand all this should be touched; yet, at the same time, I think it my Duty to *warn* the Friends, as well as *expose* the Enemies, of the Publick Weal; and to begin preaching up *Union* upon the first Suspicion that any Steps are made to disturb it.

BUT the two chief Subjects of Discontent, which, upon most great Changes, in the Management of publick Affairs, are apt to breed Differences among those who are in Possession, are what I have just now mentioned; a Desire of punishing the Corruptions of former Managers; and the rewarding *Merit*, among those who have been any Way instrumental or consenting to the Change. The first of these is a Point so nice, that I shall purposely wave it. But the latter I take to fall properly within my District: By *Merit* I here understand that Value which every Man puts upon his own Deservings from the Publick. And, I believe, there could not be a more difficult Employment found out, than that of *Pay-Master-General* to this Sort of *Merit*; or a more noisy, crowded Place, than a Court of *Judicature*, erected to settle and adjust every Man's Claim upon that Article. I imagine, if this had fallen into the Fancy of the ancient Poets, they would have drest it up after their Manner into an agreeable Fiction; and given us a Genealogy and Description of *Merit*, perhaps not very different from that which follows.

A Poetical Genealogy and Description of MERIT.

THAT, *true Merit*, was the Son of *Virtue* and *Honour*; but that there was likewise a spurious Child who usurped the Name, and whose Parents were *Vanity* and *Impudence*. That, at a Distance there was a great Resemblance between them, and they were often mistaken for each other. That, the *Bastard Issue* had a *loud shrill Voice*, which was perpetually employed in *Cravings* and *Complaints*; while the other never spoke louder than a *Whisper*; and was often so bashful that he could not speak at all. That, in great Assemblies, the *false Merit* would step before the *true*, and stand just in his Way; was constantly at Court, or great Mens *Levees*, or whispering in some Minister's Ear. That, the more you fed him, the more hungry and importunate he grew. That, he often passed for the true Son of *Virtue* and *Honour*; and the Genuine for an Impostor. That, he was born distorted and a Dwarf, but by Force of Art appeared of a handsome Shape, and taller than the usual Size; and that none but those who were wise and good, as well as vigilant, could discover his Littleness or Deformity. That, the *true Merit* had been often forced to the Indignity of applying to the *false*, for his Credit with those in Power, and to keep himself from Starving. That, the false Merit filled the *Anti-chambers* with a Crew of his Dependants and Creatures, such as *Projectors*, *Schematists*, *Occasional Converts to a Party*, *prostitute Flatterers*, *starveling Writers*, *Buffoons*, *shallow Politicians*, *empty Orators*, and the like; who all owned him for their Patron, and grew discontented if they were not immediately fed.

THIS Metaphorical Description of *false Merit*, is, I doubt, calculated for most Countries in Christendom; and as to our own, I believe it may be said, with a sufficient Reserve of Charity, that we are fully able to reward every Man among us according to his real Deservings. And, I think I may add, without Suspicion of Flattery, that never any Prince had a Ministry with a better Judgment to distinguish between false and real *Merit*, than that which is now at the Helm; or whose Inclination as well as Interest it is to encourage the latter. And it ought to be observed, that those great and excellent Persons we see at the Head of Affairs, are of the QUEEN'S *own Personal voluntary Choice*; not *forced* upon Her by any *insolent*, *overgrown Favourite*, or by the pretended *Necessity* of complying with an *unruly Faction*.

YET these are the Persons whom those Scandals to the Press, in their Daily Pamphlets and Papers, openly revile at so ignominious a Rate, as I believe was never tolerated before under any Government. For, surely no lawful Power derived from a Prince, should be so far affronted, as to leave those who are in

Authority exposed to every scurrilous Libeller. Because, in this Point, I make a mighty Difference between those who are *In*, and those who are *Out* of Power; not upon any Regard to their Persons, but the Stations they are placed in by the Sovereign. And, if my Distinction be right, I think I might appeal to any Man, whether if a Stranger were to read the Invectives which are daily published against the present Ministry; and the outrageous Fury of the Authors against me for censuring the Last; he would not conclude the *Whigs* to be at this Time in full Possession of Power and Favour, and the *Tories* entirely at Mercy? But all this now ceases to be a Wonder, since the QUEEN Her self is no longer spared; witness the Libel published some Days ago under the Title of *A Letter to Sir* Jacob Banks, where the Reflections upon Her Sacred Majesty are much more plain and direct, than ever the *Examiner* thought fit to publish against the most obnoxious Persons in a *Ministry*, discarded for endeavouring the Ruin of their Prince and Country. *Cæsar* indeed threatned to hang the *Pirates* for presuming to disturb him while he was their Prisoner aboard their Ship: But it was *Cæsar* who did so, and he did it to a Crew of *Publick Robbers*; and it became the Greatness of his Spirit; for he lived to execute what he had threatned. Had *They* been in his Power, and sent such a Message, it could be imputed to nothing but the Extreams of Impudence, Folly, or Madness.

I HAD a Letter last Week relating to Mr. *Greenshields*, an *Episcopal Clergyman* of *Scotland*; and the Writer seems to be a Gentleman of that Part of *Britain*. I remember formerly to have read a printed Account of Mr. *Greenshields*'s Case, who hath been prosecuted and silenced for no other Reason beside reading Divine Service, after the Manner of the Church of *England*, to his own Congregation, which desired it; although, as the Gentleman who writes to me says, there is no Law in *Scotland* against those Meetings; and he adds, that the Sentence pronounced against Mr. *Greenshields will soon be affirmed, if some Care be not taken to prevent it*. I am altogether uninformed in the Particulars of this Case; and besides, to treat it justly, would not come within the Compass of my Paper; therefore I could wish the Gentleman would undertake it in a Discourse by it self; and I should be glad he would inform the Publick in one Fact; Whether the *Episcopal*

Assemblies are freely allowed in *Scotland?* It is notorious that abundance of their Clergy fled from thence some Years ago into *England* and *Ireland*, as from a Persecution; but it was alledged by their Enemies, that they refused to take the Oaths to the Government, which however none of them scrupled when they came among us. It is somewhat extraordinary to see our *Whigs* and *Fanaticks* keep such a Stir about the *Sacred Act of Toleration*, while their *Brethren* will not allow a Connivance in so near a Neighbourhood; especially if what the Gentleman insists on in his Letter be true, that nine Parts in ten of the Nobility and Gentry, and two in three of the Commons, be *Episcopal*; of which one Argument he offers, is the present Choice of their Representatives in both Houses, although opposed to the utmost by the *Preachings*, *Threatnings*, and *Anathema*'s of the *Kirk*. Such Usage to a Majority may, as he thinks, be of dangerous Consequence; and I entirely agree with him. If these be the Principles of the *High-Kirk*, God preserve at least the Southern Parts from their Tyranny!

No. 31. *Thursday, March* 8, 1710.

-----------*Garrit aniles*
Ex re fabellas.

I HAD last Week sent me by an unknown Hand a Passage out of *Plato*, with some Hints how to apply it. That Author puts a Fable into the Mouth of *Aristophanes*, with an Account of the Original of *Love*. That, Mankind was at first created with four Arms and Legs, and all other Parts double to what they are now; 'till *Jupiter*, as a Punishment for his Sins, cleft him in two with a Thunderbolt; since which Time we are always looking for our other Half; and this is the Cause of *Love*. But *Jupiter* threatned, that if they did not mend their Manners, he would give them t'other Slit, and leave them to hop about in the Shape of Figures in *Basso Relievo*. The Effect of this last Threatning, my Correspondent imagines is now come to pass; and, that as the first *splitting* was the Original of *Love*, by inclining us to search out for our t'other Half, so the second was the Cause of *Hatred*, by prompting us to fly from our *other Side*, and dividing the same *Body* into two, give each Slice the Name of a Party.

I APPROVE of the Fable and Application, with this Refinement upon it. For, *Parties* do not only split a Nation, but every Individual among them, leaving each but half their Strength, and Wit, and Honesty, and good Nature; but one Eye and Ear, for their Sight and Hearing, and equally lopping the rest of the Senses: Where *Parties* are pretty equal in a State, no Man can perceive one bad Quality in his own, or good one in his Adversaries. Besides, *Party* being a dry disagreeable Subject, it renders Conversation insipid and sower, and confines Invention. I speak not here of the Leaders, but the insignificant Brood of Followers in a Party, who have been the Instruments of mixing it in every Condition, and Circumstance of Life. As the Zealots among the *Jews* bound the Law about their Foreheads and Wrists, and Hems of their Garments; so the Women among us have got the distinguishing Marks of Party in their Muffs, their Fans, and their Furbelows. The *Whig* Ladies put on their Patches in a different Manner from the *Tories*. They have made *Schisms* in the *Play-House*, and each have their particular Sides at the *Opera*: And when a Man changeth his Party, he must infallibly count upon the Loss of his Mistress. I asked a Gentleman t'other Day, how he liked such a Lady? but he would not give me his Opinion, 'till I had answered him whether she were a *Whig* or *Tory*. Mr. *** since he is known to visit the present Ministry, and lay some Time under a Suspicion of writing the *Examiner*, is no longer a Man of *Wit*; his very *Poems* have contracted a Stupidity many Years after they were printed.

HAVING lately ventured upon a Metaphorical Genealogy of *Merit*, I thought it would be proper to add another of *Party*, or rather of *Faction* (to avoid Mistake) not telling the Reader, whether it be my own or a Quotation, 'till I know how it is approved: But whether I read or dreamt it, the Fable is as follows.

LIBERTY, *the Daughter of* Oppression, *after having brought forth several fair Children, as* Riches, Arts, Learning, Trade, *and many others; was at last delivered of her youngest Daughter, called* FACTION; *whom* Juno, *doing the Office of Midwife, distorted in its Birth, out of Envy to the Mother; from whence it derived its* Peevishness *and* Sickly Constitution. *However, as it is often the Nature of Parents to grow most fond of their youngest and disagreeablest Children, so it happened with* Liberty, *who doated on this Daughter to such a Degree, that by her good Will she would never suffer the Girl to be out of her Sight. As Miss* Faction *grew up, she became so termagant and froward, that there was no enduring her any longer in* Heaven. Jupiter *gave her warning to be gone; and her Mother, rather than forsake her, took the whole Family down to* Earth. *She landed at first in* Greece, *was expelled by degrees through all the Cities by her Daughter's ill Conduct; she fled afterwards to* Italy, *and being banished thence, took Shelter among the* Goths, *with whom she passed into most Parts of* Europe; *but being driven out every where, she began to lose Esteem; and her Daughter's Faults were imputed to her self: So that at this Time she hath hardly a Place in the World to retire to. One would wonder what strange Qualities this Daughter must possess, sufficient to blast the Influence of so divine a Mother, and the rest of her Children: She always affected to keep mean and scandalous Company; valuing no Body, but just as they agreed with her in every capricious Opinion she thought fit to take up; and rigorously exacting Compliance, although she changed her Sentiments ever so often. Her great Employment was to breed* Discord *among Friends and Relations; and make up monstrous Alliances between those whose Dispositions least resembled each other. Whoever offered to contradict her, although in the most insignificant Trifle, she would be sure to distinguish by some ignominious* Appellation, *and allow them to have neither Honour, Wit, Beauty, Learning, Honesty or common Sense. She intruded into all Companies at the most unseasonable Times; mixt at Balls, Assemblies, and other Parties of Pleasure; haunted every Coffee-house and Bookseller's Shop; and by her perpetual Talking filled all Places with Disturbance and Confusion. She buzzed about the* Merchant *in the* Exchange, *the* Divine *in his Pulpit, and the* Shopkeeper *behind his Counter. Above all, she frequented* Publick Assemblies, *where she sate in the Shape of an* obscene, ominous Bird, *ready to prompt her* Friends *as they spoke.*

If I understand this Fable of Faction right, it ought to be applied to those who set themselves up against the true Interest and Constitution of their Country; which I wish the Undertakers for the late Ministry would please to take Notice of; or tell us by what Figure of Speech they pretend to call so great and unforced a Majority, with the QUEEN at the Head, by the Name of *the Faction*: Which is not unlike the Phrase of the *Nonjurors*, who dignifying one or two deprived Bishops, and half a score Clergymen of the same Stamp, with the Title of the *Church of England*; exclude all the rest as *Schismaticks*; or like the *Presbyterians*, laying the same Accusation, with equal Justice, against the Established Religion.

AND here it may be worth inquiring what are the true Characteristicks of a *Faction*; or how it is to be distinguished from that great Body of the People who are Friends to the Constitution? The Heads of a *Faction*, are usually a Set of Upstarts, or Men ruined in their Fortunes, whom some great Change in a Government, did at first, out of their Obscurity, produce upon the Stage. They associate themselves with those who dislike the old Establishment, Religious and Civil. They are full of new Schemes in Politicks and Divinity; they have an incurable Hatred against the old Nobility, and strengthen their Party by Dependents raised from the lowest of the People; they have several Ways of working themselves into Power; but they are sure to be called when a corrupt Administration wants to be supported, against those who are endeavoring at a Reformation; and they firmly observe that celebrated Maxim of preserving *Power* by the same Arts it is attained. They act with the Spirit of those who believe their Time is but short; and their first Care is to heap up immense Riches at the Publick Expence; in which they have two Ends, beside that common one of insatiable Avarice; which are to make themselves necessary, and to keep the common Wealth in Dependance: Thus they hope to compass their Design, which is, instead of fitting their Principles to the Constitution, to alter and adjust the Constitution to their own pernicious Principles.

IT is easy determining by this Test, to which Side the Name of *Faction* most properly belongs. But however I will give them any System of Lawful or Regal Government, from *William* the Conqueror to this present Time, to try whether they can tally it with their late Models; excepting only that of *Cromwell*, whom perhaps they will reckon for a Monarch.

IF the present Ministry, and so great a Majority in the Parliament and Kingdom, be only a *Faction*; it must appear by some Actions which answer the Idea we usually conceive from that Word. Have they abused the Prerogative of the Prince, or invaded the Rights and Liberties of the Subject? Have they offered at any dangerous Innovations in Church or State? Have they broached any Doctrines of Heresy, Rebellion or Tyranny? Have any of them treated their Sovereign with Insolence, engrossed and sold all Her Favours, or deceived Her by base, gross Misrepresentations of Her most faithful Servants? These are the Arts of a *Faction*; and whoever hath practised them, they and their Followers must take up with the Name.

It is usually reckoned a *Whig* Principle to appeal to the People; but that is only when they have been so wise as to poison their Understandings before-hand: Will they now stand to this Appeal, and be determined by their *Vox Populi*, to which Side their Title of *Faction* belongs? And that the People are now left to the natural Freedom of their Understanding and Choice, I believe our Adversaries will hardly deny. They will now refuse this Appeal, and it is reasonable they should; and I will further add, that if our People resembled the old *Grecians*, there might be Danger in such a Tryal. A pragmatical Orator told a great Man at *Athens*, that whenever the People were in their *Rage*, they would certainly tear him to Pieces; yes, says the other, and they will do the same to you, whenever they are in their *Wits*. But, God be thanked, our Populace is more merciful in their Nature, and at present under better Direction; and the Orators among us have attempted to confound both Prerogative and Law, in their Sovereign's Presence, and before the highest Court of Judicature, without any Hazard to their Persons.

No. 32. *Thursday, March* 15, 1710.

Non est ea medicina, cum sanæ parti corporis scalpellum adhibetur, atque integræ; carnificina est ista, & crudelitas. Hi medentur Reipublicæ qui exsecant pestem aliquam, tanquam strumam Civitatis.

I AM diverted from the general Subject of my Discourses, to reflect upon an Event of a very extraordinary and surprizing Nature: A great Minister, in high Confidence with the QUEEN, under whose Management the Weight of Affairs at present is in a great Measure supposed to lie; sitting in Council, in a Royal Palace, with a Dozen of the Chief Officers of State, is stabbed at the very Board, in the Execution of his Office, by the Hand of a *French Papist*, then under Examination for High Treason. The Assassin redoubles his Blow, to make sure Work; and concluding the * Chancellor was dispatched, goes on with the same Rage to murder a Principal Secretary of State: And that whole Noble Assembly are forced to rise, and draw their Swords in their own Defence, as if a wild Beast had been let loose among them.

THIS Fact hath some Circumstances of Aggravation not to be parallelled by any of the like kind we meet with in History. *Cæsar*'s Murder being performed in the Senate, comes nearest to the Case; but that was an Affair concerted by great Numbers of the chief Senators, who were likewise the Actors in it, and not the Work of a vile, single Ruffian. *Harry* the Third of *France* was stabbed by an Enthusiastick *Frier*, whom he suffered to approach his Person, while those who attended him stood at some Distance. His Successor met the same Fate in a Coach, where neither he nor his Nobles, in such a Confinement, were able to defend themselves. In our own Country we have, I think, but one Instance of this Sort, which hath made any Noise; I mean that of *Felton*, about fourscore Years ago: But he took the Opportunity to stab the Duke of *Buckingham* in passing through a dark Lobby, from one Room to another: The Blow was neither seen nor heard; and the Murderer might have escaped, if his own Concern

* *Mr.* HARLEY, *then Chancellor of the Exchequer.*

and Horror, as it is usual in such Cases, had not betrayed him. Besides, that Act of *Felton* will admit of some Extenuation from the Motives he is said to have had: But this Attempt of *Guiscard* seems to have outdone them all in every heightning Circumstance, except the Difference of Persons between a King and a great Minister: For I give no Allowance at all to the Difference of Success (which however is yet uncertain and depending) nor think it the least Alleviation to the Crime, whatever it may be to the Punishment.

I AM sensible, it is ill arguing from Particulars to Generals; and that we ought not to charge upon a Nation the Crimes of a few desperate Villains it is so unfortunate to produce: Yet, at the same time it must be avowed, that the *French* have for these last Centuries been somewhat too liberal of their Daggers upon the Persons of their greatest Men; such as the Admiral *de Coligny*, the Dukes of *Guise*, Father and Son, and the two Kings I last mentioned. I have sometimes wondered how a People, whose Genius seems wholly turned to singing, and dancing, and prating; to Vanity and Impertinence; who lay so much Weight upon Modes and Gestures; whose Essentialities are generally so very superficial; who are usually so serious upon Trifles, and so trifling upon what is serious; have been capable of committing such solid Villainies; more suitable to the Gravity of a *Spaniard*, or Silence and Thoughtfulness of an *Italian*: Unless it be, that in a Nation naturally so full of themselves, and of so restless Imaginations; when any of them happen to be of a morose and gloomy Constitution, that Huddle of confused Thoughts, for want of evaporating, usually terminates in Rage or Despair. *D'Avila* observes, that *Jacques Clement* was a Sort of Buffoon, whom the rest of the Friars used to make Sport with: But at last, giving his Folly a serious Turn, it ended in Enthusiasm, and qualified him for that desperate Act of murdering his King.

BUT, in the Marquis *de Guiscard* there seems to have been a Complication of Ingredients for such an Attempt: He had committed several Enormities in *France*; was extremely prodigal and vicious; of a dark melancholy Complexion, and cloudy Countenance, such as in vulgar Physiognomy is called an *Ill Look*. For the rest, his Talents were very mean, having a sort of inferior

Cunning, but very small Abilities; so that a great Man of the late Ministry, by whom he was invited over, and with much Discretion raised at first Step from a profligate *Popish Priest* to a Lieutenant-General and Colonel of a Regiment of Horse, was forced at last to drop him for Shame.

HAD such an Accident happened under that Ministry, and to so considerable a Member of it; they would have immediately charged it upon the whole Body of those they are pleased to call *the Faction*. This would have been stlyed a *High-Church Principle*; the Clergy would have been accused as Promoters and Abettors of the Fact; Committees would have been sent to promise the Criminal his Life, provided they might have Liberty to direct and dictate his Confession; and a *Black List* would have been printed of all those who had been ever seen in the Murderer's Company. But, the present Men in Power hate and despise all such detestable Arts, which they might now turn upon their Adversaries with much more Plausibility, than ever these did their Honourable Negotiations with *Greg*.

AND here it may be worth observing how unanimous a Concurrence there is between some Persons once in high Power, and a *French Papist*; both agreeing in the great End of taking away Mr. *Harley*'s Life, although differing in their Methods: The first proceeding by Subornation, the other by Violence; wherein *Guiscard* seems to have the Advantage, as aiming no further than his Life; while the others designed to destroy at once both That and his Reputation. The Malice of both against this Gentleman seems to have risen from the same Cause; his discovering Designs against the Government. It was Mr. *Harley* who detected the Treasonable Correspondence of *Greg*, and secured him betimes; when a certain Great Man who shall be nameless, had, out of the Depth of his Politicks, sent him a Caution to make his Escape; which would certainly have fixed the Appearance of Guilt upon Mr. *Harley*: But when that was prevented, they would have enticed the condemned Criminal with Promise of a Pardon, to write and Sign an Accusation against the Secretary. But to use *Greg*'s own Expression, *His Death was nothing near so ignominious, as would have been such a Life that must be saved by prostituting his Conscience*. The same Gentleman lies now stabbed by his other Enemy, a Popish Spy, whose Treason he hath discovered. God preserve the rest of Her Majesty's Ministers from such *Protestants*, and from such *Papists*!

I SHALL take Occasion to hint at some Particularities in this surprizing Fact, for the Sake of those at distance, or who may not be thoroughly informed. The Murderer confessed in *Newgate*, that his chief Design was against Mr. Secretary *St. John*, who happened to change Seats with Mr. *Harley*, for more Convenience of examining the Criminal: And being asked what provoked him to stab the Chancellor? He said, that not being able to come at the Secretary, as he intended, it was some Satisfaction to murder the Person whom he thought Mr. *St. John* loved best.

AND here, if Mr, *Harley* hath still any Enemies left, whom his Blood spilt in the Publick Service cannot reconcile; I hope they will at least admire his Magnanimity, which is a Quality esteemed even in an Enemy: And, I think there are few greater Instances of it to be found in Story. After the Wound was given, he was observed neither to change his Countenance, nor discover any Concern or Disorder in his Speech: He rose up, and walked along the Room while he was able, with the greatest Tranquility, during the Midst of the Confusion. When the Surgeon came, he took him aside, and desired he would inform him freely whether the Wound were mortal; because in that Case, he said, he had some Affairs to settle, relating to his Family. The Blade of the Penknife, broken by the Violence of the Blow against a Rib, within a Quarter of an Inch of the Handle, was dropt out (I know not whether from the Wound, or his Clothes) as the Surgeon was going to dress him; he ordered it to be taken up, and wiping it himself, gave it some body to keep, saying, he thought *it now properly belonged to him*. He shewed no Sort of Resentment, or spoke one violent Word against *Guiscard*; but appeared all the while the least concerned of any in the Company. A State of Mind, which in such an Exigency, nothing but Innocence can give; and is truly worthy of a Christian Philosopher.

IF there be really so great a Difference in Principle between the *High-flying Whigs*, and the Friends of *France*; I cannot but repeat the Question, how come they to join in the Destruction of the same Man? Can his Death be possibly for the Interest of

Both? or have they Both the same Quarrel against Him, that he is perpetually discovering and preventing the treacherous Designs of our Enemies? However it be, this great Minister may now say with St. *Paul*, that he hath been *in Perils by his own Countrymen, and in Perils by Strangers.*

In the Midst of so melancholy a Subject, I cannot but Congratulate with our own Country, that such a Savage Monster as the Marquis *de Guiscard*, is none of her Production; A Wretch perhaps more detestable in his own Nature, than even this barbarous Act hath been yet able to represent Him to the World. For, there are good Reasons to believe, from several Circumstances, that he had Intentions of a deeper Dye, than those he happened to execute; I mean such as every good Subject must tremble to think on. He hath of late been frequently seen going up the Back-stairs at Court, and walking alone in an outer Room adjoining to Her Majesty's Bedchamber. He hath often and earnestly pressed for some time to have Access to the Queen, even since his Correspondence with *France*; and he hath now given such a Proof of his Disposition, as leaves it easy to guess what was before in his Thoughts, and what he was capable of attempting.

It is humbly to be hoped that the Legislature will interpose on so extraordinary an Occasion as this, and direct a Punishment some way proportionable to so execrable a Crime.

Et quicunque tuum violavit vulnere corpus,
Morte luat merita——

No. 33. *Thursday, March* 22, 1710.

De Libertate retinenda, qua certe nihil est dulcius tibi assentior.

THE Apologies of the ancient Fathers are reckoned to have been the most useful Parts of their Writings, and to have done greatest Service to the Christian Religion; because they removed those Misrepresentations which had done it most Injury. The Mehtods these Writers took, was openly and freely to discover every Point of their Faith; to detect the Falshood of their Accusers; and to charge nothing upon their Adversaries but what they were sure to make good. This Example hath been ill followed of later Times: The *Papists* since the Reformation using all Arts to palliate the Absurdities of their Tenets, and loading the Reformers with a thousand Calumnies; the Consequence of which hath been only a more various, wide, and inveterate Separation. It is the same Thing in Civil Schisms: A *Whig* forms an Image of a *Tory*, just after the Thing he most abhors; and that Image serveth to represent the whole Body.

I AM not sensible of any material Difference there is between those who call themselves the *Old Whigs*, and a great Majority of the present *Tories*; at least by all I could ever find, from examining several Persons of each Denomination. But it must be confessed, that the present Body of *Whigs*, as they now constitute that Party, is a very odd Mixture of Mankind; being forced to enlarge their Bottom, by taking in every Heterodox Professor either in Religion or Government, whose Opinions they were obliged to encourage for fear of lessening their Number; while the Bulk of the Landed-Men and People were entirely of the old Sentiments. However, they still pretended a due Regard to the *Monarchy* and the *Church*, even at the Time when they were making the largest Steps towards the Ruin of both: But not being able to wipe off the many Accusations laid to their Charge, they endeavoured by throwing of Scandal, to make the *Tories* appear blacker than themselves; that so the People might join with *them*, as the smaller Evil of the two.

BUT, among all the Reproaches which the *Whigs* have flung upon their Adversaries, there is none hath done them more Service than that of *Passive Obedience*, as they represent it, with the Consequences of *Non-Resistance*, *Arbitrary Power*, *Indefeasible Right*, *Tyranny*, *Popery*, and what not? There is no Accusation which hath passed with more Plausibility than this; nor any that is supported with less Justice. In order therefore to undeceive those who have been misled by false Representations, I thought it would be no improper Undertaking to set this Matter in a fair Light, which, I think, hath not yet been done. A *Whig* asks, whether you hold *Passive Obedience?* You affirm it: He then immediately cries out, you are a *Jacobite*, a *Friend* of *France* and the *Pretender*; because he makes you answerable for the Definition he hath formed of that Term, however different it be from what you understand. I will therefore give two Descriptions of *Passive Obedience*; the first, as it is falsly charged by the *Whigs*; the other, as it is really professed by the *Tories*, at least by nineteen in twenty of all I ever conversed with.

Passive Obedience as charged by the WHIGS.

THE Doctrine of *Passive Obedience* is to believe, that a King, even in a limited Monarchy holding his Power only from God, is only answerable to him. That, such a King is above all Law; that the cruellest Tyrant must be submitted to in all Things; and if his Commands be ever so unlawful, you must neither fly nor resist, nor use any other Weapons than *Prayers* and *Tears*. Although he should force your Wife or Daughter, murder your Children before your Face, or cut off five hundred Heads in a Morning for his Diversion; you are still to wish him a long prosperous Reign, and to be patient under all his Cruelties, with the same Resignation as under a Plague or a famine; because, to resist him would be to resist God in the Person of his Vicegerent. If a King of *England* should go through the Streets of *London*, in order to murder every Man he met, *Passive Obedience* commands them to submit. All Laws made to limit him signify nothing, although passed by his own Consent, if he think fit to break them. God will indeed call him to a severe Account; but the whole People, united to a Man, cannot presume to hold his Hands, or offer him the least *Active Disobedience*. The People were certainly created for him, and not he for the People. His next Heir, although worse than what I have described, although a Fool or a Madman, hath a Divine indefeasible Right to succeed him, which no Law can disannul; nay, although he should kill his Father upon the Throne, he is immediately King to all Intents and Purposes; the Possession of the Crown wiping off all Stains. But, whosoever sits on the Throne without this Title, although never so peaceably, and by Consent of former Kings and Parliaments, is an *Usurper*, while there is any where in the

World another Person who hath a nearer Hereditary Right; and the whole Kingdom lies under mortal Sin until that Heir be restored; because he hath a Divine Title, which no Human Law can defeat.

THIS and a great deal more hath, in a thousand Papers and Pamphlets been laid to that Doctrine of *Passive Obedience*, which the *Whigs* are pleased to charge upon us. This is what they perpetually are instilling into the People to believe, as the undoubted Principle by which the present Ministry, and a great Majority in Parliament, do at this Time proceed. This is what they accuse the Clergy of delivering from the Pulpits, and of preaching up as a Doctrine absolutely necessary to Salvation. And whoever affirms in general, that *Passive Obedience* is due to the Supream Power, he is presently loaden by our candid Adversaries with such Consequences as these. Let us therefore see what this Doctrine is, when stript of such Misrepresentations; by describing it as really taught and practised by the *Tories*; and then it will appear what Grounds our Adversaries have to accuse us upon this Article.

Passive Obedience, as professed and practised by the TORIES.

THEY think that in every Government, whether Monarchy or Republick, there is placed a supream, absolute, unlimited Power, to which *Passive Obedience* is due. That, wherever is entrusted the Power of making Laws, that Power is without all Bounds; can repeal or enact at Pleasure whatever Laws it thinks fit; and justly demands Universal Obedience and Non-resistance. That, among us, as every Body knows, this Power is lodged in the King or Queen, together with the Lords and Commons of the Kingdom; and therefore all Decrees whatsoever, made by that Power, are to be actively or passively obeyed: That, the Administration or Executive Part of this Power is in *England* solely intrusted with the Prince; who, in administring those Laws, ought to be no more resisted than the Legislative Power it self. But, they do not conceive the same absolute *Passive Obedience* to be due to a limited Prince's Commands, when they are directly contrary to the Laws he hath consented to, and sworn to maintain. The Crown may be sued as well as a private Person; and if an arbitrary King of *England* should send his Officers to seize my Lands or Goods against Law; I can lawfully resist them. The Ministers by whom he acts are liable to Prosecution and Impeachment, although his own Person be Sacred. But, if he interpose his Royal Authority to support their Insolence, I see no Remedy, until it grows a general Grievance, or untill the Body of the People have Reason to apprehend it will be so; after which it becomes a Case of Necessity; and then I suppose, a free People may assert their own Rights, yet without any Violation to the Person or lawful Power of the Prince. But, although the *Tories* allow all this, and did justify it by the Share they had in the *Revolution*; yet they see no Reason for entring upon so ungrateful a Subject, or raising Controversies upon it, as if we were in daily Apprehensions of *Tyranny*, under the Reign of so excellent a Princess, and while we have so many Laws of late Years made to limit the Prerogative. As to the Succession; the *Tories* think an *Hereditary Right* to be the best in its own Nature, and most agreeable to our old Constitution; yet at the same Time they allow it to be defeasible by Act of Parliament; and so is *Magna Charta* too, if the Legislature think fit; which is a Truth so manifest, that no Man who understands the Nature of Government, can be in doubt concerning it.

THESE I take to be the Sentiments of a great Majority among the *Tories*, with Respect to *Passive Obedience*: And if the *Whigs* insist, from the Writings or common Talk of warm and ignorant Men, to form a Judgment of the whole Body, according to the first Account I have here given; I will engage to produce as many of their Side, who are utterly against *Passive Obedience* even to the Legislature; who will assert the last Resort of Power to be in the People, against those whom they have chosen and trusted as their Representatives, with the Prince at the Head; and who will put wild improbable Cases to shew the Reasonableness and Necessity of resisting the Legislative Power, in such imaginary Junctures. Than which however, nothing can be more idle; for I dare undertake in any System of Government, either Speculative or Practick, that was ever yet in the World, from *Plato*'s *Republick* to *Harrington*'s *Oceana*, to put such Difficulties as cannot be answered.

ALL the other Calumnies raised by the *Whigs* may be as easily wiped off: And I have Charity to wish they could as fully answer the just Accusations we have against them. *Dodwell*, *Hicks*, and *Lesley*, are gravely quoted, to prove that the *Tories* design to bring in the *Pretender*; and if I should quote them to prove that the same Thing is intended by the *Whigs*, it would be full as reasonable; since I am sure they have at least as much to do with *Nonjurors* as we. But, our Objections against the *Whigs* are built upon their constant Practice for many Years, whereof I have produced a hundred Instances, against any single one of which no Answer hath yet been attempted, although I have been curious enough to look into all the Papers I could meet with that are writ against the *Examiner*; such a Task, as I hope, no Man thinks I would undergo for any other End, but that of finding an Opportunity to own and rectify my Mistakes; as I would be ready to do upon Call of the *meanest* Adversary. Upon which Occasion, I shall take Leave to add a few Words.

I FLATTERED my self last *Thursday*, from the Nature of my Subject, and the inoffensive Manner I handled it, that I should have one Week's Respite from those merciless Pens, whose Severity will some Time break my Heart: But I am deceived, and find them more violent than ever. They charge me with two Lies, and a Blunder. The first Lie is a Truth, that *Guiscard* was invited over: But it is of no Consequence: I do not tax it as a Fault; such Sort of Men have often been serviceable: I only blamed the Indiscretion of raising a profligate Abbot, at the first Step, to a Lieutenant General and Colonel of a Regiment of Horse, without staying some reasonable Time, as is usual in such Cases, until he had given some Proofs of his Fidelity, as well as of that Interest and Credit he pretended to have in his Country: But, that is said to be another Lie, for he was a *Papist*, and could not have a Regiment. However this other Lie is a Truth too; for a Regiment he had, and paid by us, to his Agent Monsieur *Le Bas*, for his Use. The third is a *Blunder*, that I say *Guiscard*'s Design was against Mr. Secretary *St. John*; and yet my

Reasonings upon it, are, as if it were personal against Mr. *Harley*. But I say no such Thing, and my Reasonings are just; I relate only what *Guiscard* said in *Newgate*, because it was a Particularity the Reader might be curious to know (and accordingly it lies in a Paragraph by it self, after my Reflections) but I never meant to be answerable for what *Guiscard* said, or thought it of Weight enough for me to draw Conclusions from thence, when I had the Address of both Houses to direct me better: Where it is expressly said, *That Mr.* Harley*'s Fidelity to her Majesty, and Zeal for her Service, have drawn upon him the Hatred of all the Abettors of Popery and Faction.* This is what I believe, and what I shall stick to.

BUT alas, these are not the Passages which have raised so much Fury against me. One or two Mistakes in Facts of no Importance, or a single Blunder, would not have provoked them; they are not so tender of my Reputation as a Writer. All their Outrage is occasioned by those Passages in that Paper, which they do not in the least pretend to answer; and with the utmost Reluctancy are forced to mention. They take abundance of Pains to clear *Guiscard* from a Design against Mr. *Harley*'s Life; but offer not one Argument to clear their other Friends, who in the Business of *Greg*, were equally guilty of the *same Design* against the *same Person; whose Tongues were very Swords*, and whose *Penknives* were *Axes*.

No. 34. *Thursday, March* 29. 1711.

——— *Sunt hic etiam sua præmia laudi;*
Sunt lachrymæ rerum, & mentem mortalia tangunt.

I BEGIN to be heartily weary of my Employment as *Examiner*; which I wish the Ministry would consider, with half so much Concern as I do; and assign me some other with less Pains, and a Pension. There may soon be a Vacancy, either on the Bench, in the Revenue, or the Army, and I am *equally* Qualifyed for each: But this Trade of *Examining*, I apprehend, may at one time or other go near to sowr my Temper. I did lately propose that some of those *ingenious* Pens, which are engaged on the other Side, might be employed to succeed me; and I undertook to bring them over for *t'other Crown*; but it was answered, that those Gentlemen do much better Service in the Stations where they are. It was added, that abundance of Abuses yet remained to be laid open to the World, which I had often promised to do, but was too much diverted by other Subjects, that came into my Head. On the other Side; the Advice of some Friends, and the Threats of many Enemies, have put me upon considering what would become of me if *Times should alter*. This I have done very maturely, and the Result is, that I am in no manner of Pain. I grant, that what I have said upon Occasion, concerning the late Men in Power, may be called Satyr by some unthinking People, as long as that Faction is down; but if ever they come into Play again, I must give them warning beforehand, that I shall expect to be a *Favourite*, and that those pretended Advocates of theirs, will be Pillored for *Libellers*. For, I appeal to any Man, whether I ever charged that Party, or its Leaders, with one single Action or Design, which (if we may judge by their former Practices) they will not openly profess, be proud of, and score up for Merit, when they come again to the Head of Affairs? I said, they were Insolent to the QUEEN; Will they not value themselves upon That, as an Argument to prove them bold Assertors of the People's Liberty? I affirmed they were against a Peace; will they be angry with me for setting forth the Refinements of their Politicks, in pursuing the only Method left to preserve them in Power? I said, they had involved the Nation in Debts, and ingrossed much of its Money; they go beyond me, and boast they have got it *all*, and the *Credit* too. I have urged the Probability of their intending great Alterations in Religion and Government: If they destroy both at their next Coming, will they not reckon my foretelling it, rather as a Panegyrick than an Affront? I said, they had formerly a * Design against Mr. *Harly*'s Life: If they were now in Power, would they not immediately cut off his Head, and thank me for justifying the Sincerity of their Intentions? In short, there is nothing I ever said of those worthy

* *Vide* EXAMINER 32.

Patriots, which may not be as well excused: Therefore, as soon as They resume their Places, I positively design to put in my Claim; and, I think, may do it with better Grace, than many of that Party who now make their Court to the present Ministry. I know two or three great Men, at whose Levees you may Daily observe a Score of the most forward Faces, which every Body is ashamed of, except those who wear them. But I conceive my Pretensions will be upon a very different Foot: Let me offer a Parallel Case. Suppose, King *Charles* the First had entirely subdued the Rebels at *Naseby*, and reduced the Kingdom to his Obedience: Whoever had gone about to Reason, from the former Conduct of those *Saints*, that if the Victory had fallen on Their side, they would have murdered their Prince, destroyed Monarchy and the Church, and made the King's Party compound for their Estates as Delinquents; would have been called a false, uncharitable Libeller, by those very Persons who afterwards gloried in all this, and called it the *Work of the Lord*, when they happened to succeed. I remember there was a Person Fined and Imprisoned for *Scandalum Magnatum*, because he said the Duke of *York* was a Papist; but when that Prince came to be King, and made open Profession of his Religion, he had the Justice immediately to release his Prisoner, who in his Opinion had put a Compliment upon him, and not a Reproach: And therefore Colonel *Titus*, who had warmly asserted the same Thing in Parliament, was made a Privy-Counsellor.

By this Rule, if that which, for some Politick Reasons, is now called Scandal upon the late Ministry, prove one Day to be only an Abstract of such a Character as they will assume and be proud of; I think I may fairly offer my Pretensions, and hope for their Favour. And I am the more confirmed in this Notion by what I have observed in those Papers, that come weekly out against the *Examiner*: The Authors are perpetually telling me of my Ingratitude to my Masters; that I *blunder*, and betray the Cause; and write with more Bitterness against those who hire me, than against the Whigs. Now, I took all this at first only for so many Strains of Wit, and pretty Paradoxes to divert the Reader; but upon further thinking I find they are Serious. I imagined I had complimented the present Ministry for their dutiful Behaviour to the QUEEN; for their Love of the old Constitution in Church and State; for their Generosity and Justice, and for their Desire of a speedy, honourable Peace: But it seems I am mistaken, and they reckon all this for Satyr, because it is directly contrary to the Practice of all those whom they set up to defend, and utterly against all their Notions of a good Ministry. Therefore I cannot but think they have Reason on their side: For, suppose I should write the Character of an Honest, a Religious, and a learned Man, and send the first to *Newgate*, the second to the *Grecian Coffee-House*, and the last to *White*'s; would they not all pass for *Satyrs*, and justly enough, among the Companies to whom they were sent?

HAVING therefore employed several Papers in such sort of *Panegyricks*, and but very few on what they understand to be *Satyrs*; I shall henceforth upon Occasion be more Liberal of the latter; of which they are like to have a Taste in the remainder of this present Paper.

AMONG all the Advantages which the Kingdom hath received by the late Change of Ministry, the greatest must be allowed the calling of the present Parliament, upon the Dissolution of the last. It is acknowledged, that this excellent Assembly hath entirely recovered the Honour of Parliaments, which hath been unhappily prostituted for some Years past by the Factious Proceedings of an unnatural Majority, in Concert with a most corrupt Administration. It is plain, by the present Choice of Members, that the Electors of *England*, when left to themselves, do rightly understand their true Interest. The moderate *Whigs* begin to be convinced, that we have been all this while in wrong Hands; and that Things are now as they should be. And, as the present House of Commons is the best Representative of the Nation that hath ever been summoned in our Memories; so they have taken Care in their first Session, by that noble Bill of *Qualification*, that future Parliaments should be composed of Landed Men; and our Properties lie no more at Mercy of those who have none themselves, or at least only what is transient or imaginary. If there be any Gratitude in Posterity, the Memory of this Assembly will be always celebrated; if otherwise, at least we, who share in the Blessings they derive to us, ought with grateful Hearts to acknowledge them.

I DESIGN, in some following Papers, to draw up a List (for I can do no more) of the great Things this Parliament hath already performed; the many Abuses they have detected; their Justice in deciding Elections without Regard of Party; their Chearfulness and Address in raising Supplies for the War; and at the same Time providing for the Nation's Debts; their Duty to the QUEEN, and their Kindness to the Church. In the mean Time I cannot forbear mentioning two Particulars, which in my Opinion do discover, in some Measure, the Temper of the present Parliament; and bear Analogy to those Passages related by *Plutarch*, in the Lives of certain great Men; which, as himself observeth, *Although they be not of Actions which make any great Noise or Figure in History, yet give more Light into the Characters of Persons, than we could receive from an Account of their most renowned Atchievements.*

SOMETHING like this may be observed from two late Instances of *Decency* and *good Nature*, in that illustrious Assembly I am speaking of. The first was, when after that inhuman Attempt upon Mr. *Harley*, they were pleased to vote an Address to the QUEEN; wherein they express their utmost Detestation of the Fact; their high Esteem and great Concern for that able Minister; and justly impute his Misfortunes to that Zeal for her Majesty's Service, which had *drawn upon him the Hatred of all the Abettors of Popery and Faction.* I dare affirm, that so distinguishing a Mark of Honour and good Will from such a Parliament, was more acceptable to a Person of Mr. *Harley*'s generous Nature, than the most *bountiful Grant* that was ever yet made to a Subject; as her Majesty's Answer, filled with gracious Expressions in his Favour, adds more to his *real Glory*, than any *Titles* she could bestow. The Prince and Representatives of the whole Kingdom, join in their Concern for so important a Life. These are the true Rewards of Virtue; and this is the Commerce between noble Spirits, in a Coin which the *Giver* knows where to bestow, and the *Receiver* how to value, although neither *Avarice* nor *Ambition* would be able to comprehend its Worth.

THE other Instance I intended to produce of *Decency* and *good Nature*, in the present House of Commons, relates to their most worthy Speaker; who having unfortunately lost his eldest Son;

the Assembly, moved with a generous Pity for so sensible an Affliction, adjourned themselves for a Week, that so good a Servant of the Publick, might have some Interval to wipe away a Father's Tears: And indeed, that Gentleman hath too just an Occasion for his Grief by the Death of a Son, who had already acquired so great a Reputation for every amiable Quality; and who might have lived to be so great an Honour and an Ornament to his antient Family.

BEFORE I conclude, I must desire one Favour of the Reader; that when he thinks it worth his while to peruse any Paper writ against the *Examiner*, he will not form his Judgment by any mangled Quotation out of it which he finds in such Papers, but be so just to read the Paragraph referred to; which I am confident will be found a sufficient Answer to all that ever those Papers can object. At least I have seen above fifty of them, and never yet observed one single Quotation transcribed with common Candor.

No. 35. *Thursday, April* 5, 1711.

Nullo suo peccato impediantur, quo minus alterius peccata demonstrare possint.

I HAVE been considering the old Constitution of this Kingdom; comparing it with the Monarchies and Republicks whereof we meet so many Accounts in ancient Story, and with those at present in most Parts of *Europe*: I have considered our Religion, established here by the Legislature soon after the Reformation: I have likewise examined the Genius and Disposition of the People, under that reasonable Freedom they possess: Then I have turned my Reflections upon those two great Divisions of *Whig* and *Tory*, (which, some Way or other, take in the whole Kingdom) with the Principles they both profess, as well as those wherewith they reproach one another. From all this, I endeavour to determine, from which Side her present Majesty may reasonably hope for most Security to her Person and Government; and to which she ought, in Prudence, to trust the

Administration of her Affairs. If these two Rivals were really no more than *Parties*, according to the common Acceptation of the Word; I should agree with those Politicians who think, a Prince descendeth from his Dignity by putting himself at the Head of either; and that his wisest Course is, to keep them in a Balance; raising or depressing either, as it best suited with his Designs. But, when the visible Interest of his Crown and Kingdom lies on one Side; and when the other is but a *Faction*, raised and strengthned by Incidents and Intrigues, and by deceiving the People with false Representations of Things; he ought, in Prudence, to take the first Opportunity of opening his Subjects Eyes, and declaring himself in favour of those, who are for preserving the Civil and Religious Rights of the Nation, wherewith his own are so interwoven.

THIS was certainly our Case: For I do not take the Heads, Advocates, and Followers of the *Whigs*, to make up, strictly speaking, a *National Party*; being patched up of heterogeneous, inconsistent Parts, whom nothing served to unite but the common Interest of sharing in the Spoil and Plunder of the People; the present Dread of their Adversaries, by whom they apprehended to be called to an Account, and that general Conspiracy, of endeavouring to overturn the Church and State; which, however, if they could have compassed, they would certainly have fallen out among themselves, and broke in Pieces, as *their Predecessors* did, after they destroyed the Monarchy and Religion. For, how could a *Whig*, who is against all *Discipline*, agree with a *Presbyterian*, who carries it higher than the *Papists* themselves? How could a *Socinian* adjust his Models to either? Or how could any of these cement with a *Deist* or *Free-thinker*, when they came to consult upon settling Points of Faith? Neither would they have agreed better in their Systems of Government; where some would have been for a King, under the Limitations of the Duke of *Venice*; others for a *Dutch* Republick; a third Party for an *Aristocracy*; and most of them all for some new Fabrick of their own contriving.

BUT however, let us consider them as a *Party*, and under those general Tenets wherein they agreed, and which they publickly owned, without charging them with any that they pretend to deny. Then, let us *examine* those Principles of the *Tories*, which their Adversaries allow them to profess, and do not pretend to tax them with any Actions contrary to those Professions: After which, let the Reader judge from which of these two Parties a Prince hath most to fear; and whether her Majesty did not consider the Ease, the Safety, and Dignity of her Person, the Security of her Crown, and the transmission of Monarchy to her Protestant Successors, when she put her Affairs into the present Hands.

SUPPOSE the Matter were now entire; the QUEEN to make her Choice; and for that End, should order the Principles on both Sides to be fairly laid before her. First, I conceive the *Whigs* would grant, that they have naturally no great Veneration for *crowned Heads*; that they allow, the Person of the Prince may, upon many Occasions, be resisted by Arms; and that they do not condemn the War raised against King *Charles* the First, or own it to be a Rebellion, although they would be thought to blame his Murder. They do not think the *Prerogative* to be yet sufficiently limited, and have therefore taken Care (as a particular Mark of their Veneration for the illustrious House of *Hanover*) to clip it closer against the next Reign; which, consequently, they would be glad to see done in the present: Not to mention, that the Majority of them, if it were put to the Vote, would allow, that they prefer a Commonwealth before a Monarchy. As to *Religion*; their universal undisputed Maxim is, That it ought to make no Distinction at all among *Protestants*; and in the Word *Protestant* they include every Body who is not a *Papist*, and who will, by an Oath, give Security to the Government. Union in Discipline and Doctrine, the offensive Sin of Schism, the Notion of a Church and a Hierarchy, they laugh at as Foppery, Cant and *Priestcraft*. They see no Necessity at all that there should be a National Faith; and what we usually call by that Name, they only style the *Religion of the Magistrate*. Since the Dissenters and we agree in the Main, why should the Difference of a few Speculative Points, or Modes of Dress, incapacitate them from serving their Prince and Country, in a Juncture when we ought to have all Hands up against the common Enemy? And why should they be forced to take the Sacrament from our Clergy's Hands, and in our Posture; or indeed why compelled to receive it at all, when they take an Employment which has nothing to do with Religion?

THESE are the Notions which most of that Party avow, and which they do not endeavour to disguise or set off with false Colours, or complain of being misrepresented about. I have here placed them on Purpose, in the same Light which themselves do, in the very Apologies they make for what we accuse them of; and how inviting even these Doctrines are, for such a Monarch to close with, as our Law, both Statute and Common, understands a King of *England* to be, let others decide. But then, if to these we should add other Opinions, which most of their own Writers justify, and which their universal Practice hath given a Sanction to; they are no more than what a Prince might reasonably expect, as the natural Consequence of those avowed Principles. For, when such Persons are at the Head of Affairs, the low Opinion they have of Princes, will certainly lead them to violate that Respect they ought to bear; and at the same Time, their own Want of Duty to their Sovereign is largely made up, by exacting greater Submissions to themselves from their Fellow-Subjects: It being indisputably true, That the same Principle of Pride and Ambition makes a Man treat his Equals with Insolence, in the same Proportion as he affronts his Superiors; as both Prince and People have sufficiently felt from the late Ministry.

THEN, from their confessed Notions of Religion, as above related, I see no Reason to wonder, why they countenanced not only all Sorts of Dissenters, but the several *Gradations* of *Freethinkers* among us (all which were openly enrolled in their Party;) or why they were so very averse from the present established Form of Worship, which by prescribing Obedience to Princes from the Topick of Conscience, would be sure to thwart all their Schemes of Innovation.

ONE Thing I might add, as another acknowledged Maxim in that Party, and in my Opinion, as dangerous to the Constitution as any I have mentioned; I mean, That of preferring, on all Occasions, the *Moneyed* Interest before the *Landed*; which they were so far from denying, that they would gravely debate the

Reasonableness and Justice of it; and at the Rate they went on, might in a little Time have found a Majority of Representatives, fitly qualified to lay those heavy Burthens on the rest of the Nation, which themselves would not touch with one of their Fingers.

HOWEVER, to deal impartially, there are some Motives which might compel a Prince under the Necessity of Affairs, to deliver himself over to that Party. They were *said* to possess the great Bulk of Cash, and consequently of Credit in the Nation; and the Heads of them had the Reputation of presiding over those Societies who have the great Direction of both: So that all Applications for Loans to the Publick Service, upon any Emergency, must be made through them; and it might prove highly dangerous to disoblige them; because in this Case, it was not to be doubted, that they would be obstinate and malicious, ready to obstruct all Affairs, not only by shutting their own Purses, but by endeavouring to sink *Credit*, although with some present imaginary Loss to themselves, only to shew it was a *Creature* of their own.

FROM this Summary of *Whig-Principles* and Dispositions, we find what a Prince may reasonably fear and hope from that Party. Let us now very briefly consider the Doctrines of the *Tories*, which their Adversaries will not dispute. As they prefer a well-regulated Monarchy, before all other Forms of Government; so they think it next to impossible to alter that Institution here, without involving our whole Island in Blood and Desolation. They believe, that the Prerogative of a Sovereign ought, at least, to be held as sacred and inviolable as the Rights of his People; if only for this Reason; because, without a due Share of Power, he will not be able to protect them. They think, that by many known Laws of this Realm, both Statute and Common, neither the Person, nor lawful Authority of the Prince, ought, upon any Pretence whatsoever, to be resisted or disobeyed. Their Sentiments, in relation to the Church, are known enough, and will not be controverted, being just the Reverse to what I have delivered as the Doctrine and Practice of the *Whigs* upon that Article.

BUT here I must likewise deal impartially too; and add one

Principle as a Characteristick of the *Tories*, which hath much discouraged some Princes from making Use of them in Affairs. Give the *Whigs* but Power enough to insult their Sovereign, engross his Favours to themselves, and to oppress and plunder their Fellow-Subjects; they presently grow into good Humour and good Language towards the Crown; profess they will stand by it with their Lives and Fortunes; and whatever Rudenesses they may be guilty of in private, yet they assure the World, that there never was so gracious a Monarch. But, to the Shame of the *Tories*, it must be confessed, that nothing of all this hath been ever observed in them; in or out of Favour, you see no Alteration, further than a little Cheerfulness or Cloud in their Countenances; the highest Employments can add nothing to their Loyalty; but their Behaviour to their Prince, as well as their Expressions of Love and Duty, are, in all Conditions exactly the same.

HAVING thus impartially stated the avowed Principles of *Whig* and *Tory*; let the Reader determine, as he pleaseth, to which of these two a wise Prince may, with most Safety to himself and the Publick, trust his Person and his Affairs; and whether it were Rashness or Prudence in her Majesty to make those Changes in the Ministry, which have been so highly extolled by some, and condemned by others.

No. 36. *Thursday, April* 12, 1711.

Tres species tam dissimiles, tria talia texta
Una dies dedit exitio ——— ——

I WRITE this Paper for the Sake of the *Dissenters*, whom I take to be the most spreading Branch of the *Whig Party*, that *professeth Christianity*; and the only one that seems to be zealous for any particular System of it; the Bulk of those we call the *Low-Church* being generally indifferent, and undetermined in that Point; and the other Subdivisions having not yet taken either the Old or New Testament into their Scheme. By the *Dissenters* therefore, it will easily be understood, that I mean the

Presbyterians, as they include the Sects of *Anabaptists*, *Independents*, and others, which have been melted down into them since the *Restoration*. This Sect, in order to make it self National, having gone so far as to raise a Rebellion, murder their King, destroy Monarchy and the Church; was afterwards broken in Pieces by its own Divisions; which made Way for the King's Return from his Exile. However, the Zealous among them did still entertain Hopes of recovering the *Dominion of Grace*; whereof I have read a remarkable Passage, in a Book published about the Year 1661, and written by one of their own Side. As one of the Regicides was going to his Execution, a Friend asked him, *Whether he thought the* Cause *would revive?* He answered, *The* Cause *is in the Bosom of Christ; and as sure as Christ rose from the Dead, so sure will the* Cause *revive also*. And therefore the *Nonconformists* were strictly watched and restrained by Penal Laws, during the Reign of King *Charles* the Second; the Court and Kingdom looking on them as a *Faction*, ready to join in any Design against the Government in Church or State: And surely this was reasonable enough, while so many continued alive, who had voted, and fought, and preached against both, and gave no Proof that they had changed their Principles. The *Nonconformists* were then exactly upon the same Foot with our *Nonjurors* now, whom we double Tax, forbid their Conventicles, and keep under Hatches; without thinking ourselves possessed with a persecuting Spirit; because we know they want nothing but the Power to Ruin us. This, in my Opinion, should altogether silence the *Dissenters* Complaints of Persecution under King *Charles* the Second; or make them shew us wherein they differed, at that Time, from what our *Jacobites* are now.

THEIR Inclinations to the Church were soon discovered, when King *James* the Second succeeded to the Crown, with whom they unanimously joined in its Ruin, to revenge themselves for that Restraint they had most justly suffered in the foregoing Reign; not from the persecuting Temper of the Clergy, as their Clamours would suggest, but the Prudence and Caution of the Legislature. The same Indulgence against Law, was made Use of by them and the *Papists*; and they amicably employed their Power, as in Defence of one common Interest.

But the Revolution happening soon after, served to wash away the Memory of the Rebellion; upon which, the Run against *Popery*, was no doubt as just and seasonable, as that of *Fanaticism*, after the Restoration: And the Dread of *Popery*, being then our latest Danger, and consequently the most fresh upon our Spirits, all Mouths were open against That; the *Dissenters* were rewarded with an Indulgence by Law; the Rebellion and King's Murder was now no longer a Reproach; the former was only a Civil War, and whoever durst call it a *Rebellion*, was a *Jacobite*, and *Friend* to *France*. This was the more unexpected, because the Revolution being wholly brought about by Church of *England* Hands, they hoped one good Consequence of it, would be the relieving us from the Incroachments of *Dissenters*, as well as those of *Papists*; since both had equally Confederated towards our Ruin; and therefore, when the Crown was new settled, it was hoped at least that the rest of the Constitution would be restored. But this Affair took a very different Turn; the *Dissenters* had just made a Shift to save a Tide; and join with the Prince of *Orange*, when they found all was desperate with their *Protector* King *James*: And, observing a Party, then forming against the old Principles in Church and State, under the Name of *Whigs* and *Low-Churchmen*, they listed themselves of it, where they have ever since continued.

It is therefore, upon the Foot they now are, that I would apply my self to them, and desire they would consider the different Circumstances at present, from what they were under, when they began their Designs against the Church and Monarchy, about seventy Years ago. At that Juncture they made up the Body of the Party; and whosoever joined with them from Principles of Revenge, Discontent, Ambition, or Love of Change, were all forced to shelter under their Denomination; united heartily in the Pretences of a further and purer Reformation in Religion, and of advancing the *great Work* (as the *Cant* was then) *that God was about to do in these Nations*; received the Systems of Doctrine and Discipline prescribed by the *Scots*, and readily took the *Covenant*; so that there appeared no Division among them, 'till after the common Enemy was subdued.

But now their Case is quite otherwise; and I can hardly think it worth being a *Party*, upon the Terms they have been received of late Years: For, suppose the whole *Faction* should at length succeed in their Design of destroying the Church; are they so Weak to imagine, that the new Modelling of Religion, would be put into their Hands? Would their Brethren, the *Low-Churchmen* and *Freethinkers*, submit to their *Discipline*, their *Synods* or their *Classes*, and divide the Lands of Bishops, or Deans and Chapters, among Them? How can they help observing, that their Allies, instead of pretending more Sanctity than other Men, are some of them for levelling all Religion; and the rest for abolishing it? Is it not manifest, that they have been treated by their Confederates, exactly after the same manner, as they were by King *James* II; made Instruments to ruin the Church, not for their own Sakes, but under a pretended Project of universal Freedom in Opinion, to advance the dark Designs of those who employ them? For, excepting the *Antimonarchial Principle*, and a few false Notions about *Liberty*, I see but little Agreement betwixt them; and even in these, I believe it would be impossible to contrive a Frame of Government, that would please them all, if they had it now in their Power to try. But however, to be sure, the *Presbyterian* Institution would never obtain. For, suppose they should, in imitation of their Predecessors, propose to have no King but our Saviour Christ; the whole Clan of *Free-thinkers* would immediately object, and refuse his Authority. Neither would their *Low-Church* Brethren use them better, as well knowing what Enemies they are to that Doctrine of unlimitted Toleration, wherever they are suffered to preside. So that upon the whole, I do not see, as their present Circumstances stand, where the *Dissenters* can find better Quarter, than from the Church of *England*.

BESIDES, I leave it to their Consideration, whether, with all their Zeal against the Church, they ought not to shew a little Decency; and how far it consists with their Reputation, to act in Concert with such Confederates. It was reckoned a very infamous Proceeding in the present most *Christian King*, to assist the *Turk* against the *Emperor*: Policy, and Reasons of State, were not allowed sufficient Excuses for taking Part with an *Infidel* against a *Believer*. It is one of the *Dissenters* Quarrels against the

Church, that She is not enough reformed from Popery; yet they boldly entered into a League with *Papists* and a *Popish Prince*, to destroy Her. They profess much Sanctity, and object against the wicked Lives of some of our Members; yet, they have been long, and still continue, in strict Combination with *Libertines* and *Atheists*, to contrive our Ruin. What if the *Jews* should multiply, and become a formidable Party among us? Would the *Dissenters* join in Alliance with them likewise, because they agree already in some general Principles, and because the *Jews* are allowed to be a *stiff-necked and rebellious People?*

IT is the Part of Wise Men to conceal their Passions, when they are not in Circumstances of exerting them to Purpose: The Arts of getting Power, and preserving Indulgence, are very different. For the former, the reasonable Hopes of the *Dissenters*, seem to be at an End; their Comrades, the *Whigs* and *Freethinkers*, are just in a Condition proper to be forsaken; and the Parliament, as well as the Body of the People, will be deluded no longer. Besides, it sometimes happens for a Cause to be exhausted and worn out, as that of the *Whigs* in general, seems at present to be: The Nation hath felt enough of it. It is as vain to hope restoring that decayed Interest, as for a Man of Sixty to talk of entring on a new Scene of Life, that is only proper for Youth and Vigour. New Circumstances and new Men must arise, as well as new Occasions, which are not like to happen in our Time. So, that the *Dissenters* have no Game left, at present, but to secure their *Indulgence*: In order to which, I will be so bold to offer them some Advice.

FIRST, That until some late Proceedings be a little forgot, they would take Care not to provoke, by any Violence of Tongue or Pen, so great a Majority, as there is now against them; nor keep up any longer that Combination with their broken Allies; but disperse themselves, and lie dormant against some better Opportunity: I have shewn, they could have got no Advantage if the late Party had prevailed; they will certainly lose none by its Fall, unless through their own Fault. They pretend a mighty Veneration for the QUEEN, let them give Proof of it, by quitting the ruined Interest of those who have used her so ill; and by a due Respect to the Persons she is pleased to trust at present with her Affairs: When they can no longer hope to govern, when struggling can do them no good, and may possibly hurt them; what is left but to be silent and passive?

SECONDLY, Although there be no Law (beside that of God Almighty) against *Occasional Conformity*; it would be Prudence in the *Dissenters* to use it as tenderly as they can: For, besides the infamous Hypocrisy of the Thing it self; too frequent Practice would perhaps make a Remedy necessary. And after all they have said to justify themselves in this Point, it still continues hard to conceive, how those Consciences can pretend to be scrupulous, upon which an Employment hath more Power than the Love of Unity.

IN the last Place, I am humbly of Opinion, That the *Dissenters* would do well to drop that *Lesson* they have learned from their Directors, of affecting to be under horrible Apprehensions, that the *Tories* are in the Interests of the *Pretender*, and would be ready to embrace the first Opportunity of inviting him over. It is with the worst Grace in the World, that they offer to join in the Cry upon this Article: As if those, who *alone* stood in the Gap against all the Encroachments of *Popery* and *Arbitrary Power*, are not more likely to keep out both, than a Sett of *Schismaticks*, who to gratify their Ambition and Revenge, did, by the meanest Compliances, encourage and spirit up that unfortunate Prince, to fall upon such Measures, as must, at last, have ended in the Ruin of our Liberty and Religion.

I wish those who give themselves the trouble to write to the Examiner, *would consider whether what they send be proper for such a Paper to take notice of: I had one Letter last Week, written, as I suppose, by a Divine, to desire I would offer some Reasons against a Bill now before the Parliament for* Ascertaining the Tythe of Hops; *from which the Writer apprehends great Damage to the Clergy, especially the poorer* Vicars: *If it be, as he says (and he seems to argue very reasonably upon it) the* Convocation *now sitting, will, no doubt, upon due Application, represent the Matter to the House of Commons; and he may expect all Justice and Favour from that* Great Body, *who have already appeared so tender of their* Rights.

A Gentleman, likewise, who hath sent me several Letters, relating to Personal Hardships he received from some of the late Ministry; is advised to publish a Narrative of them; they being too large, and not proper for this Paper.

No. 37. *Thursday, April* 19, 1711.

Semper causæ eventorum magis movent quam ipsa eventa.

I AM glad to observe, that several among the *Whigs* have begun very much to change their Language of late. The Style is now among the reasonable part of them, when they meet a Man in Business, or a Member of a Parliament; *Well, Gentlemen, if you go on as you have hitherto done, we shall no longer have any Pretence to complain.* They find, it seems, that there have been yet no Overtures made to bring in the *Pretender*, nor any preparatory Steps towards it. They read no enslaving Votes, nor Bills brought in to endanger the Subject. The Indulgence to scrupulous Consciences, is again confirmed from the Throne, inviolably preserved, and not the least Whisper offered that may affect it. All Care is taken to support the War; Supplies chearfully granted, and Funds readily subscribed to, in spight of the little Arts made use of to discredit them. The just Resentments of some, which are laudable in themselves, and which at another Juncture it might be proper to give way to, have been softened or diverted by the Calmness of others. So that upon the Article of present Management, I do not see how any Objection of Weight can well be raised.

HOWEVER, our Adversaries still alledge, that this great Success was wholly unexpected, and out of all probable View. That, in publick Affairs, we ought, least of all others, to judge by Events; That, the Attempt of changing a Ministry, during the Difficulties of a long War, was rash and inconsiderate: That, if the QUEEN were disposed by her Inclinations, or from any personal Dislike, for such a Change, it might have been done with more Safety in a Time of Peace: That, if it had miscarried by any of those Incidents, which in all Appearance might have intervened, the Consequences would perhaps have ruined the whole Confederacy; and therefore, however it hath now succeeded, the Experiment was too dangerous to try.

BUT this is what we can by no means allow them. We never will admit Rashness or Chance to have produced all this Harmony and Order. It is visible to the World, that the several Steps towards this Change were slowly taken, and with the utmost Caution. The *Movers* observed as they went on, how Matters would bear; and advanced no farther at first, than so as they might be able to stop or go back, if Circumstances were not mature. Things were grown to such a Height, that it was no longer the Question, whether a Person who aimed at an Employment were a *Whig* or a *Tory*; much less, whether he had Merit or proper Abilities for what he pretended to: He must owe his Preferment only to the Favourites; and the Crown was so far from *Nominating*, that they would not allow it a *Negative*. This, the QUEEN was resolved no longer to endure; and began to break into their *Prescription*, by bestowing one or two Places of Consequence, without consulting her *Ephori*; after they had fixed them for others, and concluded as usually, that all their Business was to signify their Pleasure to her Majesty. But, although the Persons the QUEEN had chosen, were such as no Objection could well be raised against, upon the Score of Party, yet the *Oligarchy* took the Alarm; their Sovereign Authority was, it seems, called in Question; they grew into Anger and Discontent, as if their undoubted Rights were violated. All former Obligations to their Sovereign now became cancelled; and they put themselves upon the Foot of People, who were hardly used after the most eminent Services.

I BELIEVE, all Men who know any thing in Politicks, will agree, that a Prince thus treated by those he hath most confided in, and perpetually loaded with his Favours, ought to extricate himself as soon as possible; and is then only blameable in his Choice of Time, when he defers one Minute after it is in his Power; because, from the monstrous Encroachments of exorbitant Avarice and Ambition, he cannot tell how long it may continue to be so. And it will be found, upon enquiring into History, that most of those Princes, who have been ruined by Favourites, have owed their Misfortune to the Neglect of early Remedies; deferring to struggle until they were quite sunk.

THE *Whigs* are every Day cursing the ungovernable Rage, the haughty Pride, and unsatiable Covetousness of a *certain Person*, as the Cause of their Fall; and are apt to tell their Thoughts, that *one single Removal* might have set all Things right. But the Interests of that *single Person* were found upon Experience, so complicated and woven with the rest, by *Love*, by *Awe*, by *Marriage*, by *Alliance*; that they would rather confound Heaven and Earth, than dissolve such an Union.

I HAVE always heard and understood, that a King of *England*, possessed of his People's Hearts; at the Head of a Free Parliament, and in full Agreement with a great Majority, made the true Figure in the World that such a Monarch ought to do; and pursued the real Interest of himself and his Kingdom, Will they allow her Majesty to be in those Circumstances at present? And was it not plain by the Addresses sent from all Parts of the Island, and by the visible Disposition of the People, that such a Parliament would undoubtedly be chosen? And so it proved, without the Court's using any Arts to influence Elections.

WHAT People then, are these in a Corner, to whom the Constitution must truckle? If the whole Nation's Credit cannot supply Funds for the War, without humble Application from the entire Legislature to a few *Retailers* of Money; it is high time we should sue for a Peace. What new Maxims are these, which neither we nor our Forefathers ever heard of before, and which no wise Institution would ever allow? Must our Laws from henceforward pass the *Bank* and *East-India* Company, or have their *Royal Assent* before they are in Force?

TO hear some of these worthy Reasoners talking of *Credit*; that she is so nice, so squeamish, so capricious; you would think they were describing a Lady troubled with Vapours or the Cholick, to be only removed by a *Course of Steel*, or *swallowing a Bullet*. By the narrowness of their Thoughts, one would imagine they conceived the World to be no wider than *Exchange-Alley*. It is probable *They* may have such a sickly Dame among them; and it is well if she hath no worse Diseases, considering what Hands she passes through. But, the *National Credit* is of another Complexion; of sound Health, and an even Temper; her Life and Existence being a Quintessence drawn from the Vitals of the whole Kingdom. And we find these *Money-Politicians*, after all their Noise, to be of the same Opinion, by the Court they paid her, when she lately appeared to them in the Form of a *Lottery*.

As to that mighty Error in Politics they charge upon the QUEEN, for changing her Ministry in the Heighth of a War, I suppose it is only looked upon as an Error under a *Whiggish Administration*; otherwise the late King had much to answer for, who did it pretty frequently. And it is well known, that the late Ministry, of *Famous Memory*, was brought in during the present War; only with this Circumstance, that two or three of the Chief did first change their own Principles, and then took in suitable Companions.

BUT however, I see no Reason why the *Tories* should not value their Wisdom by Events, as well as the *Whigs*. Nothing was ever thought a more precipitate rash Counsel, than that of *altering the Coin* at the Juncture it was done; yet the Prudence of the Undertaking was sufficiently justified by the Success. Perhaps it will be said, that the Attempt was necessary, because the whole Species of Money was so grievously Clipped and Counterfeit. And, is not her Majesty's Authority as Sacred as her Coin? And hath not that been most scandalously Clipped and Mangled; and often Counterfeited too?

IT is another grievous Complaint of the *Whigs*, that their late Friends, and the whole Party, are treated with Abundance of Severity in Print; and in particular by the *Examiner*. They think it hard, that when they are wholly deprived of Power, hated by the People, and out of all Hope of re-establishing themselves; their Infirmities should be so often displayed, in order to render them yet more odious to Mankind. This is what they employ their Writers to set forth in their Papers of the Week; and it is Humoursome enough to observe one Page taken up in railing at the *Examiner* for his Invectives against a discarded Ministry; and the other Side filled with the falsest and vilest Abuses, against those who are now in the highest Power and Credit with their Sovereign; and whose least Breath would scatter them into Silence and Obscurity. However, although I have indeed often wondered to see so much Licentiousness taken and connived at, and am sure it would not be suffered in any other Country of

Christendom; yet, I never once invoked the Assistance of the *Goal* or the *Pillory*, which upon the least Provocation, was the usual Style during their Tyranny. There hath not passed a Week these twenty Years without some malicious Paper scattered in every Coffee-House by the Emissaries of that Party, whether it were *down* or *up*. I believe, they will not pretend to object the same Thing to us. Nor do I remember any constant Weekly Paper, with Reflections on the late Ministry or Junta. They have many weak, defenceless Parts; they have not been used to a regular Attack, and therefore it is, that they are so ill able to endure one, when it comes to be their Turn. So that they complain more of a few Months Truths from us, than we did of all their Lies, and for twice as many Years.

I CANNOT forbear observing upon this Occasion, that those worthy Authors I am speaking of, seem to me not fairly to represent the Sentiments of their Party; who, in disputing with us, do generally give up several of the late Ministry; and freely own many of their Failings. They confess the monstrous *Debt upon the Navy*, to have been caused by most scandalous Mismanagement: They allow the *Insolence* of *some*, and the *Avarice* of *others*, to have been insupportable: But these Gentlemen are most liberal in their Praises to those Persons, and upon those very Articles, where their wisest Friends give up the Point. They gravely tell us, that *such a one* was the most faithful Servant ever any Prince had; *another* the most dutiful, a third the most generous, and a fourth of the greatest Integrity. So that I look upon these Champions, rather as retained by a *Cabal* than a *Party*; which I desire the reasonable Men among them would please to consider.

No. 38. *Thursday, April* 26, 1711.

Indignum est in eâ civitate, quæ legibus continetur, discedi a legibus.

I HAVE been often considering how it comes to pass, that the Dexterity of Mankind in Evil, should always outgrow, not only the Prudence and Caution of private Persons, but the continual Expedients of the wisest Laws contrived to prevent it. I cannot imagine a Knave to possess a greater Share of natural Wit or Genius, than an honest Man. I have known very notable Sharpers at Play, who upon all other Occasions, were as great Dunces, as Human Shape can well allow; and, I believe, the same might be observed among the other Knots of Thieves and Pick-Pockets about this Town. The Proposition however is certainly true, and to be confirmed by an hundred Instances. A Scrivener, an Attorney, a Stock-Jobber, and many other *Retailers of Fraud*, shall not only be able to over-reach others, much wiser than themselves; but find out new Inventions, to elude the Force of any Law made against them. I suppose the Reason of this may be, that as the *Aggressor* is said to have generally the Advantage of the *Defender*; so, the Makers of the Law, which is to defend our Rights, have usually not so much Industry or Vigour, as those whose Interest leads them to attack it. Besides, it rarely happens that Men are rewarded by the Publick for their Justice and Virtue; neither do those who act upon such Principles, expect any Recompence until the next World: Whereas Fraud, where it succeeds, gives present Pay; and this is allowed the greatest Spur imaginable both to Labour and Invention. When a Law is made to stop some growing Evil, the Wits of those, whose Interest it is to break it with Secrecy or Impunity, are immediately at Work; and even among those who pretend to fairer Characters, many would gladly find Means to avoid, what they would not be thought to violate. They desire to reap the Advantage, if possible, without the Shame, or, at least, without the Danger. This Art is what I take that dextrous Race of Men, sprung up soon after the Revolution, to have studied with great Application ever since; and to have arrived at great Perfection in it. According to the Doctrine of some *Romish* Casuists, they have found out *Quam prope ad peccatum sine peccato possint accedere*. They can tell how to go within an Inch of an Impeachment, and yet come back untouched. They know what Degree of Corruption will just forfeit an Employment, and whether the Bribe you receive be sufficient to set you right, and put something in your Pocket besides. How much, to a Penny, you may safely cheat the QUEEN, whether forty, fifty, or sixty *per Cent*. according to the Station you are in, and the Dispositions of the Persons in Office, below and above you. They have computed the Price you may securely take or give for a Place, or what Part of the Salary you ought to reserve. They can discreetly distribute five hundred Pounds in a small Borough, without any Danger from the Statutes, against bribing Elections. They can manage a Bargain for an Office, by a third, fourth, or fifth Hand; so that you shall not know whom to accuse; they can win a thousand Guineas at Play, in spight of the Dice, and send away the Loser satisfied: They can pass the most exorbitant Accounts, overpay the Creditor with half his Demands, and sink the rest.

It would be endless to relate, or rather indeed impossible to discover, the several Arts which curious Men have found out to enrich themselves, by defrauding the Publick, in defiance of the Law. The Military Men, both by Sea and Land, have equally cultivated this most useful Science: Neither hath it been altogether neglected by the other Sex; of which, on the contrary, I could produce an Instance, that would make ours Blush to be so far out-done.

Besides, to confess the Truth, our Laws themselves are extremely defective in many Articles, which I take to be one ill Effect of our best Possession, Liberty. Some Years ago, the Ambassador of a great Prince was arrested, and Outrages committed on his Person in our Streets, without any Possibility of Redress from *Westminster-Hall*, or the Prerogative of the Sovereign; and the Legislature was forced to provide a Remedy against the like Evil in Times to come. A Commissioner of the Stamped Paper was lately discovered to have notoriously cheated the Publick of great Sums for many Years, by counterfeiting the Stamps, which the Law had made Capital: But the Aggravation of his Crime, provèd to be the Cause that saved his Life; and that additional heightning Circumstance of betraying his Trust, was found to be a legal Defence. I am assured, that the notorious Cheat of the Brewers at *Portsmouth*, detected about two months ago in Parliament, cannot by any Law now in Force be punished in a Degree, equal to the Guilt and Infamy of it. Nay, what is almost incredible, had *Guiscard* survived his detestable Attempt upon Mr. *Harley*'s Person, all the inflaming Circumstances of the Fact, would not have sufficed, in the Opinion of many Lawyers, to have punished him with Death; and the Publick must have lain under this *Dilemma*, either to condemn him by a Law, *ex post Facto* (which would have been of dangerous Consequence, and form an ignominious Precedent) or undergo the Mortification to see the greatest Villain upon Earth escape unpunished, to the infinite Triumph and Delight of *Popery* and *Faction*. But even this is not to be wondred at, when we consider, that of all the Insolences offered to the QUEEN since the Act of Indemnity, (at least, that ever came to my Ears) I can hardly instance above two or three, which, by the Letter of the Law could amount to High Treason.

FROM these Defects in our Laws, and the Want of some discretionary Power safely lodged, to exert upon Emergencies; as well as from the great Acquirements of able Men, to elude the Penalties of those Laws they break; it is no wonder that the Injuries done to the Publick are so seldom redressed. But besides, no Individual suffers, by any Wrong he doth to the Commonwealth, in Proportion to the Advantage he gains by doing it. There are seven or eight Millions who contribute to the Loss, while the whole Gain is sunk among a few. The Damage suffered by the Publick, is not so immediately or heavily felt by particular Persons; and the Zeal of Prosecution is apt to drop and be lost among Numbers.

BUT, imagine a Set of Politicians for many Years at the Head of Affairs, the Game visibly their own, and by Consequence acting with great Security; may not these be sometimes tempted to forget their Caution, by length of Time, by excess of Avarice and Ambition, by the Insolence or Violence of their Nature, or perhaps by a meer Contempt for their Adversaries? May not such Motives as these put them often upon Actions directly against the Law, such as no Evasions can be found for, and which will lay them fully open to the Vengeance of a prevailing Interest, whenever they are out of Power? It is answered in the Affirmative. And here we cannot refuse the late Ministry their due Praises; who foreseeing a Storm, provided for their own Safety by two admirable Expedients, by which, with great Prudence, they have escaped the Punishments due to pernicious

Councils and corrupt Management. The first, was to procure, under Pretences hardly specious, a general Act of Indemnity, which cuts off all Impeachments. The second, was yet more refined: Suppose, for Instance, a Counsel is to be pursued, which is necessary to carry on the dangerous Designs of a prevailing Party, to preserve them in Power, to gratify the unmeasurable Appetites of a few *Leaders*, Civil and Military, although by hazarding the Ruin of the whole Nation: This Counsel, desperate in it self, unprecedented in the Nature of it, they procure a Majority to form into an Address, which makes it look like the Sense of the Nation. Under that Shelter they carry on the Work, and lie secure against After-Reckonings.

I MUST be so free to tell my Meaning in this; that among other Things, I understand it of the Address made to the QUEEN about three Years ago, to desire that her Majesty would not consent to a Peace, without the entire Restitution of *Spain*. A Proceeding, which to People abroad, must look like the highest Strain of Temerity, Folly, and Gasconade. But we at home, who allow the Promoters of that Advice to be no Fools, can easily comprehend the Depth and Mystery of it. They were assured by this Means, to pin down the War upon us; consequently to increase their own Power and Wealth, and multiply Difficulties on the QUEEN and Kingdom, until they had fixed their Party too firmly to be shaken, whenever they should find themselves disposed to reverse their Address, and give us Leave to wish for a Peace.

IF any Man entertain a more favourable Opinion of this monstrous Step in Politicks, I would ask him what we must do, in Case we find it impossible to recover *Spain?* Those among the *Whigs* who believe a GOD, will confess, that the Events of War lie in his Hands; and the rest of them, who acknowledge no such Power, will allow, that *Fortune* hath too great a Share in the good or ill Success of Military Actions, to let a wise Man reason upon them, as if they were entirely in his Power. If Providence shall think fit to refuse Success to our Arms; with how ill a Grace, with what Shame and Confusion shall we be obliged to recant that precipitate Address, unless the World will be so charitable to consider, that Parliaments among us, differ as much as Princes; and, that by the fatal Conjunction of many unhappy Circumstances, it is very possible for our Island to be represented some Times by those who have the least Pretensions? So little Truth or Justice there is in what some pretend to advance, that the Actions of former Senates, ought always to be treated with Respect by the latter; that those Assemblies are all equally venerable, and no one to be preferred before another: By which Argument, the Parliament that began the Rebellion against King *Charles the First*, voted his Tryal, and appointed his Murderers, ought to be remembered with Respect.

BUT to return from this Digression; it is very plain, that considering the Defectiveness of our Laws, the variety of Cases, the Weakness of the Prerogative, the Power or the Cunning of ill-designing Men, it is possible, that many great Abuses may be visibly committed, which cannot be legally punished: Especially if we add to this, that some Enquiries might probably involve those, whom upon other Accounts, it is not thought convenient to disturb. Therefore, it is very false Reasoning, especially in the Management of Public Affairs, to argue that Men are Innocent, because the Law hath not pronounced them Guilty.

I AM apt to think, it was to supply such Defects as these, that Satyr was first introduced into the World; whereby those whom neither Religion, nor natural Virtue, nor fear of Punishment, were able to keep within the Bounds of their Duty, might be with-held by the Shame of having their Crimes exposed to open View in the strongest Colours, and themselves rendered odious to Mankind. Perhaps all this may be little regarded by such hardened and abandoned Natures as I have to deal with; but, next to taming or binding a Savage-Animal, the best Service you can do the Neighbourhood, is to give them warning, either to arm themselves, or not come in its Way.

COULD I have hoped for any Signs of Remorse from the Leaders of that Faction, I should very gladly have changed my Style, and forgot or passed by their Million of Enormities. But they are every Day more fond of discovering their impotent Zeal and Malice: Witness their Conduct in the City about a Fortnight ago, which had no other End imaginable, beside that of perplexing our Affairs, and endeavouring to make Things desperate, that themselves may be thought necessary. While they continue in this frantick Mood, I shall not forbear to treat them as they deserve; that is to say, as the inveterate, irreconcilable Enemies to our Country and its Constitution.

No. 39. *Thursday, May* 3, 1711.

Quis tulerit Gracchos de seditione querentes?

THERE have been certain Topicks of Reproach, liberally bestowed for some Years past, by the *Whigs* and *Tories*, upon each other. We charge the former with a Design of destroying the *Established Church*, and introducing *Fanaticism* and *Free-thinking* in its stead. We accuse them as Enemies to Monarchy; as endeavouring to undermine the present Form of Government, and to build a Commonwealth, or some new Scheme of their own, upon its Ruins. On the other Side, their Clamours against us, may be summed up in those three formidable Words, *Popery*, *Arbitrary Power*, and the *Pretender*. Our Accusations against them we endeavour to make good by certain Overt-Acts; such as their perpetually abusing the whole Body of the Clergy; their declared Contempt for the very Order of Priesthood; their Aversion against Episcopacy; the publick Encouragement and Patronage they gave to *Tindall*, *Toland*, and other Atheistical Writers; their appearing as professed Advocates, retained by the Dissenters; excusing their Separation, and laying the Guilt of it to the Obstinacy of the Church; their frequent Endeavours to repeal the Test, and their setting up the Indulgence to scrupulous Consciences, as a Point of greater Importance than the established Worship. The Regard they bear to our *Monarchy*, hath appeared by their open ridiculing the *Martyrdom* of King *Charles* the First, in their *Calves-head Clubs*, their common Discourses and their Pamphlets: Their denying the unnatural War raised against that Prince, to have been a Rebellion; their justifying his Murder in the allowed Papers of the Week; their Industry in publishing and spreading Seditious and Republican Tracts; such as *Ludlow*'s Memoirs, *Sidney* of Government, and many others; their endless lopping of the Prerogative, and mincing into nothing her Majesty's Titles to the Crown.

WHAT Proofs they bring for our endeavouring to introduce *Popery*, *Arbitrary Power*, and the *Pretender*, I cannot readily tell, and would be glad to hear; however, those important Words having, by dextrous Management, been found of mighty Service to their Cause, although applied with little Colour, either of Reason or Justice; I have been considering whether they may not be adapted to more proper Objects.

AS to *Popery*, which is the first of these; to deal plainly, I can hardly think there is any Sett of Men among us, except the Professors of it, who have any direct Intention to introduce it here: But the Question is, whether the Principles and Practices of us, or the *Whigs*, be most likely to make Way for it? It is allowed on all Hands, that among the Methods concerted at *Rome*, for bringing over *England* into the Bosom of the Catholick Church; one of the Chief was, to send Jesuits and other Emissaries, in Lay-Habits; who personating *Tradesmen* and *Mechanicks*, should mix with the People, and under the Pretence of a further and purer *Reformation*, endeavour to divide us into as many Sects as possible; which would either put us under the Necessity of returning to our old Errors, to preserve *Peace* at home; or by our *Divisions* make Way for some powerful Neighbour, with the Assistance of the *Pope*'s Permission, and a consecrated Banner, to *convert* and *enslave* us at once. If this hath been reckoned good Politicks (and it was the best the *Jesuit-Schools* could invent) I appeal to any Man, whether the *Whigs*, for many Years past, have not been employed in the very same Work? They professed on all Occasions, that they knew no Reason why any one System of *Speculative Opinions* (as they termed the Doctrines of the Church) should be established by Law more than another; or why Employments should be confined to the Religion of the Magistrate, and that called *the Church Established*. The grand Maxim they laid down, was, That no Man, for the Sake of a few *Notions* and *Ceremonies*, under the Names of *Doctrine* and *Discipline*, should be denied the Liberty of serving his

Country: As if Places would go a begging, unless *Brownists*, *Familists*, *Sweet-Singers*, *Quakers*, *Anabaptists* and *Muggletonians*, would take them off our Hands.

I HAVE been sometimes imagining this Scheme brought to Perfection, and how diverting it would look to see half a Dozen *Sweet-Singers* on the Bench in their Ermins, and two or three *Quakers* with their white Staves at Court. I can only say, this Project is the very Counter-part of the late King *James*'s Design, which he took up as the best Method for introducing his *own Religion*, under the Pretext of an *universal Liberty of Conscience*; and that no Difference in Religion should make any in his Favour. Accordingly, to save Appearances, he dealt some Employments among *Dissenters* of most Denominations; and what he did was, no doubt, in pursuance of the best Advice he could get at Home or Abroad; but the Church thought it the most dangerous Step he could take for her Destruction. It is true, King *James* admitted *Papists* among the rest, which the *Whigs* would not; but this is sufficiently made up by a material Circumstance, wherein they seem to have much out-done that Prince, and to have carried their *Liberty of Conscience* to a higher Point; having granted it to all the Classes of *Free-thinkers*, which the nice Conscience of a *Popish Prince* would not give him leave to do; and was therein mightily overseen; because it is agreed by the Learned, that there is but a very narrow Step from *Atheism*, to the other Extream, *Superstition*. So that upon the whole, whether the *Whigs* had any real Design of bringing in *Popery* or no, it is very plain, that they took the most effectual Step towards it; and if the *Jesuits* had been their immediate Directors, they could not have taught them better, nor have found apter Scholars.

THEIR second Accusation is, That we encourage and maintain Arbitrary Power in Princes; and promote enslaving Doctrines among the People. This they go about to prove by Instances, producing the particular Opinions of certain Divines in King *Charles the Second*'s Reign; a Decree of *Oxford-University*, and some few Writers since the *Revolution*. What they mean is the Principle of *Passive-Obedience* and *Non-Resistance*, which those who affirm, did, I believe, never intend should include

Arbitrary Power. However, although I am sensible that it is not reckoned prudent in a Dispute, to make any Concessions without the last Necessity; yet I do agree, that, in my own private Opinion, some Writers did carry that Tenet of *Passive-Obedience* to a Height, which seemed hardly consistent with the Liberties of a Country, whose Laws can be neither enacted nor repealed, without the Consent of the whole People, I mean not those who affirm it due in general, as it certainly is to the Legislature; but such as fix it entirely in the Prince's Person. This last hath, I believe, been done by a very few; but when the *Whigs* quote Authors to prove it upon us, they bring in all who mention it as a Duty in general, without applying it to Princes, abstracted from their Senate.

By thus freely declaring my own Sentiments of *Passive-Obedience*, it will at last appear, that I do not write for a Party: Neither do I, upon any Occasion, pretend to speak their Sentiments, but my own. The Majority of the two Houses, and the present Ministry (if those be a Party) seem to me, in all their Proceedings, to pursue the real Interest of Church and State: And if I shall happen to differ from particular Persons among them in a single Notion about Government, I suppose they will not, upon that Account, explode me and my Paper. However, as an Answer once for all, to the tedious Scurrilities of those idle People, who affirm, I am hired and directed what to write; I must here inform them, that their *Censure* is an Effect of their *Principles*: The present Ministry are under no Necessity of employing prostitute Pens; they have no dark Designs to promote, by advancing *Heterodox Opinions*.

But, (to return) suppose two or three private Divines, under *King Charles the Second*, did a little over-strain the *Doctrine of Passive-Obedience* to Princes; some Allowance might be given to the Memory of that *unnatural Rebellion* against his Father, and the dismal Consequences of *Resistance*. It is plain, by the Proceedings of the Churchmen before and at the Revolution, that this Doctrine was never designed to introduce arbitrary Power.

I look upon the *Whigs* and *Dissenters* to be exactly of the same political Faith; let us, therefore, see what Share each of them had in advancing *Arbitrary Power*. It is manifest, that the

Fanaticks made *Cromwell* the most absolute Power in *Christendom*: The *Rump* abolished the *House of Lords*; the *Army* abolished the *Rump*; and by this Army of *Saints* he governed. The *Dissenters* took Liberty of Conscience and Employments from the late King *James*, as an Acknowledgment of his *dispensing Power*; which makes the King of *England* as absolute as the *Turk*. The *Whigs*, under the late King, perpetually declared for keeping up a standing Army in Times of Peace; which hath in all Ages been the first and great Step to the Ruin of Liberty. They were, besides, discovering every Day their Inclinations to destroy the Rights of the Church; and declared their Opinion in all Companies, against Bishops sitting in the *House of Peers*; which was exactly copying after their Predecessors of *Forty One*. I need not say, their real Intentions were to make the King absolute; but whatever be the Designs of innovating Men, they usually end in a Tyranny: As we may see by an hundred Examples in *Greece*, and in the later Commonwealths of *Italy* mentioned by *Machiavel*.

IN the third Place, the *Whigs* accuse us of a Design to bring in the *Pretender*; and to give it a greater Air of Probability, they suppose the QUEEN to be a Party in this Design; which, however, is no very extraordinary Supposition in those who have advanced such singular Paradoxes concerning *Greg* and *Guiscard*. Upon this Article their Charge is general, without ever offering to produce an Instance. But I verily think and believe, it will appear no Paradox, that if ever he be brought in, the *Whigs* are his Men. For, first, it is an undoubted Truth, that a Year or two after the *Revolution*, several Leaders of that Party had their Pardons sent them by the late King *James*; and had entred upon Measures to restore him, on Account of some Disobligations they received from King *William*. Besides, I would ask, whether those who are under the greatest Ties of Gratitude to King *James*, are not at this Day become the most zealous *Whigs?* And of what Party those are now, who kept a long Correspondence with St. *Germains?*

IT is likewise very observable of late, that the *Whigs* upon all Occasions, profess their Belief of the *Pretender*'s being no *Impostor*, but a real *Prince*, born of the late QUEEN's Body: Which, whether it be true or false, is very unseasonably advanced, considering the Weight such an Opinion must have with the Vulgar, if they once thoroughly believe it. Neither is it at all improbable, that the *Pretender* himself puts his chief Hopes in the Friendship he expects from the *Dissenters* and *Whigs*; by his Choice to invade the Kingdom when the latter were most in Credit: And he had Reason to count upon the former, from the gracious Treatment they received from his supposed Father, and their joyful Acceptance of it. But further; what could be more consistent with the *Whiggish* Notion of a *Revolution-Principle*, than to bring in the *Pretender?* A *Revolution-Principle*, as their Writings and Discourses have taught us to define it, is a Principle perpetually disposing Men to *Revolutions*: this is suitable to the famous Saying of a great *Whig*, *That the more Revolutions the better*; which how odd a Maxim soever in Appearance, I take to be the true Characteristick of the Party.

A Dog loves to turn round often; yet after certain *Revolutions*, he lies down to *Rest*: But Heads, under the Dominion of the *Moon*, are for perpetual *Changes*, and perpetual *Revolutions*: Besides, the *Whigs* owe all their Wealth to *Wars* and *Revolutions*; like the Girl at *Bartholomew*-Fair, who gets a Penny by turning round a hundred Times, with Swords in her Hands.

To conclude, the *Whigs*, have a natural Faculty of bringing in *Pretenders*, and will therefore probably endeavour to bring in the great One at last: How many *Pretenders* to Wit, Honour, Nobility, Politicks, have they brought in these last twenty Years? In short, they have been sometimes able to procure a Majority of *Pretenders* in Parliament; and wanted nothing to render the Work compleat, except a *Pretender* at their Head.

No. 40. *Thursday*, *May* 10, 1711.

Dos est magna parentium virtus.

I TOOK up a Paper some Days ago in a Coffee-House; and if the Correctness of the Style, and a superior Spirit in it, had not immediately undeceived me, I should have been apt to imagine, I had been reading an *Examiner*. In this Paper there were several important Propositions advanced. For Instance, That *Providence raised up Mr.* Harley *to be an Instrument of great Good, in a very critical Juncture, when it was much wanted.* That, his *very Enemies acknowledge his eminent Abilities, and distinguishing Merit, by their unwearied and restless Endeavours against* his *Person and Reputation:* That, *they have had an inveterate Malice against both:* That, he *hath been wonderfully preserved from* SOME *unparalled Attempts*; with more to the same Purpose. I immediately computed by Rules of Arithmetick, that in the last cited Words there was something more intended than the Attempt of *Guiscard*, which I think can properly pass but for *One* of the SOME. And, although I dare not pretend to guess the Author's Meaning, yet the Expression allows such a Latitude, that I would venture to hold a Wager, most Readers, both *Whig* and *Tory*, have agreed with me, that this Plural Number must in all Probability, among other Facts, take in the Business of *Greg*.

SEE now the Difference of Styles. Had I been to have told my Thoughts on this Occasion; instead, of saying how Mr. *Harley was treated by some Persons*, and *preserved from some unparalleled Attempts*, I should, with intolerable Bluntness and ill Manners, have told a formal Story, of a Committee sent to a condemned Criminal in *Newgate*, to bribe him with a Pardon, on Condition he would swear High Treason against his Master; who discovered his Correspondence, and secured his Person, when *a certain grave Politician* had given him Warning to make his Escape: And by this Means I should have drawn a whole swarm of Hedge-Writers to exhaust their Catalogue of Scurrilities against me as a Lyar, and a Slanderer. But with Submission to the Author of that forementioned Paper, I think he hath carried that Expression to the utmost it will bear: For, after all this Noise, I know of but *two Attempts* against Mr. *Harley*, that can really be called *unparalleled*; which are those aforesaid of *Greg* and *Guiscard*: For, as to the rest, I will engage to *parallel* them from the Story of *Cataline*, and others I could produce.

HOWEVER, I cannot but observe with infinite Pleasure, that a great Part of what I have charged upon the late prevailing Faction, and for affirming which, I have been adorned with so many decent Epithets, hath been sufficiently confirmed at several Times, by the Resolutions of one or the other House of Parliament. I may therefore now say, I hope, with good Authority, that *there have been some unparalleled Attempts against Mr.* Harley. That, the late Ministry were justly to blame in some Management, which occasioned the unfortunate Battle of *Almanza*, and the Disappointment at *Toulon*. That, the Publick hath been grievously wronged by most notorious Frauds, during the *Whig Administration*. That, those who advised the bringing in the *Palatines*, were Enemies to the Kingdom. That, the late Managers of the Revenue have not duly passed their Accounts, for a great Part of thirty five Millions; and ought not to be trusted in such Employments any more. Perhaps in a little Time I may venture to affirm some other Paradoxes of this kind, and produce the same Vouchers. And perhaps also, if it had not been so busy a Period, instead of one *Examiner*, the late Ministry might have had above four hundred, each of whose little Fingers would be heavier than my Loins. It makes me think of *Neptune*'s Threat to the Winds; *Quos ego——sed motos præstat componere fluctus*. Thus, when the Sons of *Æolus* had almost sunk the Ship with the Tempests they raised, it was necessary to smooth the Ocean, and secure the Vessel, instead of pursuing the Offenders.

But, I observe the general Expectation at present, instead of dwelling any longer upon Conjectures who is to be punished for past Miscarriages, seems bent upon the Rewards intended to those who have been so highly instrumental in rescuing our Constitution from its late Dangers. It is the Observation of *Tacitus*, in the Life of *Agricola*, that his eminent Services had raised a general Opinion of his being designed, by the Emperor, for *Prætor* of *Britain*. *Nullis in hoc suis sermonibus*, *sed quia par videbatur*: And then he adds, *Non semper errat Fama*, *aliquando &* *eligit*. The Judgment of a wise Prince, and the general Disposition of the People, do often point at the same Person; and sometimes the popular Wishes do even foretel the Reward intended for some superior Merit. Thus, among several deserving Persons, there are *Two*, whom the publick Vogue hath in a peculiar Manner singled out, as designed very soon to receive the choicest Marks of the Royal Favour. *One* of them to be placed in a very high Station, and *Both* to increase the Number of our

Nobility. This, I say, is the general Conjecture; for I pretend to none, nor will be chargeable if it be not fulfilled; since it is enough for their Honour, that the Nation thinks them worthy of the greatest Rewards.

UPON this Occasion I cannot but take Notice, That of all the Heresies in Politicks, profusely scattered by the Partisans of the *late Administration*, none ever displeased me more, or seemed to have more dangerous Consequences to *Monarchy*, than that pernicious Talent so much affected, of discovering a Contempt for *Birth*, *Family*, and *ancient Nobility*. All the Threadbare Topicks of *Poets* and *Orators* were displayed to discover to us, that *Merit* and *Virtue* were the only *Nobility*; and that the Advantages of *Blood* could not make a *Knave* or a *Fool* either Honest or Wise. Most popular Commotions we read of in Histories of *Greece* and *Rome*, took their Rise from unjust Quarrels to the *Nobles*; and in the latter, the *Plebeians* Encroachments on the P*atricians*, were the first Cause of their Ruin.

SUPPOSE there be nothing but *Opinion* in the Difference of Blood; every Body knows, that *Authority* is very much founded on *Opinion*. But surely, that Difference is not wholly imaginary. The Advantages of a liberal Education, of chusing the best Companions to converse with; not being under the Necessity of practicing little mean Tricks by a scanty Allowance; the enlarging of Thought, and acquiring the Knowledge of Men and Things by Travel; the Example of Ancestors inciting to great and good Actions. These are usually some of the Opportunities that fall in the Way of those who are born, of what we call the better Families; and, allowing *Genius* to be equal in them and the Vulgar, the Odds are clearly on their Side. Nay, we may observe in some, who by the Appearance of Merit, or Favour of Fortune, have risen to great Stations, from an obscure Birth, that they have still retained some sordid Vices of their *Parentage* or *Education*, either *insatiable Avarice*, or *ignominious Falshood* and *Corruption*.

TO say the Truth, the great Neglect of Education in several noble Families, whose Sons are suffered to pass the most improveable Seasons of their Youth in Vice and Idleness, have too much lessened their Reputation: But, even this Misfortune we owe, among all the rest, to that *Whiggish* Practice of reviling the *Universities*, under the Pretence of their instilling *Pedantry*, *narrow Principles*, and *High-Church Doctrines*.

I WOULD not be thought to undervalue *Merit* and *Virtue*, where ever they are to be found; but will allow them capable of the highest Dignities in a State, when they are in a very great Degree of Eminence. A Pearl holds its Value although it be found in a Dunghill; but however, that is not the most probable Place to search for it. Nay, I will go farther, and admit, that a Man of Quality without *Merit*, is just so much the worse for his Quality; which at once sets his Vices in a more publick View, and reproacheth him for them. But on the other Side, I doubt, those who are always undervaluing the Advantages of Birth, and celebrating personal Merit, have principally an Eye to their own, which they are fully satisfied with, and which no Body will dispute with them about; whereas they cannot, without Impudence and Folly, pretend to be nobly born; because this is a Secret too easily discovered: For, no Mens Parentage is so nicely enquired into, as that of assuming Upstarts; especially when they affect to make it better than it is, as they often do; or behave themselves with Insolence.

BUT whatever may be the Opinion of others upon this Subject, whose Philosophical Scorn for *Blood* and *Families* reacheth even to those that are *Royal*, or perhaps took its Rise from a *Whiggish* Contempt of the latter; I am pleased to find *two* such Instances of extraordinary Merit, as I have mentioned, joined with ancient and honourable Birth; which, whether it be of real or imaginary Value, hath been held in Veneration by all wise, polite States, both Ancient and Modern. And, as much a Foppery as Men pretend to think it, nothing is more observable in those who rise to great Place or Wealth, from mean Originals, than their mighty Solicitude to convince the World that they are not so low as is commonly believed. They are glad to find it made out by some strained Genealogy, that they have a remote Alliance with better Families. *Cromwell* himself was pleased with the Impudence of a Flatterer, who undertook to prove him descended from a Branch of the Royal Stem. I know a *Citizen* who adds or alters a Letter in his Name with every *Plumb* he acquires: He now wants only the Change of a * Vowel, to be allied to a Sovereign Prince in *Italy*; and that perhaps he may contrive to be done, by a *Mistake* of the Graver upon his *Tombstone*.

WHEN I am upon this Subject of *Nobility*, I am sorry for the Occasion given me, to mention the Loss of a *Person* who was so great an Ornament to it, as the late † *Lord President*; who began early to distinguish himself in the *Publick Service*; and passed through the highest Employments of State, in the most difficult Times, with great *Abilities* and untainted *Honour*. As he was of a good old Age, his Principles of Religion and Loyalty had received no Mixture from *late Infusions*, but were instilled into him by his illustrious Father, and other noble Spirits, who had exposed their Lives and Fortunes for the *Royal Martyr*.

——————Pulcherrima proles,
Magnanimi Heroes nati melioribus annis.

HIS first great Action was, like *Scipio*, to defend his Father, when oppressed by Numbers; and his Filial Piety was not only rewarded with long Life, but with a Son, who, upon the like Occasion, would have shewn the same Resolution. No Man ever preserved his Dignity better when he was out of Power, nor shewed more Affability while he was in. To conclude: His Character (which I do not here pretend to draw) is such, as his nearest Friends may safely trust to the most impartial Pen; nor wants the least of that Allowance which, they say, is required for those who are Dead.

No. 41. *Thursday*, *May* 17, 1711.

————Quem cur distringere coner,
Tutus ab infestis latronibus?

I NEVER let slip an Opportunity of endeavouring to convince the World, that I am not Partial; and to confound the idle Reproach of my being hired or directed what to write in Defence of the present Ministry, or for detecting the Practices of

---

* *Sir* H. FURNESE. † *Earl of* ROCHESTER.

the former. When I first undertook this Paper, I firmly resolved, that if ever I observed any gross Neglect, Abuse or Corruption in the publick Management, which might give any just Offence to reasonable People; I would take Notice of it with that innocent Boldness which becometh an honest Man, and a true Lover of his Country; at the same Time preserving the Respect due to Persons so highly entrusted by so wise and excellent a QUEEN. I know not how such a Liberty might have been resented; but I thank GOD there hath been no Occasion given me to exercise it; for, I can safely affirm, that I have with the utmost Rigour examined all the Actions of the present Ministry, as far as they fall under general Cognizance, without being able to accuse them of one ill or mistaken Step. Observing indeed some Time ago, that Seeds of Dissention had been plentifully scattered from a *certain Corner*; and fearing they began to rise and spread, I immediately writ a Paper on the Subject; which I treated with that Warmth, I thought it required: But the Prudence of those at the Helm soon prevented this growing Evil; and at present it seems likely to have no Consequences.

I HAVE had indeed for some Time a small Occasion of Quarrelling, which I thought too inconsiderable for a formal Subject of Complaint, although I have hinted at it more than once. But, it is grown at present to as great Height, as a Matter of that Nature can possibly bear; and therefore I conceive it high Time that an effectual Stop should be put to it. I have been amazed at the flaming Licentiousness of several Weekly Papers, which for some Months past, have been chiefly employed in barefaced Scurrilities against those who are in the greatest Trust and Favour with the QUEEN, with the first and last Letters of their Names frequently printed; or some Periphrasis describing their Station, or other Innuendo's, contrived too plain to be mistaken. The Consequence of which is, (and it is natural it should be so) that their long Impunity hath rendered them still more audacious.

AT this Time I particularly intend a Paper called the *Medley*; whose indefatigable, incessant Railings against me, I never thought convenient to take Notice of, because it would have diverted my Design, which I intended to be of Publick Use.

Besides, I never yet observed that Writer, or those Writers, (for it is every Way a *Medley*) to argue against any one material Point or Fact that I had advanced; or make one fair Quotation. And after all, I knew very well how soon the World grows weary of Controversy. It is plain to me, that three or four Hands at least have been joined at Times in this worthy Composition; but the Out-lines, as well as the Finishing, seem to have been always the Work of the same Pen, as it is visible from half a score Beauties of Style inseperable from it. But who these *Medlers* are, or where the judicious Leaders have picked them up, I shall never go about to conjecture. Factious Rancour, false Wit, abandoned Scurrility, impudent Falshood, and servile Pedantry, having so many Fathers, and so few to own them, that Curiosity her self would not be at the Pains to guess. It is the first Time I ever did my self the Honour to mention that admirable Paper: Nor could I imagine any Occasion likely to happen, that would make it necessary for me to engage with such an Adversary. This Paper is Weekly published, and as appears by the Number, hath been so for several Months; and is next to the *Observator*, allowed to be the best Production of that Party. Last Week my Printer brought me that of *May* 7, Number 32, where there are two Paragraphs relating to the *Speaker* of the House of Commons, and to Mr. *Harley*; which, as little as I am inclined to engage with such an Antagonist, I cannot let pass, without failing in my Duty to the Publick: And if those in Power will suffer such infamous Insinuations to pass with Impunity, they act without Precedent from any Age or Country of the World.

I DESIRE to open this Matter, and leave the *Whigs* themselves to determine upon it. The House of Commons resolved, *Nemine Contradicente*, that the *Speaker* should congratulate Mr. *Harley*'s Escape and Recovery in the Name of the House, upon his first Attendance on their Service. This is accordingly done; and the Speech, together with the Chancellor of the *Exchequer*'s, are printed by Order of the House. The Author of the *Medley* takes this Speech to Task the very next Week after it is published; telling us, in the aforesaid Paper, That *the* Speaker'*s commending Mr*. Harley, *for being an* Instrument of great Good to the Nation, *was ill-chosen Flattery; because Mr*. Harley *had brought the*

Nation under great Difficulties, to say no more: He says, *that when the* Speaker *tells Mr.* Harley, that Providence hath wonderfully preserved him from some unparalleled Attempts, (for that the *Medley* alludes to) *he only revives a false and groundless Calumny upon other Men; which is an Instance of impotent, but inveterate Malice, that makes him* [the *Speaker*] *still appear more vile and contemptible.* This is an Extract from his first Paragraph. In the next this Writer says, *That the Speaker's praying to God for the Continuance of Mr.* Harley'*s Life, as an invaluable Blessing, was a fulsome Piece of Insincerity, which exposeth him to Shame and Derision; because he is known to bear ill Will to Mr.* Harley*; to have an extream bad Opinion of him, and to think him an Obstructor of those fine Measures he would bring about.*

I NOW appeal to the *Whigs* themselves, whether a great Minister of State, in high Favour with the QUEEN, and a *Speaker* of the House of Commons, were ever publickly treated after so extraordinary a Manner, in the most licentious Times? For, this is not a clandestine Libel stolen into the World, but openly Printed and Sold, with the Bookseller's Name and Place of Abode at the Bottom. And the Juncture is admirable, when Mr. *Harley* is generally believed upon the very Point to be made an *Earl*, and promoted to the most important Station of the Kingdom: Nay, the very Marks of Esteem he hath so lately received from the whole Representative Body of the People, are called *ill-chosen Flattery, and a fulsome Piece of Insincerity, exposing the* Donors *to Shame and Derision.*

DOES this intrepid Writer think he hath sufficiently disguised the Matter, by that stale Artifice of altering the Story, and putting it as a supposed Case? Did any Man who ever saw the Congratulatory Speech, read either of those Paragraphs in the *Medley*, without interpreting them just as I have done? Will the Author declare upon his great Sincerity, that he never had any such Meaning? Is it enough, that a Jury at *Westminster-Hall* would, perhaps, not find him guilty of defaming the *Speaker* and Mr. *Harley* in that Paper? Which, however, I am much in doubt of too; and must think the Law very defective, if the Reputation of such Persons must lie at the Mercy of such Pens. I do not remember to have seen any Libel, supposed to be writ with

Caution and double Meaning, in order to prevent Prosecution, delivered under so thin a Cover, or so unartificially made up as this; whether it were from an Apprehension of his Reader's Dulness, or an Effect of his own. He hath transcribed the very Phrases of the *Speaker*, and put them in a different Character, for fear they might pass unobserved; and to prevent all Possibility of being mistaken. I shall be pleased to see him have Recourse to the old Evasion, and say, that I who make the Application, am chargeable with the Abuse: Let any Reader of either Party be Judge. But I cannot forbear asserting, as my Opinion, that for a Ministry to endure such open Calumny, without calling the Author to Account, is next to deserving it. And, this is an Omission I venture to charge upon the present Ministry, who are too apt to despise little Things, which however have not always little Consequences.

WHEN this Paper was first undertaken, one Design, among others, was, to *examine* some of those Writings so frequently published with an evil Tendency, either to Religion or Government; but I was long diverted by other Enquiries, which I thought more immediately necessary; to animadvert upon Mens Actions, rather than their Speculations; to shew the Necessity there was of changing the Ministry, that our Constitution in Church and State might be preserved; to expose some dangerous Principles and Practices under the former Administration; and prove by many Instances, that those who are now at the Helm, are entirely in the true Interest of Prince and People. This I may modestly hope, hath in some Measure been already done, sufficient to answer the End proposed, which was to inform the Ignorant and those at Distance; and to convince such as are not engaged in a Party, from other Motives than that of Conscience. I know not whether I shall have any Appetite to continue this Work much longer; if I do, perhaps some Time may be spent in exposing and overturning the false Reasonings of those who engage their Pens on the other Side; without losing Time in vindicating my self against their Scurrilities, much less in retorting them. Of this Sort there is a certain humble Companion, a * *French Maitre de Langues*, who every Month publisheth an

* *One* A. BOYER.

Extract from Votes, News-Papers, Speeches and Proclamations, larded with some insipid Remarks of his own; which he calls, *The Political State of* Great-Britain: This ingènious Piece he tells us himself, is constantly translated into *French*, and printed in *Holland*, where the *Dutch*, no doubt, conceive most noble Sentiments of us, conveyed through such a Vehicle. It is observable in his Account for *April*, that the Vanity, so predominant in many of his Nation, hath made him more concerned for the Honour of *Guiscard*, than the Safety of Mr. *Harley*: And for fear we should think the worse of his Country upon that *Assassin*'s Account, he tells us, there have been more Murders, Paracides and Villainies, committed in *England*, than any other Part of the World. I cannot imagine how an illiterate Foreigner, who is Neither Master of our Language, or indeed of common Sense; and who is devoted to a Faction, I suppose, for no other Reason, but his having more *Whig*-Customers than *Tories*, should take it into his Head to write Politick Tracts of our Affairs. But I presume, he builds upon the Foundation of having been called to an Account for his Insolence in one of his former Monthly Productions; which is a Method that seldom fails of giving some Vogue to the foolishest Composition. If such a Work must be done, I wish some tolerable Hand would undertake it; and that we would not suffer a little whiffling *Frenchman* to neglect his Trade of teaching his Language to our Children, and presume to instruct Foreigners in our Politicks.

No. 42. *Thursday, May* 24, 1711.

Delicta majorum immeritus lues,
Romane; donec templa refeceris,
Ædesq; labentes deorum;———

SEVERAL Letters have been lately sent me, desiring I would make honourable mention of the pious Design of building fifty Churches, in several Parts of *London* and *Westminster*, where they are most wanted; occasioned by an Address of the *Convocation* to the QUEEN, and recommended by her Majesty to the House of Commons; who immediately promised, they *would enable* her *to accomplish so excellent a Design*; and are now preparing a Bill accordingly. I thought, to have deferred any Notice of this important Affair until the End of this Session; at which Time I proposed to deliver a particular Account of the great and useful Things already performed by this present Parliament. But in Compliance to those who give themselves the Trouble of advising me; and partly convinced by the Reasons they offer; I am content to bestow a Paper upon a Subject, that indeed so well deserveth it.

THE Clergy, and whoever else have a true Concern for the Constitution of the Church, cannot but be highly pleased with one Prospect in this new Scene of publick Affairs. They may very well remember the Time, when every Session of Parliament was like a Cloud hanging over their Heads; and, if it happened to pass without bursting into some Storm upon the Church, we thanked GOD, and thought it an happy Escape, until the next Meeting; upon which we resumed our secret Apprehensions, although we were not allowed to believe any Danger. Things are now altered; the Parliament takes the Necessities of the Church into Consideration; receives the Proposals of the Clergy met in Convocation; and amidst all the Exigencies *of a long expensive War*, and *under the Pressure of heavy Debts*, finds a Supply for erecting fifty Edifices to the Service of GOD. And, it appears by the Address of the Commons to her Majesty upon this Occasion, (wherein they discovered a true Spirit of Religion) that the applying the Money granted *to accomplish so excellent a Design*, would, in their Opinion, be the most effectual Way of carrying on the War: That, it would (to use their own Words) *be a Means of drawing down Blessings on her Majesty's Undertakings, as it adds to the Number of those Places, where the Prayers of her devout and faithful Subjects, will be daily offered up to God, for the Prosperity of her Government at Home, and the Success of her Arms Abroad.*

I AM sometimes hoping, that we are not naturally so bad a People, as we have appeared for some Years past. *Faction*, in order to support it self, is generally forced to make Use of such abominable Instruments, that as long as it prevails, the Genius of a Nation is over-pressed, and cannot appear to exert it self: But, when that is broke and suppressed; when Things return to the old Course; Mankind will naturally fall to act from Principles of Reason and Religion. The *Romans*, upon a great Victory, or Escape from publick Danger, frequently built a Temple in Honour of some God, to whose peculiar Favour they imputed their Success or Delivery: And sometimes the *General* did the like, *at his own Expence*, to acquit himself of some pious Vow he had made. How little of any Thing resembling this hath been done by us after all our Victories! And perhaps for that Reason, among others, they have turned to so little Account. But what could we expect? We acted all along as if we believed nothing of a GOD or his Providence; and therefore it was consistent to offer up our Edifices only to *Those*, whom we looked upon as *Givers of all Victory*, in his stead.

I HAVE computed, that Fifty Churches may be built by a Medium, at Six Thousand Pound for a Church; which is somewhat *under* the Price of a *Subject*'s *Palace*: Yet perhaps the Care of above two hundred thousand Souls, with the Benefit of their Prayers for the Prosperity of their QUEEN and Country, may be almost put in the Balance with the domestick Convenience, or even Magnificence of any *Subject* whatsoever.

SIR *William Petty*, who under the Name of Captain *Graunt*, published some Observations upon Bills of Mortality about five Years after the *Restoration*; tells us, the Parishes in *London* were even then so unequally divided, that some were two hundred times larger than others. Since that Time, the Encrease of Trade, the Frequency of Parliaments, the Desire of living in the Metropolis, together with that Genius for Building, which began after the *Fire*, and hath ever since continued; have prodigiously enlarged this Town on all sides, where it was capable of Encrease: And those Tracts of Land built into Streets, have generally continued of the same Parish they belonged to, while they lay in Fields; so that the Care of above thirty thousand Souls hath been sometimes committed to one Minister, whose Church would hardly contain the twentieth part of his Flock: Neither, I think, was any Family in those Parishes obliged to pay above a Groat a Year to their Spiritual Pastor. Some few of those

Parishes have been since divided; in others were erected Chapels of Ease, where a Preacher is maintained by general Contribution. Such poor Shifts and Expedients, to the infinite Shame and Scandal of so vast and flourishing a City, have been thought sufficient for the Service of God and Religion; as if they were Circumstances wholly indifferent.

THIS Defect, among other Consequences of it, hath made *Schism* a Sort of necessary Evil; there being at least three hundred thousand Inhabitants in this Town, whom the Churches would not be able to contain, if the People were ever so well disposed: And in a City not overstocked with Zeal, the only way to preserve any Degree of Religion, is to make all Attendance upon the Duties of it, as easy and cheap as possible: Whereas, on the contrary, in the larger Parishes, the Press is so great, and the Pew-keeper's Tax so exorbitant, that those who love to save Trouble and Money, either stay at home, or retire to the *Conventicles*. I believe there are few Examples in any *Christian* Country of so great a Neglect for Religion; and the Dissenting Teachers have made their Advantages largely by it; *Sowing Tares among the Wheat while Men slept*; being much more expert at procuring Contributions, which is a Trade they are bred up in, than Men of a liberal Education.

AND to say Truth, the Way practised by several Parishes in and about this Town, of maintaining their Clergy by voluntary Subscriptions, is not only an Indignity to the Character, but hath many pernicious Consequences attending it; such a precarious Dependance, subjecting a Clergyman, who hath not more than ordinary Spirit and Resolution, to many Inconveniences, which are obvious to imagine: But this Defect, will no doubt, be remedied by the Wisdom and Piety of the present Parliament; and a Tax laid upon every House in a Parish, for the Support of their Pastor. Neither indeed can it be conceived, why a House, whose Purchase is not reckoned above one third less than Land of the same yearly Rent, should not pay a twentieth Part annually (which is half Tyth) to the Support of the Minister. One thing I could wish; that in fixing the Maintenance to the several Ministers in these new intended Parishes, no determinate Sum of Money may be named, which in all Perpetuities ought by any means to be avoided; but rather a Tax in Proportion to the Rent of each House, although it be but a Twentieth or even a thirtieth part. The contrary of this, I am told, was done in several Parishes of the City after the *Fire*; where the Incumbent and his Successors were to receive for ever a certain Sum; for Example, one or two hundred Pounds a Year. But the Lawgivers did not consider, that what we call at present, one hundred Pounds, will in Process of Time, have not the intrinsick Value of twenty; and twenty Pounds now are hardly equal to forty Shillings, three hundred Years ago. There are a thousand Instances of this all over *England*, in reserved Rents applied to Hospitals; in old Chiefries; and even among the Clergy themselves, in those Payments which, I think, they call a *Modus*.

As no Prince had ever better Dispositions than her present Majesty, for the Advancement of true Religion; so, there was never any Age that produced greater Occasions to employ them on. It is an unspeakable Misfortune, that any Designs of so excellent a Queen, should be checked by the Necessities of a long and ruinous War, which the Folly or Corruption of *modern Politicians* have involved us in, against all the Maxims whereby our Country flourished so many hundred Years: Else her Majesty's Care of Religion would certainly have reached even to her *American* Plantations. Those noble Countries, stocked by Numbers from hence, whereof too many are in no very great Reputation for Faith or Morals, will be a perpetual Reproach to us, until some better Care be taken for cultivating *Christianity* among them. If the Governors of those several Colonies were obliged, at certain Times, to transmit an exact Representation of the State of Religion, in their several Districts; and the Legislature here would, in a time of Leisure, take that Affair under their Consideration; it might be perfected with little Difficulty, and be a great Addition to the Glories of her Majesty's Reign.

But, to wave further Speculations upon so remote a Scene, while we have Subjects enough to employ them on at home; It is to be hoped, the Clergy will not let slip any proper Opportunity of improving the pious Dispositions of the Queen and Kingdom, for the Advantage of the Church; when by the Example of Times past, they consider how rarely such Con-junctures are like to happen. What if some Method were thought on towards repairing of Churches? For which there is like to be too frequent Occasions; those ancient *Gothick* Structures, throughout this Kingdom, going every Year to decay. That Expedient of repairing or rebuilding them by charitable Collections, seems in my Opinion not very suitable, either to the Dignity and Usefulness of the Work, or to the Honour of our Country; since it might be so easily done, with very little Charge to the Publick, in a much more decent and honourable Manner, while Parliaments are so frequently called. But, these and other Regulations must be left to a Time of *Peace*, which I shall humbly presume to wish may soon be our Share, however offensive it may be to any, either *abroad* or *at home*, who are Gainers by the War.

No. 43. *Thursday, May* 31, 1711.

Scilicet, ut posses curvo dignoscere rectum.

HAVING been forced in my Papers to use the Cant-words of *Whig* and *Tory*, which have so often varied their Significations, for twenty Years past; I think it necessary to say something of the several Changes those two Terms have undergone since that Period; and then to tell the Reader what I have always understood by each of them, since I undertook this Work. I reckon, that these Sorts of conceited Appellations, are usually invented by the Vulgar; who not troubling themselves to examine through the Merits of a Cause, are consequently the most violent Partisans of what they espouse; and in their Quarrels, usually proceed to their beloved Argument of *calling Names*, until at length they light upon one which is sure to stick; and in time, each Party grows proud of that Appellation, which their Adversaries at first intended for a Reproach. Of this kind were the *Prasini* and *Veneti*, the *Guelfs* and *Gibelines*, *Huguenots* and *Papists*, *Round-heads* and *Cavaliers*; with many others, of ancient and modern Date. Among us of ate there seems to have been a Barrenness of Invention in this

Point; the Words *Whig* and *Tory*, although they be not much above thirty Years old, having been pressed to the Service of many Successions of Parties, with very different Idea's fastened to them. This Distinction, I think, began towards the latter part of King *Charles* the Second's Reign; was dropt during that of his Successor, and then revived at the *Revolution*; since which it hath perpetually flourished, although applied to very different kinds of Principles and Persons. In that Convention of Lords and Commons, some of both Houses were for a *Regency* to the Prince of *Orange*, with a Reservation of Style and Title to the absent King, which should be made Use of in all publick Acts. Others, when they were brought to allow the Throne vacant, thought the Succession should immediately go to the next Heir, according to the Fundamental Laws of the Kingdom, as if the last King were actually dead. And, although the Dissenting Lords (in whose House the chief Opposition was) did at last yield both those Points, took the Oaths to the new King, and many of them Employments; yet they were looked upon with an Evil Eye by the warm Zealots of the other Side; neither did the Court ever heartily favour any of them, although some were of the most eminent for Abilities and Virtue; and served that Prince, both in his Councils and his Army, with untainted Faith. It was apprehended, at the same Time, and perhaps it might have been true, that many of the Clergy would have been better pleased with the Scheme of a *Regency*, or at least an uninterrupted lineal Succession, for the Sake of those whose Consciences were truly *Scrupulous*; and they thought there were some Circumstances, in the Case of the deprived Bishops, that looked a little hard, or at least deserved Commiseration.

THESE, and other the like Reflections did, as I conceive, revive the Denominations of *Whig* and *Tory*.

SOME Time after the Revolution, the Distinction of *High* and *Low*-Church came in; which was raised by the Dissenters, in order to break the Church Party, by dividing the Members into *High* and *Low*; and the Opinion raised, That the *High* joined with the Papists, inclined the *Low* to fall in with the Dissenters.

AND here I shall take Leave to produce some Principles, which in the several Periods of the late Reign, served to denote a Man of one or the other Party. To be against a Standing Army in Time of Peace, was all *High-Church*, *Tory* and *Tantivy*. To differ from a Majority of Bishops was the same. To raise the Prerogative above Law for serving a Turn, was *Low-Church* and *Whig*. The Opinion of the Majority in the House of Commons, especially of the Country-Party or Landed Interest, was *High-flying* and *rank Tory*. To exalt the King's Supremacy beyond all Precedent, was *Low-Church*, *Whiggish* and *Moderate*. To make the least Doubt of the pretended Prince being Supposititious, and a Tyler's Son, was, in their Phrase, *Top and Top-gallant*, and perfect *Jacobitism*. To resume the most exorbitant Grants that were ever given to a Set of profligate Favourites, and apply them to the Publick, was the very Quintescence of *Toryism*; notwithstanding those Grants were known to be acquired, by sacrificing the Honour and the Wealth of *England*.

In most of these Principles, the two Parties seem to have shifted Opinions, since their Institution under King *Charles* the Second; and indeed to have gone very different from what was expected from each, even at the Time of the *Revolution*. But, as to that concerning the *Pretender*, the *Whigs* have so far renounced it, that they are grown the great Advocates for his Legitimacy: Which gives me the Opportunity of vindicating a noble * Duke who was accused of a Blunder in the House, when, upon a certain Lord's mentioning the *Pretended Prince*, his Grace told the Lords, He *must be plain with them, and call that Person, not the Pretended Prince, but the Pretended Impostor*: Which was so far from a Blunder in that Polite Lord, as his Ill-willers give out, that it was only a refined Way of delivering the avowed Sentiments of his whole Party.

But to return. This was the State of Principles when the Queen came to the Crown; sometime after which, it pleased *certain great Persons*, who had been all their Lives in the Altitude of *Tory*-Profession, to enter into a Treaty with the *Whigs*; from whom they could get better Terms than from their old Friends, who began to be resty, and would not allow Monopolies of Power and Favour; nor consent to carry on the War intirely at

* *The Duke of* [Incomplete note in F.]

the Expence of this Nation, that they might have Pensions from Abroad; while another People, more immediately concerned in the War, Traded with the Enemy as in Times of Peace. Whereas, the other Party, whose Case appeared then as desperate, was ready to yield to any Conditions that would bring them into Play. And I cannot help affirming. That this Nation was made a Sacrifice to the unmeasurable Appetite of Power and Wealth in *a very few*, who shall be nameless, who in every Step they made, acted directly against what they had always professed. And if his Royal Highness the Prince had died some Years sooner (who was a perpetual Check in their Career) it is dreadful to think how far they might have proceeded.

SINCE that Time, the Bulk of the *Whigs* appeareth rather to be linked to a certain Sett of *Persons*, than any certain Set of *Principles*: So that if I were to define a Member of that Party, I would say, he was one *who believed in the late Ministry*. And therefore, whatever I have affirmed of *Whigs* in any of these Papers, or objected against them, ought to be understood either of those who were Partisans of the late Men in Power, and privy to their Designs; or such who joined with them, from a Hatred to our Monarchy and Church; as Unbelievers and *Dissenters* of all Sizes: Or Men in Office, who had been guilty of much Corruption, and dreaded a Change; which would not only put a Stop to further Abuses for the Future, but might perhaps, introduce Examinations of what was past: Or those who had been too highly obliged, to quit their Supporters with any common Decency. Or lastly, the *Money-Traders*, who could never hope to make their Markets so well of *Præmiums* and Exorbitant Interest, and high Remittances, by any other Administration.

UNDER these Heads, may be reduced the whole Body of those whom I have all along understood for *Whigs*: For, I do not include within this Number, any of those, who have been misled by Ignorance, or seduced by plausible Pretences, to think better of that Sort of Men than they deserve, and to apprehend mighty Dangers from their Disgrace: Because, I believe, the greatest Part of such well-meaning People, are now thoroughly converted.

AND indeed, it must be allowed, that the two fantastick

Names of *Whig* and *Tory*, have at present very little Relation to those Opinions, which were at first thought to distinguish them. Whoever formerly professed himself to approve the *Revolution*, to be against the *Pretender*, to justify the Succession in the House of *Hanover*, to think the *British* Monarchy not absolute, but limited by Laws, which the Executive Power could not dispense with; and to allow an Indulgence to scrupulous Consciences; such a Man was content to be called a *Whig*. On the other side, whoever asserted the QUEEN'S Hereditary Right; that the Persons of Princes were Sacred; their lawful Authority not to be resisted on any Pretence; nor even their Usurpations, without the most extream Necessity: That, Breaches in the Succession were highly dangerous; that, *Schism* was a great Evil, both in it self and its Consequences; that, the Ruin of the *Church*, would probably be attended with that of the *State*; that, no Power should be trusted with those who are not of the established Religion; such a Man was usually called a *Tory*. Now, although the Opinions of both these are very consistent, and I really think are maintained at present by a great Majority of the Kingdom; yet, according as Men apprehend the Danger greater, either from the *Pretender* and his Party, or from the Violence and Cunning of *other Enemies* to the Constitution; so, their common Discourses and Reasonings, turn either to the first or second Sett of these Opinions I have mentioned; and are consequently styled either *Whigs* or *Tories*. Which is, as if two *Brothers* apprehended their House would be set upon, but disagreed about the Place from whence they thought the *Robbers* would come; and therefore would go on different Sides to defend it; they must needs weaken and expose themselves by such a *Separation*; and so did we, only our Case was worse: For, in order to keep off a *weak*, *remote Enemy*, from whom we could not suddenly apprehend any Danger, we took a *nearer* and a *stronger* one into the *House*. I make no Comparison at all between the two Enemies: *Popery* and *Slavery* are without doubt the greatest and most dreadful of any; but I may venture to affirm, that the Fear of these, have not, at least since the *Revolution*, been so close and pressing upon us, as that from *another Faction*; excepting only one short Period, when the Leaders of that very Faction, invited the abdicating King to return; of which I have formerly taken Notice.

Having thus declared what Sort of Persons I have always meant, under the Denomination of *Whigs*, it will be easy to shew whom I understand by *Tories*. Such whose Principles in Church and State, are what I have above related; whose Actions are derived from thence, and who have no Attachment to any Sett of *Ministers*, further than as these are Friends to the Constitution in all its Parts; but will do their utmost to save their Prince and Country, *whoever* be at the Helm.

By these Descriptions of *Whig* and *Tory*, I am sensible those Names are given to several Persons very undeservedly; and, that many a Man is called by one or the other, who hath not the least Title to the Blame or Praise I have bestowed on each of them throughout my Papers.

No. 44. *Thursday, June* 7, 1711.

Magna vis est, magnum nomen, unum & idem Sentientis Senatus.

WHOEVER calls to mind the Clamour and the Calumny, the artificial Fears and Jealousies, the shameful Misrepresentation of Persons and of Things, that were raised and spread by the Leaders and Instruments of a *certain Party*, upon the Change of the last Ministry, and Dissolution of Parliament; if he be a true Lover of his Country, must feel a mighty Pleasure, although mixed with some Indignation, to see the Wishes, the Conjectures, the Endeavours of an inveterate Faction intirely disappointed; and this important Period wholly spent, in restoring the Prerogative to the Prince, and Liberty to the Subject; in reforming past Abuses, preventing future, supplying old Deficiences, providing for Debts, restoring the Clergy to their Rights, and taking Care of the Necessities of the Church: And, all this unattended with any of those Misfortunes which some Men *hoped* for, while they pretended to *fear*.

For my own part, I must confess, the Difficulties appeared so great to me, from such a Noise and Shew of Opposition, that

I thought nothing but the absolute Necessity of Affairs, could ever justify so daring an Attempt. But, a wise and good Prince, at the Head of an able Ministry, and of a Senate freely chosen, all united to pursue the true Interest of their Country, is a Power, against which, the little inferior Politicks of any Faction, will be able to make no long Resistance. To this we may add one additional Strength, which in the Opinion of our Adversaries, is the greatest and justest of any; I mean the *Vox Populi*, so indisputably declarative on the same Side. I am apt to believe, when these discarded Politicians begin seriously to consider all this, they will think it proper to give out; and reserve their Wisdom for some more convenient Juncture.

It is pleasant enough to observe, that those who were the chief Instruments of raising the Noise; who started Fears, bespoke Dangers, and formed ominous Prognosticks, in order to scare the *Allies*, to spirit the *French*, and fright ignorant People at home; made use of those very Opinions themselves had broached, for Arguments to prove, that the Change of Ministers was dangerous and unseasonable. But, if a House be *Swept*, the more Occasion there is for such a Work, the more *Dust* it will raise; if it be going to *Ruin*, the *Repairs*, however necessary, will *make a Noise*, and *disturb the Neighbourhood* awhile. And as to the Rejoicings made in *France*, if it be true, that they had any, upon the News of those Alterations among us; their Joy was grounded upon the *same Hopes* with that of the *Whigs*, who comforted themselves, that a Change of Ministry and Parliament, would infallibly put us all into Confusion; increase our Divisions, and destroy our Credit; wherein, I suppose, by this time they are *equally* undeceived.

But this long Session, being in a manner ended, which several Circumstances, and one *Accident*, altogether unforeseen, have drawn out beyond the usual Time; it may be some small piece of Justice to so excellent an Assembly, barely to mention a few of those great Things they have done for the Service of their Queen and Country; which I shall take notice of, just as they come to my Memory.

The Credit of the Nation began mightily to suffer by a Discount upon *Exchequer* Bills, which have been generally reckoned the surest and most sacred of all Securities. The present Lord Treasurer, then a Member of the House of Commons, proposed a Method, which was immediately complied with, of raising them to a *Par* with *Specie*; and so they have ever since continued.

THE *British* Colonies of *Nevis* and St. *Christophers*, had been miserably Plundered by the *French*; their Houses burnt, their Plantations destroyed, and many of the Inhabitants carried away Prisoners: They had often, for some Years past, applyed in vain for Relief from hence; until the present Parliament, considering their Condition as a Case of Justice and Mercy, voted them one hundred thousand Pounds by Way of Recompence, in some Manner, for their Sufferings.

SOME Persons, whom the Voice of the Nation authorizeth me to call her *Enemies*, taking Advantage of the general Naturalization Act, had invited over a great Number of Foreigners of all Religions, under the Name of *Palatines*; who understood no Trade or Handicraft; yet rather chose to beg than labour; who besides infesting our Streets, bred contagious Diseases, by which we lost in *Natives*, thrice the Number of what we gained in *Foreigners*. The House of Commons, as a Remedy against this Evil, brought in a Bill for repealing that Act of general Naturalization; which, to the Surprize of most People, was rejected by the Lords. And upon this Occasion, I must allow my self to have been justly rebuked by one of my Weekly Monitors, for pretending in a former Paper, to hope that Law would be repealed; wherein the Commons being disappointed, took care, however, to send many of the *Palatines* away, and to represent their being invited over, as a pernicious Council.

THE *Qualification*-Bill, incapacitating all Men to serve in Parliament, who have not some Estate in Land, either in Possession or certain Reversion, is perhaps the greatest Security that ever was contrived for preserving the Constitution, which otherwise might, in a little time, lie wholly at the Mercy of the *Monyed* Interest. And, since much the greatest Part of the Taxes is paid, either immediately from Land, or from its Productions; it is but common Justice, that those who are the Proprietors, should appoint what Portion of it ought to go to the Support of the Publick; otherwise, the Engrossers of Money, would be apt to lay heavy Loads on others, which themselves never touch with one of their Fingers.

THE Publick Debts were so prodigiously encreased, by the Negligence and Corruption of those who had been Managers of the Revenue; that the late Ministers, like careless Men, who run out their Fortunes, were so far from any Thoughts of Payment; that they had not the Courage to state or compute them. The Parliament found that thirty Five Millions had never been accounted for; and that the Debt on the Navy, wholly unprovided for, amounted to nine Millions. * The late Chancellor of the *Exchequer*, suitable to his transcendant Genius for publick Affairs, proposed a Fund to be Security for that immense Debt, which is now confirmed by a Law; and is likely to prove the greatest Restoration and Establishment of the Kingdom's Credit. Nor content with this, the Legislature hath appointed Commissioners of Accompts, to inspect into past Mismanagements of the publick Money, and prevent them for the Future.

I HAVE, in a former Paper, mentioned the Act for building fifty new Churches in *London* and *Westminster*, with a Fund appropriated for that pious and noble Work. But, while I am mentioning Acts of Piety, it would be unjust to conceal my Lord High Treasurer's Concern for Religion, which hath extended even to another Kingdom: His Lordship having some Months ago, obtained of her Majesty the first Fruits and Tenths to the Clergy of *Ireland*, as he is known to have already done for that Reverend Body here.

THE Act for carrying on a Trade to the *South-Sea*, proposed by the same great Person, whose Thoughts are perpetually employed, and ever with Success, on the Good of his Country; will, in all Probability, if duly executed, be of mighty Advantage to the Kingdom, and an everlasting Honour to the present Parliament.

I MIGHT go on further, and mention that seasonable Law against excessive Gaming; the putting a Stop to that scandalous Fraud of false Musters in the Guards; the diligent and effectual Enquiry made by the Commons into several gross Abuses. I might produce many Instances of their impartial Justice in de-

* *Earl of* OXFORD.

ciding controverted Elections, against *former Example*, and great Provocations to retaliate. I might shew their chearful Readiness in granting such vast Supplies; their great Unanimity, not to be broken by all the Arts of a malicious and cunning Faction; their unfeigned Duty to the QUEEN; and lastly, that Representation made to her Majesty from the House of Commons, discovering such a Spirit and Disposition in that noble Assembly, to redress all those Evils, which a long Male-Administration had brought upon us.

IT is probable, that trusting only to my Memory, I may have omitted many Things of great Importance; neither do I pretend further in the Compass of this Paper, than to give the World some general, however imperfect Idea, how worthily this great Assembly hath discharged the Trust of those who so freely chose them; and what we may reasonably hope and expect from the Piety, Courage, Wisdom, and Loyalty of such excellent Patriots, in a Time so fruitful of Occasions to exert the greatest Abilities.

AND now I conceive the main Design I had in writing these Papers, is fully executed. A great Majority of the Nation is at Length thoroughly convinced, that the QUEEN proceeded with the highest Wisdom, in changing her Ministry and Parliament. That, under a former Administration, the greatest Abuses of all Kinds were committed; and the most dangerous Attempts against the Constitution for some Time intended. The whole Kingdom finds the present Persons in Power, directly and openly pursuing the true Service of their QUEEN and Country; and to be such whom their most bitter Enemies cannot tax with Bribery, Covetousness, Ambition, Pride, Insolence, or any pernicious Principles in Religion or Government.

FOR my own particular, those little barking Pens which have so constantly pursued me, I take to be of no further Consequence to what I have writ, than the scoffing Slaves of old, placed behind the Chariot, to put the General in Mind of his Mortality; which was but a Thing of Form, and made no Stop or Disturbance in the Show. However, if those perpetual Snarlers against me, had the same Design, I must own they have effectually compassed it; since nothing can well be more mortifying, than to reflect, that I am of the same Species with Creatures capable of uttering so much Scurrility, Dulness, Falshood and Impertinence, to the Scandal and Disgrace of Human Nature.

No. 45. *Thursday, June* 14, 1711.

Melius non tangere Clamo.

WHEN a General hath conquered an Army, and reduced a Country to Obedience; he often finds it necessary to send out small Bodies, in order to take in petty Castles and Forts; and beat little straggling Parties, which are otherwise, apt to make Head and infest the Neighbourhood: This Case exactly resembles mine; I count the main Body of the *Whigs* entirely subdued; at least, until they appear with new Reinforcements, I shall reckon them as such; and therefore do now find my self at Leisure to *examine* inferior Abuses. The Business I have left, is to fall on those Wretches who would still be keeping the War on Foot, when they have no Country to defend, no Forces to bring into the Field, nor any Thing remaining, but their bare good-Will towards *Faction* and *Mischief*: I mean, the present Sett of Writers, whom I have suffered without Molestation, so long to infest the Town. If there were not a Concurrence from Prejudice, Party, weak Understanding, and Misrepresentation, I should think them too inconsiderable in themselves to deserve Correction: But, as my Endeavour hath been to expose the gross Impositions of the *Fallen Party*, I will give a Taste in the following Petition, of the Sincerity of their *Factors*; to shew how little those Writers for the *Whigs* were guided by Conscience or Honour; their Business being only to gratify a private Interest.

To the Right Honourable the present Ministry, the humble Petition of the Party-Writers to the late Ministry.

Humbly Sheweth,

T*HAT your Petitioners have served their Time to the Trade of writing* Pamphlets *and* Weekly Papers, *in Defence of the* Whigs, *against the Church of* England, *and the Christian* R*eligion, and her Majesty's Prerogative, and her Title to the Crown:*

That, since the late Change of Ministry, and meeting of this Parliament, the said Trade is mightily fallen off, and the Call for the said Pamphlets and Papers, much less than formerly; and it is feared, to our further Prejudice, that the Examiner *may discontinue Writing; whereby some of your Petitioners will be brought to utter Distress; for as much as through false Quotations, noted Absurdities, and other legal Abuses, many of your Petitioners, to their great Comfort and Support, were enabled to pick up a Weekly Subsistance out of the said* Examiner.

That, your said poor Petitioners, did humbly offer your Honours to write in Defence of the late Change of Ministry and Parliament, much cheaper than they did for your Predecessors; which your Honours were pleased to refuse.

Notwithstanding which Offer, your Petitioners are under daily Apprehension, that your Honours will forbid them to follow the said Trade *any longer; by which your Petitioners, to the Number of four Score, with their Wives and Families, will inevitably starve; having been bound to no other Calling.*

YOUR Petitioners desire your Honours will tenderly consider the Premisses, and suffer your said Petitioners to continue their Trade (those who set them at Work, being still willing to employ them, although at lower Rates) and your said Petitioners will give Security to make Use of the *same Stuff*, and dress it in the *same Manner*, as they always did, and no other.

And your Petitioners, &c.

A Short

CHARACTER

OF

His Ex. *T.* E. of *W.*

L. L. of *I*——.

WITH

An Account of ſome ſmaller Facts, during His Government, which will not be put into the Articles of Impeachment,

---

LONDON:

Printed for *William Coryton*, Bookſeller, at the *Black-Swan* on *Ludgate-hill.* 1711.

Price *d.*

A short Character of his Excellency THOMAS Earl of WHARTON, Lord Lieutenant of IRELAND

With an Account of some smaller Facts during his Government, which will not be put into the Articles of Impeachment.

London, *Aug*. 30, 1710.

THE Kingdom of *Ireland*, being governed by Deputation from hence, its Annals, since the *English* Establishment, are usually digested under the Heads of the several Governors: But, the Affairs and Events in that Island, for some Years past, have been either so insignificant, or so annexed to those of *England*, that they have not furnished Matter of any great Importance to History. The Share of Honour, which Gentlemen from thence have had by their Conduct and Employments in the Army, turneth all to the Article of this Kingdom; the rest which relateth to Politics, or the Art of Government, is inconsiderable to the last Degree, however it may be represented at Court by those who preside there, and would value themselves upon every Step they make, towards finishing the Slavery of that People, as if it were gaining a mighty Point to the Advantage of *England*.

GENERALLY speaking, the Times which afford most plentiful Matter for Story, are those in which a Man would least chuse to live; such as under the various Events and Revolutions of War, the Intrigues of a ruined Faction, or the Violence of a prevailing one, and lastly the arbitrary, unlawful Acts of oppressing Governors. In the War, *Ireland* hath no Share but in Subordination to us; the same may be said of their Factions, which, at present, are but imperfect Transcripts of ours: But the third Subject for History, which is arbitrary Power, and Oppression; as it is that by which the People of *Ireland* have for some Time, been distinguished from all her * Majesty's Subjects, so being

* *Queen* ANNE.

now at its greatest Height under his Excellency *Thomas* Earl of *Wharton*, a short Account of his Government, may be of some Use or Entertainment to the present Age, although, I hope, it will be incredible to the next: And, because this Account may be judged rather an History of his Excellency, than of his Government, I must here declare that I have not the least View to his Person in any Part of it. I have had the Honour of much Conversation with his Lordship, and am thoroughly convinced how indifferent he is to Applause, and how insensible of Reproach: Which is not a Humour put on to serve a Turn, or keep a Countenance, nor arising from the Consciousness of Innocence, or any Grandeur of Mind, but the meer unaffected Bent of his Nature.

HE is without the Sense of Shame or Glory, as some Men are without the Sense of Smelling; and, therefore, a good Name to him is no more than a precious Ointment would be to these. Whoever, for the Sake of others, were to describe the Nature of a Serpent, a Wolf, a Crocodile or a Fox, must be understood to do it without any personal Love or Hatred for the Animals themselves.

IN the same Manner, his Excellency is one whom I neither personally love nor hate. I see him at Court, at his own House, and sometimes at mine (for I have the Honour of his Visits) and when these Papers are public, it is Odds but he will tell me, as he once did upon a like Occasion, that he is damnably mauled; and then with the easiest Transition in the World, ask about the Weather, or Time of the Day? So that I enter on the Work with more Chearfulness, because I am sure, neither to make him angry, nor any Way hurt his Reputation; a Pitch of Happiness and Security to which his Excellency hath arrived, which no Philosopher before him could reach.

I INTEND to execute this Performance by first giving a Character of his Excellency, and then relating some Facts during his Government, which will serve to confirm it.

I KNOW very well that Mens Characters are best known from their Actions; but these being confined to his Administration in *Ireland*, his Character may, perhaps, take in something more, which the Narrowness of the Time, or the Scene hath not given him Opportunity to exert.

THOMAS, Earl of *Wharton*, Lord Lieutenant of *Ireland*, by the Force of a wonderful Constitution hath some Years passed his Grand Climacteric, without any visible Effects of old Age, either on his Body or his Mind, and in Spight of a continual Prostitution to those Vices which usually wear out both. His Behaviour is in all the Forms of a young Man at five and twenty. Whether he walketh or whistleth, or sweareth, or talketh Bawdy, or calleth Names, he acquitteth himself in each beyond a Templar of three Years standing. With the same Grace, and in the same Style he will rattle his Coachman in the Middle of the Street, where he is Governor of the Kingdom; and, all this is without Consequence, because it is in his Character, and what every Body expecteth. He seemeth to be but an ill Dissembler, and an ill Liar, although they are the two Talents he most practiseth, and most valueth himself upon. The Ends he hath gained by Lying appear to be more owing to the Frequency, than the Art of them: His Lies being sometimes detected in an Hour, often in a Day, and always in a Week. He tells them freely in mixed Companies, although he knows half of those that hear him to be his Enemies, and is sure they will discover them the Moment they leave him. He sweareth solemnly he loveth, and will serve you; and your Back is no sooner turned, but he tells those about him you are a Dog and a Rascal. He goeth constantly to Prayers in the Forms of his Place, and will talk Bawdy and Blasphemy at the Chapel Door. He is a Presbyterian in Politics, and an Atheist in Religion; but he chuseth at present to whore with a Papist. In his Commerce with mankind his general Rule is, to endeavour to impose on their Understanding, for which he hath but one Receipt, a Composition of Lies and Oaths: And this he applieth indifferently, to a Freeholder of forty Shillings, and a Privy-Counsellor; by which the Easy and the Honest are often either deceived or amused, and either Way he gaineth his Point. He will openly take away your Employment To-day, because you are not of his Party; To-morrow he will meet or send for you, as if nothing at all had passed, lay his Hands with much Friendship on your Shoulders, and with the greatest Ease and Familiarity, tell you that the Faction are driving at something in the House; that you must be sure to attend, and to speak to all your Friends to be there, although he knoweth at the same Time, that you and your Friends are against him in the very Point he mentioneth: And however absurd, ridiculous and gross this may appear, he hath often found it successful, some Men having such an aukward Bashfulness, they know not how to refuse on a sudden, and every Man having something to hope or fear, which often hinders them from driving Things to Extremes with Persons of Power, whatever Provocations they may have received. He hath sunk his Fortune by endeavouring to ruin one Kingdom *, and hath raised it by going far in the Ruin of another †. With a good natural Understanding, a great Fluency in Speaking, and no ill Taste of Wit, he is generally the worst Companion in the World; his Thoughts being wholely taken up between Vice and Politics, so that Bawdy, Prophaneness and Business, fill up his whole Conversation. To gratify himself in the two first he maketh use of suitable Favourites, whose Talents reach no higher than to entertain him with all the Lewdness that passeth in Town. As for Business, he is said to be very dextrous at that Part of it which turneth upon Intrigue, and he seemeth to have transferred those Talents of his Youth for intriguing with Women, into public Affairs. For, as some vain young Fellows, to make a Gallantry appear of Consequence, will chuse to venture their Necks by climbing up a Wall or Window at Midnight to a common Wench, where they might as freely have gone in at the Door, and at Noon-Day; so his Excellency, either to keep himself in Practice, or advance the Fame of his Politics, affects the most obscure, troublesome, and winding Paths, even in the most common Affairs, those which would be brought about as well in the ordinary Forms, or would follow of Course whether he intervened or not.

HE bears the Gallantries of his Lady with the Indifference of a Stoic, and thinks them well recompenced by a Return of Children to support his Family without the Fatigues of being a Father. He has three predominant Passions, which you will seldom find united in the same Man, as arising from different Dispositions of Mind, and naturally thwarting each other: These

* *England.* † *Ireland.*

are Love of Power, Love of Money, and Love of Pleasure; they ride him sometimes by Turns, and sometimes all together: Since he went into *Ireland*, he seemeth most disposed to the second, and hath met with great Success, having gained by his Government, of under two Years, five and forty thousand Pounds by the most favourable Computation, half in the regular Way, and half in the prudential.

HE was never yet known to refuse or keep a Promise; as I remember he told a Lady, but with an Exception to the Promise he then made (which was to get her a Pension) yet he broke even that, and I confess, deceived us both. But here I desire to distinguish between a Promise and a Bargain; for he will be sure to keep the latter when he has the fairest Offer.

THUS much for his Excellency's Character: I shall now proceed to his Actions, only during the Time he was Governor of *Ireland*, which were transmitted to me by an eminent Person in Business there, who had all Opportunities of being well informed, and whose Employment did not lie at his Excellency's Mercy.

THIS Intelligence being made up of several Facts independent of each other, I shall hardly be able to relate them in due Order of Time, my Correspondent omitting that Circumstance, and transmitting them to me just as he recollected them; so that the Gentlemen of that Kingdom, now in Town, will, I hope, pardon me any Slips I shall make in that or any other Kind, while I keep exactly to the Truth.

THOMAS PROBY, Esq; Chirurgeon-General of *Ireland*, a Person universally esteemed, and whom I have formerly seen here, had built a Country-House, half a Mile from *Dublin*, adjoining to the Phœnix Park. In a Corner of the Park, just under his House, he was much annoyed with a Dog-kennel which belonged to the Government; upon which he applied to *Thomas*, Earl of *Pembroke*, then Lord Lieutenant, and to the Commissioners of the Revenue, for a Lease of about five Acres of that Part of the Park. His Petition was referred to the Lord Treasurer here, and sent back for a Report, which was in his Favour, and the Bargain so hard, that the Lord Treasurer struck off some Part of the Rent. He had a Lease granted him, for which he was to build another Kennel, provide Ice yearly for the Government, and pay a certain Rent; the Land might be worth about thirty Shillings an Acre. His Excellency, soon after his Arrival in *Ireland*, was told of this Lease, and by his absolute Authority commanded Mr. *Proby* to surrender up the Land; which he was forced to do, after all the Expence he had been at, or else, must have expected to lose his Employment; at the same Time he is under an Obligation to pay his Rent, and, I think, he doth it to this Day. There are several Circumstances in this Story which I have forgot, having not been sent to me with the rest; but, I had it from a Gentleman of that Kingdom, who some Time ago was here.

UPON his Excellency's being declared Lord Lieutenant, there came over to make his Court one Dr. *Lloyd*, Fellow of Trinity College, *Dublin*, noted in that Kingdom for being the only Clergyman that declared for taking off the Sacramental Test, as he did openly in their Convocation of which he was a Member. The Merit of this, and some other Principles suitable to it, recommended by *Tom Broderick*, so far ingratiated him with his Excellency, that being provided of a proper Chaplain already, he took him however into a great Degree of Favour: The Doctor attended his Excellency to *Ireland*, and observing a cast Wench in the Family to be in much Confidence with my Lady, he thought by addressing there, to have a short open Passage to Preferment. He met with great Success in his Amour; and walking one Day with his Mistress after my Lord and Lady in the Castle-Garden, my Lady said to his Excellency, "What do you think? we are going to lose poor *Foydy*," a Name of Fondness they usually gave her. "How do you mean?" said my Lord. "Why the Doctor behind us is resolved to take her from us." "Is he, by G—d? why then (G—d d—mn me) he shall have the "first Bishoprick that falls *."

THE Doctor, thus encouraged, grew a most violent Lover, returned with his Excellency for *England*; and soon after, the Bishoprick of *Cork* falling void, to shew he meant fair, he mar-

* *It was confidently reported, as a Conceit of his Excellency, that, talking upon this Subject, he once said with great Pleasure, that he hoped to make his W——e a Bishop.*

ried his Damsel publickly here in *London*, and his Excellency as honourably engaged his Credit to get him the Bishoprick; but, the Matter was reckoned so infamous, that both the Archbishops here, especially his Grace of *York*, interposed with the Queen, to hinder so great a Scandal to the Church, and Dr. *Brown*, Provost of *Dublin* College, being then in Town, her Majesty was pleased to nominate him; so that Dr. *Lloyd* was forced to sit down with a moderate Deanery in the Northern Parts of that Kingdom, and the additional Comfort of a sweet Lady, who brought this her first Husband no other Portion, than a Couple of Olive Branches for his Table, though she herself hardly knoweth by what Hand they were planted.

THE Queen reserveth all the great Employments of *Ireland* to be given by herself, though often by the Recommendation of the chief Governor, according to his Credit at Court. The Provostship of *Dublin* College is of this Number, which was now vacant, upon the Promotion of Dr. *Brown*; Dr. *Benjamin Pratt*, a Fellow of that College, and Chaplain to the House of Commons of that Kingdom, as well as domestic Chaplain to the Duke of *Ormond*, was at that Time here, in Attendance upon the Duke. He is a Gentleman of good Birth and Fortune in *Ireland*, and lived here in a very decent Figure: He is a Person of Wit and Learning, hath travelled and conversed in the best Company, and was very much esteemed among us here when I had the Pleasure of his Acquaintance: But, he had the original Sin of being a reputed Tory, and a Dependent on the Duke of *Ormond*; however, he had many Friends among the Bishops and other Nobility to recommend him to the Queen; at the same Time there was another Fellow of that College, one Dr. *Hall*, who had much the Advantage of *Pratt* in Point of Seniority; this Gentleman had very little introduced himself into the World, but lived retired, although otherwise said to be an excellent Person, and very deserving for his Learning and Sense: He had been recommended from *Ireland* by several Persons, and his Excellency, who had never before seen nor thought of him, after having tried to injure the College by recommending Persons from this Side, at last set up *Hall*, with all imaginable Zeal against *Pratt*. I tell this Story the more fully, because it is affirmed, by his

Excellency's Friends, that he never made more Use of his Court Skill, than at this Time, to stop Dr. *Pratt's* Promotion; not only from the Personal Hatred he had to the Man, on Account of his Patron and Principles, but that he might return to *Ireland* with some little Opinion of his Credit at Court; which had mightily suffered by many Disappointments, especially that of his Chaplain Dr *Lloyd*. It would be incredible to relate the many Artifices he used to this End, of which the Doctor had daily intelligence, and would fairly tell his Excellency so at his Levees, who sometimes could not conceal his Surprize, and then would promise with half a dozen Oaths, never to concern himself one Way or other; these were broke every Day, and every Day detected. One Morning, after some Expostulation between the Doctor and his Excellency, and a few additional Oaths, that he would never oppose him more, his Excellency went immediately to the Bishop of *Ely*, and prevailed on him to go to the Queen, from him, and let her Majesty know, that he never could consent, as long as he lived, that Dr. *Pratt* should be Provost, which the Bishop barely complied with, and delivered his Message; although at the same Time he did the Dr. all the good Offices he could. The next Day the Doctor was again with his Excellency, and gave him Thanks for so open a Proceeding; the Affair was now past dissembling, and his Excellency, owned he did not oppose him directly, but confessed he did it collaterally. The Doctor, a little warmed, said, "No, my Lord, you mean directly you did not, but indirectly you did." The Conclusion was, that the Queen named the Doctor to the Place; and, as a further Mortification, just upon the Day of his Excellency's Departure for *Ireland*.

BUT here I must desire the Reader's Pardon, if I cannot digest the following Facts in so good a Manner as I intended; because it is thought expedient, for some Reasons, that the World should be informed of his Excellency's Merits as soon as possible. I will therefore only transcribe the several Passages as they were sent me from *Dublin*, without either correcting the Style, or adding any Remarks of my own. As they are, they may serve for Hints to any Person, who may hereafter have a Mind to write Memoirs of his Excellency's Life.

SOME
REMARKS
UPON A
Pamphlet,
ENTITL'D,

[*A Letter to the Seven Lords of the Committee, appointed to Examine* GREGG.]

By the Author of the EXAMINER.

LONDON,
Printed for *John Morphew*, near *Stationers-Hall*. 1711. (Price 3 *d*.)

SOME REMARKS, &c.

THOSE who have given themselves the trouble to write against me, either in single Papers, or Pamphlets, (and they are pretty numerous) do all agree in discovering a violent Rage, and at the same time affecting an Air of Contempt toward their Adversary; which, in my humble Opinion, are not very consistent; and therefore it is plain, that their Fury is real and hearty, their Contempt only personated. I have pretty well studied this Matter, and would caution Writers of their Standard, never to engage in that difficult Attempt of Despising, which is a Work to be done in cold Blood, and only by a superior Genius to one at some distance beneath him. I can truly affirm, I have had a very sincere Contempt for many of those who have drawn their Pens against me; yet I rather chose the cheap way of discovering it by silence and neglect, than be at the pains of new Terms to express it: I have known a Lady value her self upon a haughty disdainful Look, which very few understood, and no Body alive regarded. Those Common-place Terms of *Infamous Scribler*, *Prostitute Libeller*, and the like, thrown abroad without Propriety or Provocation, do ill personate the true Spirit of Contempt, because they are such as the meanest Writer whenever he pleases, may use, towards the best. I remember indeed a Parish Fool, who, with a great deal of Deformity carried the most disdainful Look I ever observed in any Countenance; and it was the most prominent part of his Folly; but he was thoroughly in earnest, which these Writers are not: For there is another thing I would observe, that my Antagonists are most of them *so*, in a literal Sense; breathe *real* Vengeance, and extend their Threats to my Person, if they knew where to find it; wherein they are so far from despising, that I am sensible they do me too much Honour. The Author of *the Letter to the seven Lords*, takes upon him the three Characters of a *Despiser*, a *Threatner*, and a *Railer*; and succeeds so well in the two last, that it has made him miscarry in the first. It is no unwise Proceeding which the Writers of that side have taken up, to scatter their Menaces in every Paper they publish; it may perhaps look absurd, ridiculous and impudent in People at mercy to assume such a Style; but the

Design is right, to endeavour persuading the World that it is *They* who are the injured Party, that *They* are the Sufferers, and have a right to be angry.

However, there is one Point wherein these Gentlemen seem to stretch this wise Expedient a little farther than it will allow. I, who for several Months undertook to Examine into the late Management of Persons and Things, was content sometimes to give only a few Hints of certain Matters, which I had Charity enough to wish might be buried for ever in Oblivion, if the Confidence of these People had not forced them from me. One Instance whereof, among many, is the Business of *Gregg*, the Subject of a Letter I am now considering. If this Piece hath been written by Direction, as I should be apt to suspect; yet I am confident, they would not have us think so, because it is a sort of Challenge, to let the World into the whole Secret of *Gregg*'s Affair. But I suppose they are confident, it is what I am not Master of; wherein it is odds but they may be mistaken; for I believe, the Memorials of that Transaction are better preserved than they seem to be aware of, as perhaps may one Day appear.

This Writer is offended because I have said so many severe Things with Application to particular Persons. The *Medley* has been often in the same Story: If they condemn it as a Crime in general, I shall not much object, at least I will allow it should be done with Truth and Caution; but by what Argument will they undertake to prove that it is pardonable on one side, and not on the other? Since the late Change of Ministry, I have observed many of that Party take up a new Style, and tell us, That *this way of personal Reflection ought not to be endured*; *they could not approve of it*; *it was against Charity and good Manners*. When the *Whigs* were in Power, they took special Care to keep their *Adversaries* silent; then all kind of Falshood and Scurrility, was *doing good service to the Cause*, *and detecting of evil Principles*. Now, that the Face of Things is changed, and we have liberty to retort upon them, they are for calling down Fire from Heaven upon us; though by a sort of Indulgence which they were Strangers to, we allow them equal liberty of the Press with ourselves; and they even now make greater Use of it against Persons in highest Power and

Credit, than we do against those who have been discarded for the most infamous Abuse of both.

Who encouraged and rewarded the *Observator* and *Review* for many Years together, in charging the whole Body of the Clergy with the most odious Crimes and Opinions? In declaring all who took Oaths to the Government, and called themselves *Tories*, to be worse than *Papists* and *Nonjurors*? in exposing the Universities, as Seminaries of the most pernicious Principles in Church and State? in defending the Rebellion, and the Murder of King *Charles* I. which they asserted to be altogether as justifiable as the late Revolution? Is there a great Man now in Power, or in any Credit with the Queen, whom those worthy Undertakers have not treated by Name in the most ignominious Manner? Even since this great Change of Affairs, with what amazing Licentiousness hath the Writer of the *Medley* attacked every Person of the present Ministry, the Speaker of the House of Commons, and the whole Senate? He has turned into Ridicule the Results of the Council and the Parliament, as well as the just and generous Endeavours of the latter to pay the Debts and restore the Credit of the Nation, almost ruined by the Corruption and Management of his own Party.

And are these the People who complain of personal Reflections? Who so confidently invoke the Men in Power (whom they have so highly obliged) to punish or silence me for reflecting on their exploded Heroes? Is there no difference between Men chosen by the Prince, reverenced by the People for their Virtue, and others rejected by both for the highest Demerits? Shall the *Medley* and his Brothers fly out with Impunity against those who preside at the Helm; and am I to be torn in pieces because I censure others, who for endeavouring to split the Vessel against a Rock, are put under the *Hatches*.

I now proceed to the Pamphlet which I intend to consider; It is a Letter written to seven Great Men, who were appointed to Examine *Gregg* in *Newgate*. The Writer tells their Lordships, that the *Examiner* hath charged them for *endeavouring by Bribery and Subornation of that Criminal to take away Mr.* Harley*'s Life*. If there be anything among the Papers I have writ, which may be applied to these Persons, it would have become this Author to have cleared them fully from the Accusation, and then he might at leisure have fallen upon me as a Lyar and Misrepresenter; but of that he has not offered a Syllable: The Weight of his Charge lies here; that such an Author as the *Examiner* should presume, by certain Innuendo's, to accuse any great Persons of such a Crime. My Business in those Papers was to represent Facts, and I was as sparing as possible of reflecting upon particular Persons; but the Mischief is, that the Readers have always found Names to tally with those Facts; and I know no Remedy for this. As for Instance in the Case here before us. An under Clerk in the Secretary's Office, of 50*l.* a Year, is discovered to hold Correspondence with *France*, and apprehended by his Master's Order, before he could have Opportunity to make his Escape, by the private warning of a certain Person, a profest Enemy to the Secretary. The Criminal is condemned to dye. It is found, upon his Tryal, that he was a poor profligate Fellow; the Secretary at that time was under the mortal hatred of a violent prevailing Party, who dreaded him for his great Abilities, and his avowed Design to break their destructive Measures. It was very well known, that a Secretary of State hath little or no Intercourse with the lower Clerks, but with the Under Secretaries, who are the more immediate Masters of those Clerks, and are, and ought to be, as they then were, Gentlemen of Worth: However, it would pass well enough in the World, that *Gregg* was employed in Mr. Secretary *Harley*'s Office, and was consequently one of his Clerks, which would be Ground enough to build upon it what Suggestions they pleased. Then for the Criminal, he was Needy and Vicious: He owed his Death to the Secretary's watchful Pursuit of him, and would therefore probably incline to hearken to any Offers that would save his Life, gratify his Revenge, and make him easy in his Fortune: So that if a work of Darkness were to be done, it must be confest, here were proper Motives, and a proper Instrument. But ought we to suspect any Persons of such a diabolical Practice? Can all Faith, and Honour, and Justice be thus violated by Men? Questions proper for a Pulpit, or well becoming a Philosopher; but what if it were *Regnandi causa*? (and that perhaps in a literal Sense). Is this an Age of the World to think Crimes improbable because they are great?

Perhaps it is: But what shall we say to some of those Circumstances which attended this Fact? Who gave Rise to this Report against Mr. *Harley*? Will any of his Enemies confess in cold Blood that they did either believe, suspect or imagine, the Secretary, and one of the under Clerks, to be joined in corresponding with *France*? Some of them, I should think, knew better what belonged to such a Correspondence, and how it ought to be managed. The Nature of *Gregg*'s Crime was such, as to be best performed without any Accomplices at all: It was, to be a Spy here for the *French*, and to tell them all he knew; and it appears by his Letters that he never had it in his Power to let them into any thing of Importance. The Copy of the Queen's Letter to the *Emperor*, which he sent to the Enemy, and hath made such a noise, was only to desire, that Pr. *Eugene* might be employed to command in *Spain*, which for six Weeks before had been mentioned in all the Gazettes of *Europe*. It was evident from the Matter of his Letters, that no Man of Consequence could have any share in them. The whole Affair had been Examined in the *Cabinet*, two Months before, and there found and reported as only affecting the Person of *Gregg*, who to supply his Vices and his Wants was tempted to engage in that Correspondence; it is therefore hard to conceive, how that Examination should be resumed after such a distance of Time, with any fair or honourable Intention. Why were not *Gregg*'s Examinations published, which were signed by his own Hand, and had been taken in *Cabinet* two Months before the Committee of the House was appointed to re-examin him? Why was he pressed so close to cry out with Horror, *Good God, would you have me accuse Mr.* Harley *when he is wholly innocent*? why were all the Answers returned to the Queries sent him, immediately burned? I cannot in my Conscience but think, that the Party was bound in Honour to procure *Gregg* a Pardon, which was openly promised him, upon Condition of making an *ingenuous* Confession, unless they had some other Notions of what is *ingenuous*, than is commonly meant by that Word. A Confession may be never the less *ingenuous*, for not answering the Hopes or Designs of those who take it; but though the Word was publickly used, the Definition of it was reserved to *private Interpretation*, and by a capricious humour of Fortune, a most flagitious, though repenting Villain, was hanged for his Virtue. It could not indeed consist with any kind of Prudence then in Fashion, to spare his Life, and thereby leave it in his Power at any time to detect their Practices, which he might afterwards do at any time, with so much Honour to himself.

But I have the luck to be accused by this Author in very good Company; the two Houses of Parliament in general, and the *Speaker* of the House of Commons in particular; whom he taxes with *Falshood* and *Absurdity*, as well as my self, though in a more respectful manner, and by a sort of Irony. The whole Kingdom had given the same Interpretation that I had done, to some certain Passages in the Address from both Houses, upon the Attempt of *Guiscard*; Friends and Enemies agreed in applying the word *Faction*. But the *Speaker* is much clearer; talks (as I have mentioned in another Place) of SOME *unparalelled Attempts*, and uses other Terms that come pretty home to the Point. As to what the Parliament affirms, this Author makes it first as absurd and impracticable as he can, and then pretends to yield, as *pressed by so great an Authority*, and explains their Meaning into Nonsense, in order to bring them off from reflecting upon his Party. Then for the *Speaker*, this Writer says, *he is but a single Man*, and because his Speech was in Words too direct to avoid, he advises him to *save his Honour and Virtue, by owning a Solecism in Speech*, and to *write less Correctly*, *rather than mean Maliciously*. What an Expedient this Advocate hath found to remove the Load of an Accusation! He answers, the Crime is horrible, that Great Men ought not to be thus insolently Charged: We reply, that the Parliament and Speaker appear, in many Points, to be of the same Opinion: He rejoins, that *he is pressed by too great an Authority*; that perhaps those wise Assemblies, and that Honourable Gentleman, (who besides *is but a single Man*) may probably speak Nonsense; they must either deliver a Solecism, or be Malicious, and in good Manners he rather thinks it may be the former.

The Writer of the Letter having thus dispatched the *Examiner*, falls next upon a Paper called *Secret Transactions*, &c. written, as he tells us, by one *Francis Hoffman*, and the *Ordinary* of

Newgate, Persons whom I have not the Honour to be known to, (whatever my *Betters* may be) nor have yet seen their Productions; but by what is cited from them in the Letter, it should seem, they have made some untoward Observations; however, the same Answer still serves, not a Word to controul what they say, only they are a couple of daring, insolent Wretches, to *reflect upon the greatest and best Men in England*; and there's an End. I have no sort of Regard for that same *Hoffman*, to whose Character I am a perfect Stranger; but methinks the *Ordinary* of *Newgate* should be treated with more Respect, considering what *Company* he has kept, and what *Visitors* he may have had. However I shall not enter into a Point of Controversy whether *the Lords were acquainted with the Ordinary*, or the *Ordinary with the Lords*, since this Author leaves it undecided. Only one Thing I take to be a little hard; It is now confessed on all Hands, that Mr. *Harley* was most unjustly suspected of joining with an under Clerk in corresponding with *France*: The Suspicion being in it self unreasonable, and without the least probable Grounds, wise Men began to consider what violent Enemies that Gentleman had; they found the Report most industriously spread, the *Whigs* in common Discourse discovering their Wishes, that he might be found guilty; the management of the whole Affair was put into the Hands of such, as it is supposed would at least not be sorry to find more than they expected; The Criminals dying Speach is unfortunately published, wherein he thanks God he was not tempted *to save his Life by falsly accusing his Master*, with more to the same purpose: From all this put together, it was no very unnatural Conjecture, that there might have been some tampering; now, I say, it is a little hard that Mr. *Harley*'s Friends must not be allowed to have their Suspicions, as well as his Enemies: And this Author, if he intended to deal fairly, should have spent one Paragraph in railing at those who had the Impudence and Villainy to suspect Mr. *Harley*, and then proceed in due method to defend his Committee of *Examiners*: But that Gentleman being, as this Author says of the Speaker, *but a single Man*; I suppose, his Reputation and Life were esteemed but of little Consequence.

There is one State of the Case in this Letter, which I cannot well omit, because the Author, I suppose, conceives it to be extremely cunning and malicious; that it cuts to the quick, and is wonderfully Severe upon Mr. *Harley*, without exposing the Writer to any Danger. I say this to gratify him, to let him know, I take his meaning, and discover his Inclinations. His parallel Case is this; *Supposing* Guiscard *had been intimate with some great Officer of State, and had been suspected to communicate his most secret Affairs with that Minister*; then he asks, *Whether it would have been Subornation, or Seeking the Life and Blood of that Officer, in these great Lords of the Council, if they had narrowly examined this Affair, inquired with all Exactness what he knew of this great Officer, what Secrets he had imported to him, and whether he were privy to his corresponding*? &c. In this Parallel, *Guiscard*'s Case is supposed to be the same with *Greg*'s; and That of the great Officer with Mr. *Harley*'s. So that here he lays down as a Thing granted, that *Gregg* was *intimate with* Mr. *Harley*, and *suspected to communicate his most Secret Affairs to him*. Now did ever any rational Man suspect, that Mr. *Harley*, first Principal Secretary of State, was intimate with an under Clerk, or upon the Foot of having *most Secret Affairs communicated to Him* from such a Councellor, from one in so inferior a Station, whom perhaps he hardly knew by sight? Why was that Report raised, but for the Uses which were afterwards made of it? Or, why should we wonder that they, who were so wicked to be Authors of it, would be scrupulous in applying it to the only Purpose for which it could be raised?

Having thus considered the main Design of this Letter, I shall make a few Remarks upon some particular Passages in it.

First, Though it be of no Consequence to this Dispute, I cannot but observe a most evident Falshood, which he repeats three or four times in his Letter, that I *make the World believe I am set on work by Great People*. I remember my self to have several Times affirmed the direct contrary, and so I do still; and if I durst tell him my Name, which he is so desirous to know, he would be convinced that I am of a Temper to think no Man great enough to set me on Work; nay I am content to own all the scurrilous Titles he gives me, if he be able to find one *Innuendo* through all those Papers that can any way favour this Calumny: The Malice of which is not intended against *Me*, but the present Ministry, to make the World believe, that what I have published, is the utmost Effort of all they can say or think against the last: Whereas it is nothing more than the common Observations of a private Man, deducing Consequences and Effects from very natural and visible Causes.

He tells us, with great Propriety of Speech, That the Seven Lords and their Friends are treated as *Subverters of the Constitution, and such as have been long endeavouring to destroy both Church and State*. This puts me in mind of One, who first murdered a Man, and afterwards endeavoured to kill him: And therefore I here solemnly deny them to have been *Subverters of the Constitution*: But that *some People* did their best Endeavours, I confidently believe.

He tells *Me* particularly, that I *acquit* Guiscard *by a blunder of a Design against Mr.* Harley's *Life*. I declare he injures me, for I look upon *Guiscard* to be full as guilty of the Design, as even those were who tampered in the Business of *Gregg*; and both (to avoid all cavelling) as guilty as ever any Man was that suffered Death by Law.

He calls the Stabbing of Mr. *Harley*, a *sore Blow*, but I suppose he means His *Recovery*; That indeed was a *sore Blow* to the *Interests* of his Party: But I take the Business of *Gregg* to have been a much *sorer Blow* to their *Reputation*.

This Writer wonders how I *should know their Lordship*'s *Hearts, because he hardly knows his own*. I do not well see the Consequence of this: Perhaps he never examines into his own Heart, perhaps it keeps no correspondence with his Tongue or his Pen: I hope at least, it is a Stranger to those foul Terms he has strowed throughout his Letter; otherwise I fear I *know it too well:* For *out of the abundance of the Heart, the Mouth speaketh*. But however, Actions are pretty good Discoverers of the Heart, though Words are not; and whoever has once endeavoured to take away my Life, if he has still the same, or rather much greater Cause, whether it be a just one or no, and has never shewn the least Sign of Remorse; I may venture, without being a Conjurer, to know so much of his Heart, as to believe he would repeat his Attempt, if it were in his Power. I must needs quote some following Lines in the same Page, which are of an extraordinary Kind, and seem to describe the blessed Age we should live in, under the return of the late Administration. *It is very well* (saith he) *that Peoples Heads are to stand on their Shoulders, as long as the Laws will let them; if it depended upon any thing besides, it may be your Lordships seven Heads might be as soon cut off, as that one Gentleman's, were you in Power.* Then he concludes the Paragraph with this charitable Prayer, in the true Moderation-Style, and in Italick Letter, *May the Head that has done the Kingdom the greatest Mischief, fall first, let it be whose it will.* The plain meaning of which is this: If the late Ministry were in Power, they would act just as the present Ministry would, if there were no Law, which perhaps may be true: But I know not any Ministry upon Earth, that I durst confide in without Law; and if at their coming in again, they design to make their *Power* the *Law*, they may as easily cut off *Seven Heads* as *One*. As for *the Head that has done the greatest Mischief to the Kingdom*, I cannot consent it should fall, untill he and I have settled the meaning of the word *Mischief*. Neither do I much approve this renewing an old Fashion of whipping off *Heads* by a *Prayer*; it began from what *some of us* think an ill Precedent. Then that unlimitted Clause, *let it be whose it will*, perplexes me not a little: I wish in compliance with an old Form, he had excepted *my Lord-Mayor*: Otherwise, if it were to be determined by their Vote, *whose Head it was that had done the greatest Mischief*; which way can we tell how far *their Predecessor's* Principles may have influenced them? God preserve the Queen and Her Ministers from such undistinguishing disposers of Heads.

His Remarks upon what the *Ordinary* told *Hoffman*, are singular enough. The *Ordinary*'s Words are, that *so many Endeavours were used to corrupt* Gregg's *Conscience*, &c. *that he felt as much uneasiness lest* Gregg *should betray his Master, as if it had been his own Case.* The Author of the Letter says to this, that *for ought the* Ordinary *knew, he might confess what was exactly true of his Master; and that therefore, an indifferent Person might as well be uneasy, for fear* Gregg *should discover something of his Master, that would touch his Life, and yet might have been True.* But if these were really the *Ordinary*'s Thoughts at that time, they were honest and reasonable. He knew it was highly improbable that a Person of Mr. *Harley*'s Character and Station should make use of such a Confederate in Treason: If he had suspected his *Loyalty*, he could not have suspected his *Understanding*; and knowing how much Mr. *Harley* was feared and hated by the Men in Power, and observing that *Resort to* Greg *at unseasonable Hours, and that strange Promises were often made him by Men of Note*; all this put together, might naturally incline the *Ordinary* to think, the Design could be nothing else, but that Mr. *Harley* should be accused in spight of his Innocence.

This Charge of *Subornation* is, it seems, so extraordinary a Crime, that the Author *challenges all the Books in the* new Lord's *Library* (*because* he hears *it is the largest*) *to furnish us with an Instance like it*. What if this Charge should be true? Then I, in my turn, would challenge all the Books in *another* Lord s Library, which is ten times larger (though perhaps not so often disturbed) to furnish us with an Instance like this. If it be so monstrous a Thing to accuse others of *Subornation*, what Epithet is left to bestow upon those who are really guilty of the Crime it self? I think it beyond Controversy, that Subornation was practised in the Business of *Greg*: This manifestly appears from those few Facts I have mentioned: Let the *Whigs* agree among them where to fix it. Nay it is plain, by the great Endeavours made to stifle his last Speech, that they would have suborned the poor Man even after he was dead: And is this a Matter now to be called in question, much less to be denied?

He compares the Examination of *Guiscard* with that of *Greg*, talks of several great Persons who Examined the former in Prison, and promised him the Queen's Pardon if he would make a full Discovery. Then the Author puts the Case, *How wicked it would be to charge these honourable Counsellors with suborning* Guiscard *by Promises of Life*, &c. *to accuse the Innocent*, *and betray his Friends*. Does it any where appear that those Noble Persons who examined *Guiscard*, put *leading Questions* to him, or pointed out where they would have him *fix* an Accusation? Did they name *some mortal Enemy* of their own, and then *drop Words of Pardon and Reward*, *if he would accuse him*? Did *Guiscard* leave any Paper behind him, to justify the Innocence of *some great Person* whom he was *tempted* to accuse! Yet perhaps I could think of certain People, who were much more likely to act in Concert with *Guiscard*, than ever Mr. *Harley* was to be Confederate with *Greg*. I can imagine several who *wished* the Pen-knife in Mr. *Harley*'s Heart, though *Guiscard* alone was desperate enough to attempt it. Who were those, that by their Discourses, as well as Countenances, discovered their Joy when the Blow was struck? Who were those that went out, or stood silent, when the *Address* and *Congratulation* were voted? And who were those that refined so far as to make Mr. *Harley* Confederate with his own *Assassin*?

There is one Point which this Author affirms more than once or twice in a transient way, as if he would have us suppose it a Thing granted; but is of such a weight, that it wants nothing but Truth to make the late Change of Ministry a very useless and dangerous Proceeding: For so it must be allowed, if, as he affirms, *Affairs are still under the like Management, and must be so, because there is no better;* that *this Sett of Men must take the same courses in their Ministration with their Predecessors, or ten times worse; that the new Servants go on in the old Methods, and give the same Council and Advice, on the like Occasions, with the old ones*; with more to the same Purpose. A Man may affirm, without being of the *Cabinet*, that every Syllable of this is absolutely false; unless he means, that Mony is still raised by Parliament, and borrowed upon new Funds; that the Duke of *Marlborough* still Commands the Army; that we have a Treasurer, Keeper, President, and Secretaries, as we had before; and that because the Council meets much about the same Times and Places as formerly, therefore they *give the same Advice*, and *pursue the same Measures*. What does he think of finding Funds to pay the old unprovided-for Debt of the Navy, and erecting a Company for the *South-sea* Trade? What does he think of Mr. *Hill*'s Expedition to preserve our Trade in the *West-Indies*? What, of the Methods taken to make our Allies pay their *Quota*'s to the War, which was a thing so scandalously either neglected, connived at, or encouraged? What, of the Care to retrench the exorbitant Expences of the *Spanish* War? What, of those many Abuses and Corruptions at home, which have been so narrowly enquired into, and in a good part redressed? Evils so deeply radicated, must require some time to remedy them, and cannot be all set right in a few Months. Besides, there are some Circumstances known by the Names of

Honour, Probity, good Sense, great Capacity for Business; as likewise, certain Principles of Religion and Loyalty, the Want or Possession of all which, will make a mighty Difference even in the Pursuit of the same Measures. There is also one Characteristick which will ever distinguish the late Ministry from the Present, That the former sacrificing all Regards to the Increase of their Wealth and Power, found Those were no otherwise to be preserved, but by Continuance of the War; whereas the Interest, as well as Inclinations of the present, dispose them to make use of the first Opportunities for a safe and honourable Peace.

The Writer goes on upon another parallel Case, which is, the modern way of reflecting upon a Prince and Ministry. He tells us, That *the Queen was brought to discard her old Officers through the multitude of Complaints, secret Teazings, and importunate Clamors of a Rout of People, led by their Priests, and spirited underhand by crafty Emissaries.* Would not any one who reads this imagine, that the whole Rabble, with the Clergy at their Head, were whispering in the Queen's Ear, or came in Disguise to *desire a Word with her Majesty*, like the Army of the two Kings of *Brentford*? The unbiassed Majority of the Nobility and Gentry of the Kingdom, are called, by this Son of Obscurity, a *Rout of People*, and the *Clergy* their *Leaders*. We have often accused that Party for their evil Talent of Railing perpetually against the Clergy, which they discovered at first without any visible Reason or Provocation, as conscious of the Designs they had in view, and therefore wisely began by villifying those whom they intended to destroy. I have observed formerly, that the Party-Malice against the Clergy hath been so blind and furious, as to charge them with Crimes wholly inconsistent. I find they are still in the same Disposition, and that this Writer hath received *Direction from his Superiors*, to pursue the old Stile upon that Article. Accordingly, in the Paragraph I am now upon, he represents that Reverend Body as *Leaders*, *Cullies*, and *Tools*. First he says, That *Rout of secret Teazers* (meaning the Nobility and Gentry of the Kingdom) were *led by the Priests*. Then he assures us, that the Queen will, in a Year or two, begin to consider, *Who it was that cheated those poor Priests*. And in case Her Majesty should have a mind to bring in the old Ministry again, he comforts his Party, That *the Priests are seldom wanting to become the Tools of cunning Managers.* I desire to know in what Sense he would have us to understand, that *these poor Priests* have been cheated: Are they cheated by a Fund established for Building 50 Churches? Or by the Queen's Letter empowering them to proceed on the Business proper for a Convocation? What one single Advantage could they possibly lose by this Change? They are still indeed abused every Day in Print, but it is by those who are without the Power to hurt them; the Serpent has lost his Sting, is trodden under Foot, and its *hissing* is contemned. But he confidently affirms, That when it shall be thought fit to restore the old Ministry, *the Priests will not be wanting to become the Tools of their cunning Managers.* This I cannot by any Means allow, unless they have some hidden Reserve of Cunning which hath never yet been produced. The cunningest Managers I ever knew among them, are of all others most detested by the Clergy: Neither do I remember they have been ever able to make any of them *Tools*, except by making them *Bishops*; even those few they were able to seduce, would not be their *Tools* at a lower Rate.

But because this Author, and others of his Standard, affect to make use of that Word *Tool*, when they have a mind to be Shrewd and Satyrical; I desire once for all to set them right. A *Tool* and an *Instrument*, in the metaphorical Sense, differ thus: the Former, is an Engine in the Hands of *Knaves*, the latter in those of wise and honest Men. The greatest Ministers are *Instruments* in the Hands of Princes, and so are Princes themselves in the Hands of God; and in this Sense the Clergy are ready to be *Instruments* of any Good to the Prince or People. But that the Clergy of England, since the *Reformation*, have at any Time been the *Tools* of a Party, is a Calumny which History and constant Experience, will immediately confute. *Scismatick* and *Fanatick* Preachers, have indeed been perpetually employed that way with good Success; by the Faction against K. *Charles* I. to Murder their Prince, and ruin the Monarchy; by K. *James* II. to bring in Popery: And ever since the Revolution, to advance the unmeasurable Appetite of Power and Wealth, among a Set of profligate Upstarts. But in all these three Instances, the established Clergy (except a very few, like *Tares among Wheat*, and those generally *Sown by the Enemy*) were so far from being *Tools*, that in the first, they were persecuted, imprisoned and deprived; and in the two others, they were great *Instruments*, under God, for preserving Our Religion and Liberty.

In the same Paragraph, which contains a Project for turning out the present Ministry, and restoring the last; he owns, that the Queen is *now Served with more obsequious Words, more humble Adorations, and a more seeming Resignation to her Will and Pleasure, then she was before*. And indeed if this be not true, her Majesty has the worst Luck of any Prince in Christendom. The Reverse of these Phrases I take to be *Rude Expressions, Insolent Behaviour*, and a *real Opposition to her Majesty's most just and reasonable Commands*, which are the mildest Terms that the Demeanor of some *late Persons* towards their Prince can deserve, in return of the highest Favours that Subjects ever received, whereof a hundred Particulars might be produced. So that according to our Authors way of Reasoning, I will put a parallel Case in my Turn. I have a Servant to whom I am exceeding Kind, I reward him infinitely above his Merit. Besides which, he and his Family snap every thing they can lay their Hands on; they will let none come near me, but themselves and Dependants; they misrepresent my best Friends as my greatest Enemies; besides, they are so saucy and malapert, there is no Speaking to them; so far from any Respect, that they treat me as an Inferior. At last I pluck up Spirit, turn them all out of doors, and take in new ones, who are content with what I allow them, though I have less to spare than formerly; give me their best Advice when I ask it, are constantly in the way, do what I bid them, make a Bow when they come in and go out, and always give me a respectful Answer. I suppose the Writer of the Letter would tell me that my present Domesticks were indeed a *little more Civil*, but the former were *better Servants*.

There are two Things wherewith this Author is peculiarly Angry. First, at the *licentious way of the Scum of Mankind treating the greatest Peers in the Nation*. Secondly, that *these Hedge-Writers* (a Phrase I unwillingly lend him, because it cost me some Pains to invent) *seldom speak a Word against any of the late Ministry, but they presently fall to Compliment my Lord Treasurer, and others in great Places*. On the first, he brings but one Instance, but I could produce a good many hundred; what does he think of the *Observator*, the *Review* and the *Medley*? In his own impartial judgment, may not they as fairly bid for being the *Scum of Mankind*, as the *Examiner*? and have they not treated *at least* as many, and *almost* as *great Peers*, in as infamous a manner? I grant indeed, that through the great defect of Truth, Genius, Learning, and common Sense among the Libellers of that Party, they being of no Entertainment to the World, after serving the present Turn, were immediately forgotten. But this we can remember in gross, that there was not a great Man in *England*, distinguished for his Love to the Monarchy or the Church, who under the Appellations of *Tory*, *Jacobite*, *High-flyer*, and other *Cant Words*, was not represented as a publick Enemy, and loaden by name with all manner of Obloquy. Nay have they not even disturbed the Ashes, and endeavoured to blast the Memories of the Dead, and chiefly of those who lost their Lives in the Service of the Monarchy and the Church? His other Quarrel is at our *Flattering my Lord Treasurer, and other Great Persons in Power*. To which I shall only say; for every Line written in Praise of the present Ministry, I will engage to furnish the Author with three Pages of the most fulsom Panegyricks on the least deserving Members of the last; which is somewhat more than by the Proportion of Time, while they were in Power, could fall to their share. Indeed I am apt to think that the Men of Wit at least, will be more sparing in their Incense of this Kind for the future, and say no more of any Great Man now at the Helm, than they believe he deserves. Poems, Dedications, and other publick Encomiums, might be of use to those, who were obliged to keep up an unnatural Spirit in the Nation, by supplying it with Art; and consequently the Authors deserved, and sometimes met Encouragment and Reward. But those Great Patriots, now at the Head of Affairs, are sufficiently supported by the *uncompelled* Favour of the Queen, and the *natural* Disposition of the People. We can do them no *Service* by our Applauses, and therefore can expect no *Payment*: So that I look upon this kind of Stock to have fallen at least 90 *per. cent.* since the great Changes at Court.

He puts a few Questions, which I am in some pain to answer. *Cannot* (says he) *the Successors be excellent Men, unless the Predeces-*

sors be Villains? Cannot the Queen change her Ministers, but they must presently be such as neither God nor Man can endure? Do Noble Men fall from all Honour, Vertue and Religion, because they are so unhappy as to fall from their Prince's Favour? I desire to say something in the first place, to this last Question, which I answer in the Negative. However he will own, that *Men should fall from their Prince's Favour, when they are so unhappy as to fall from all Honour, Vertue and Religion*; though I must confess my Belief at the same time, that *some certain Persons* have lately *fallen from Favour*, who could not, for a very manifest Reason, be said, properly speaking, to *fall from any of the other three*. To his other Questions I can only say, that the constant Language of the Whig-Pamphleteers, has been this Twelvemonth past, to tell us how dangerous a Step it was to change the Ministry at so nice a Juncture; to shake our Credit, disoblige our Allies, and encourage the French. Then, this Author tells us, that those discarded Politicians *were the greatest Ministers we ever had*: His Brethren have said the same thing a hundred times. On the other side, the Queen, upon long Deliberation, was resolved to part with them: The universal Voice of the People was against them: Her Majesty is the most mild and gracious Prince that ever reigned: We have been constantly victorious, and are ruined; the Enemy flourishes under his perpetual Losses. If these be the Consequences of an *able*, *faithful*, *diligent* and *dutiful* Administration; *of that astonishing Success*, he says, *Providence hath crowned us with*, what can be those of one directly contrary? But, not to enter into a wide Field at present, I faithfully promise the Author of the Letter, his Correspondents, his Patrons, and his Brethren, that this Mystery of Iniquity shall be very shortly laid open to the view of the World; when the most ignorant and prejudiced Reader will, I hope, be convinced by Facts not to be controuled, how miserably this poor Kingdom has been deluded to the very brink of Destruction.

He would have it, that the People of *England* have *lost their Senses*; are *bewitched* and *cheated*, *mad* and *without Understanding*: But that all this *will go off by degrees*, and then his *Great Men will recover their Esteem and Credit*. I did, in one of my Papers, overthrow this idle affected Opinion, which has been a thousand times urged by those who most wished and least believed it: I there shewed the difference between *a short Madness of the People*, and their *natural Bent or Genius*. I remember when King *James* II. went from *England*, he left a Paper behind him, with Expressions much to the same purpose; *hoping*, among other things, that *God would open the Eyes of the Nation*. Too much Zeal for his Religion brought us then in danger of *Popery* and *arbitrary Power*; too much *Infidelity*, *Avarice* and *Ambition*, brought us lately into *equal* danger of *Atheism* and *Anarchy*. The People have not yet *opened their Eyes*, to see any Advantage in the two former; nor I hope will ever *find their Senses* enough to discover the Blessings of the two latter. Cannot I see things in another Light than this Author and his Party do, without being *blind*? Is my *Understanding lost* when it differs from theirs? Am I *cheated, bewitched* and *out of my Senses*, because I think those to have been Betrayers of our Country, whom they call Patriots?

He hopes his seven Correspondents *will never want their Places*; but is in pain for the poor Kingdom, lest *their Places should want them*. Now I have examined this matter, and am not at all discouraged. Two of them hold their Places still, and are likely to continue in them. Two more were Governours of Islands; I believe the Author does not imagin those to be among the *Places* which will *want Men* to fill them. God be thanked, a Man may Command the *Beef-Eaters* without being a Soldier; I will at any time undertake to do it my self. Then, it would be a little hard, if the Queen should be at a Loss for a *Steward* to Her Family. So that upon the whole, I see but one great Employment which is in any danger of wanting a sufficient Person to execute it. We must do as well as we can: Yet I have been told, that the bare Business of *Presiding* in Council, does not require such very transcendent Abilities; and I am mistaken, if till within these late Years, we have not been some Ages without that Office. So that I hope Things may go well enough, provided the *Keeper*, *Treasurer*, and both the *Secretaries* will do their Duties; and it is happy for the Nation that none of *their seven Lordships* left any of *those Places* to *want* them.

The Writer of the Letter concludes it with an *Appeal to all the Princes and States of Europe*, *Friends and Enemies* by Name, *to give their Judgment*, *whether they think the late Ministry were wanting in*

Faithfulness, Abilities, or Diligence to serve their Prince and Country. Now, if he speaks by Order of his Party, I am humbly of Opinion, they have incurred a *Premunire*, for appealing to a Foreign Jurisdiction, and Her Majesty may seize their Goods and Chattels whenever she pleases. In the mean time, I will not accept his Appeal; which has been rejected by the Queen and both Houses of Parliament. But let a fair Jury be Impanelled in any County of *England*, and I will be determined by their Verdict. First, he names the King of *France* and all his Counsellors, with the *Pretender* and all his Favourers and Abettors. These I except against: I know they will readily judge the late Ministry to be faithful, able and diligent in serving *their Prince* and Country. The Councils of *some People* have, in their way, served very much to promote the Service of the *Pretender*, and to enable the *French King* to assist him; and is not he, in that Monarch's Opinion, as well as his own, *their lawful Prince*? I except against the *Emperor* and the *States*; because it can be proved upon them, that the *Plaintiffs* and they have an *Understanding* together. I except against any Prince who makes unreasonable Demands, and threatens to recal his Troops if they be not complyed with; because they have been forced of late to change their Language, and may perhaps be shortly obliged to observe their Articles more strictly. I should be sorry, for the Appealers sakes, to have their Case referred to the Kings of *Sweden* and *Denmark*, who infallibly would decree them to be all hanged up for their Insolence to their Sovereign. But above all, the King of *Spain* would certainly be against them, when he considers, with how scandalous a Neglect his Interests have been managed; and that the full Possession of his Kingdom was made a Sacrifice to those, whose private or Party-Interest swayed them to the continuance of the War. The Author had reason to omit the *Grand Signior* and the *Czar* in the List of his Judges; The Decrees of those Princes are too sudden and sanguinary, and their Lessons to instruct Subjects in Behaviour to their Princes, by strangling them with a Bowstring, or flinging them to be devoured alive by Hogs, were enough to deter him from submitting to their Jurisdiction.

FINIS.

A NEW
Journey to PARIS:
Together with some
Secret Transactions
Between the
Fr---h K---g,
AND AN
Eng—— Gentleman.

By the Sieur du BAUDRIER.

Translated from the French.

The Second Edition, Corrected.

LONDON,
Printed for *John Morphew*, near *Stationers-Hall.* 1711. (Price 2 *d.*)

THE TRANSLATOR TO THE READER.

THE *Original of the following Discourse was transmitted to me three Days ago from the* Hague, *to which Town it was sent from* France; *but in the Title-Page there was no mention of the Place where it was Printed, only the Author's Name at length, and the Year of our Lord. That the Tract is genuine, I believe no Person will doubt. You see all along the Vanity of That Nation, in a mean Man, giving himself the Airs of a Secretary, when it appears, by several Circumstances, that he was received only as a menial Servant. It were to be wished, the Author had been one of more Importance, and farther trusted in the Secrets of his Master's Negotiation; but to make amends, he informs us of several Particulars, which one of more Consequence would not have given himself the trouble about: And these Particulars are such, as we at home will perhaps be curious to know; not to mention that he gives us much Light into some Things that are of great moment; and by his not pretending to know more, we cannot doubt the Truth of what he relates.*

It is plain, he waited at Table, carried his Master's Valise, *and attended in his Bed-chamber; though he takes care to tell us, that Monsieur* Prior *made many Excuses and Apologies, because these mean Offices appear very inconsistent with the Character of Secretary, which he would seem to set up for.*

I shall make no Reflections on this important Affair, nor upon the Consequences we may expect from it: To reason upon Secrets of State, without knowing all the Springs and Motions of them, is too common a Talent among us, and the Foundation of a thousand Errors. Here is room enough for Speculations; but I advise the Reader *to let them serve for his own Entertainment, without troubling the World with his* Remarks.

TO

Monsieur Monsieur,

AT

*ESTAPLE.

SIR,

I DOUBT not but you are curious, as many others are, to know the Secret of Monsieur *Prior*, an *English* Gentleman's late Journey from *London* to *Paris*. Perhaps, living retired as you do, you may not have heard of this Person, though some Years ago he was very much distinguished at *Paris*, and in good Esteem even with our August Monarch. I must let you so far into his Character, as to tell you, that Monsieur *Prior* has signalized himself, both as an eminent Poet, and Man of Business; was very much valued by the late King *William*, who employed him in important Affairs, both in *England* and *Holland:* He was Secretary to the *English* Ambassy, at the Treaty of *Reswick*; and afterwards, to my Lords the Counts of *Portland* and *Jersey*; and, in the Absence of the latter, managed, for some time, the Affairs of *England* at our Court by himself. Since the Reign of Queen *Anne* he was employed as Commissioner of Trade; but the Ministry changing soon after Queen *Anne*'s coming to the Crown, Monsieur *Prior*, who was thought too much attached to the ¶*Rigides*, was laid aside, and lived privately at || *Cambridge*, where he is a Professor, till he was recalled by the present Ministry.

ABOUT two Months ago, our King, resolving once more to give Peace to *Europe*, notwithstanding the flourishing Condition of his Fleets and Armies, the good Posture of his Finances, that

* A Sea-Port Town in the *Bolognois*.

¶ *Tories*.

|| A Mistake of the Author; for, Monsieur *Prior* did not retire to *Cambridge*, nor is a Professor, but a Fellow.

his Grandson was almost entirely settled in the quiet Possession of *Spain*, and that the Affairs of the *North* was changing every Day to his Advantage; offered the Court of *England* to send a Minister as far as *Bologn*, who should be there met by some Person from *England*, to treat the Overtures of a Peace. Upon the first Notice that this was agreed to, the King immediately dispatched Monsieur *de Torcy*, in whom he very much confides, to *Bologn*, where he took Lodgings at a private House in the *Faux Bourg*, at one Mr. *de Marais*, *Marchand de Soy*, who is married to an *English* Woman, that formerly had been a *Suivante* to one of the forementioned *English* Ambassador's Ladies, over against the *Hostelerie de St. Jean*. Monsieur stayed six Days with much Impatience, when, late at Evening, on *Wednesday* the 14th of *July**, a Person, whom we afterwards knew to be Monsieur *Prior*, came directly to the Door, and enquired for Monsieur *De la Bastide*, (the Name and Place, I suppose, having been before concerted:) He was immediately shewn unto Monsieur *de Torcy*, where, as I am informed, they were shut up for three Hours together, without any Refreshment, though Monsieur *Prior* had rid Post from *Calais* that Day in a great deal of Rain. The next Morning I was sent for, in all haste, by Monsieur *de Marais*, who told me, that a Person of Quality, as he suspected, lately come from *England*, had some occasion for a Secretary; and, because he knew I understood the Languages, wrote a tolerable Hand, had been conversant with Persons of Quality, and formerly trusted with Secrets of Importance, had been so kind to recommend me to the said Gentleman, to serve him in that Quality. I was immediately called up, and presented to Mr. *Prior*, who accosted me with great Civility, and after some Conversation was pleased to tell me, I had fully answered the Character Monsieur *de Marais* had given me. From this time, to the Day Monsieur *Prior* left *Calais*, in order to return to *England*, I may pretend to give you a faithful Account of all his Motions, and some probable Conjectures of his whole Negotiation between *Bologn* and *Versailles*.

BUT perhaps, Sir, you may be farther curious to know the

* New Style.

Particulars of Monsieur *Prior*'s Journey to *Bologn*. It is reported that sometime before the Peace of *Ryswick*, King *William* did dispatch this very Gentleman to *Paris*, upon the same account for which he now came: This possibly might be the Motive (besides the known Abilities of Monsieur *Prior*) to send him a second time. The following Particulars I heard in Discourse between *Madamoiselle de Marais* and her Husband, which being no great Secrets on our side the Water, I suppose were told without Consequence.

MONSIEUR *Prior* having received his Instructions from the *English* Court, under pretence of taking a short Journey of Pleasure, and visiting the *Chevalier de Hanmer* in the Province of *Suffolk*, left his House on *Sunday* night, the 11th of *July*, N.S. taking none of his Servants with him. Monsieur *Moore*, who had already prepared a Bark, with all Necessaries, on the Coast of *Dover*, took Monsieur *Prior* disguised in his Chariot: They lay on *Monday* Night, the 12th of *July*, at the Count de *Jersey*'s House in *Kent*; arrived in good time the next Day at *Dover*, drove directly to the Shoar, made the Sign by waving their Hats; which was answered by the Vessel; and the Boat was immediately sent to take him in, which he entered, wrapt in his Cloak, and soon got Aboard. He was six hours at Sea, and arrived at *Calais* about eleven at Night; went immediately to the Governour, who received him with great Respect, where he lay all Night; and set out pretty late the next Morning, being somewhat incommoded with his Voyage, and then took Post for *Bologn*, as I have before related.

IN the first Conversation I had the Honour to have with Monsieur *Prior* he was pleased to talk, as if he would have occasion for my Service but a very few Days; and seemed resolved, by his Discourse, that after he had dispatched his Commission with Monsieur *de la Bastide* (for so we shall from henceforward call that Minister) he would return to *England*; by this I found I should have but little Employment in Quality of Secretary; however, having heard so great a Character of him, I was willing to attend him in any Capacity he pleased. Four Days we continued at *Bologn*, where Monsieur *de la Bastide* and Monsieur *Prior* had two long Conferences every Day from Ten to One at Noon, and from Six till Nine in the Evening. Monsieur *Prior* did me the Honour to send me some Meat and Wine constantly from his own Table; upon the third Morning I was ordered to attend early, observed Monsieur *Prior* to have a pleasant Countenance, he asked me what I thought of a Journey to *England?* and commanded me to be ready at an hours Warning. But upon the fourth Evening all this was changed; and I was directed to hire the best Horse I could find for my self.

WE set out early the next Day, *Sunday* the 18th, for *Paris*, in Monsieur *de la Bastide*'s Chaize, whose two Attendants and my self, made up the Equipage; but a small *Valise*, which I suppose contained Monsieur *Prior*'s Instructions, he was pleased to trust to my Care to carry on Horseback; which Trust I discharged with the utmost Faithfulness.

SOMEWHAT above two Leagues from *Bologn*, at a small Village called *Neile*, the Axletree broke, which took us two hours to mend; we baited at *Montreuil*, and lay that Night at *Abbeville*. But I shall not give you any detail of our Journey, which passed without any considerable Accident, till we arrived within four Leagues of *Paris*; when about three in the Afternoon, two Cavaliers, well mounted, and armed with Pistols, crossed the Road, then turned short and rode up briskly to the Chaize, commanding the Coachman to stop. Monsieur *de la Bastide*'s two Attendants were immediately up with them; but I, who guessed at the Importance of the Charge that Monsieur *Prior* had intrusted me with, though I was in no fear for my own Person, thought it most prudent to advance with what speed I could, to a small Village, about a quarter of a League forward, to wait the Event. I soon observed the Chaize to come on without any Disturbance, and I ventured to meet it; when I found that it was only a Frolick of two young Cadets of Quality, who had been making a Debauch at a Friend's House hard by, and were returning to *Paris*; one of them was not unknown to Monsieur *de la Bastide*. The two Cavaliers began to rally me, said I knew how to make a Retreat, with some other Pleasantries; but Monsieur *Prior*, (who knew the Cause) highly commended my Discretion. We continued our Journey very merrily, and arrived at *Paris* on *Tuesday* the 20th, in the Cool of the Evening.

At the Entrance of the Town our two Cavaliers left us, and Monsieur *de la Bastide* conducted Monsieur *Prior* to a private Lodging in the *ruë St. Louis*, which, by all Circumstances, I concluded to be prepared before for his Reception. Here I first had Orders to say that the Gentleman to whom I had the Honour to belong, was called Monsieur *Matthews*; I then knew no otherwise; afterwards, at *Versailles*, I overheard in Conversation with Monsieur *de la Bastide*, that his real Name was *Prior*.

Monsieur *Bastide* would have had Monsieur *Matthews* to have gone with him next Morning to *Versailles*, but could not prevail with him to comply; of which I could never be able to learn the Reason. Our Minister was very importunate, and Monsieur *Prior* seemed to have no Fatigue remaining from his Journey; perhaps he might conceive it more suitable to his Dignity that Monsieur *de la Bastide* should go before, to prepare the King, by giving Notice of his Arrival: However it were, Monsieur *Bastide* made all haste to *Versailles*, and returned the same Night. During his Absence, Monsieur *Prior* never stirred out of his Chamber; and after Dinner, did me the Honour to send for me up, that I might bear him Company, as he was pleased to express it. I was surprized to hear him wondering at the Misery, he had observed in our Country, in his Journey from *Calais*, at the Scarcity and Poverty of the Inhabitants, which he said, did much exceed even what he had seen in his former Journey; for he owned that he had been in *France* before. He seemed to value himself very much upon the Happiness of his own Island, which, as he pretended, had felt no Effects, like these, upon Trade or Agriculture.

I made bold to return for Answer, That in our Nation we only consulted the Magnificence and Power of our Prince; but that in *England*, as I was informed, the Wealth of the Kingdom was so divided among the People, that little or nothing was left to their Sovereign; and that it was confidently told (though hardly believed in *France*) that some Subjects had Palaces more Magnificent than Queen *Anne* her self: That I hoped, when he went to *Versailles*, he would allow the Grandeur of our Potent Monarch to exceed, not only that of *England*, but any other in *Europe*, by which he would find that what he called the Poverty of our Nation, was rather the Effect of Policy in our Court, than any real Want or Necessity. Monsieur *Prior* had no better Answer to make me, than that he was no Stranger to our Court, the Splendor of our Prince, and the Maxims by which he governed; but for his part, he thought those Countries were happier, where the Productions of it were more equally divided: Such unaccountable Notions is the Prejudice of Education apt to give! In these and the like Discourses we wore away the time till Mons. *de la Bastide*'s return; who after an hour's private Conference with Monsieur *Prior*, which I found by their Countenances had been warmly pursued on both sides, a Chariot and six Horses(to my great surprize)were instantly ordered,wherein the two Ministers entered, and drove away with all Expedition, my self only attending on Horseback, with my important *Valise*.

WE got to *Versailles* on *Wednesday* the 21st, about Eleven at Night; but instead of entering the Town, the Coachman drove us a back way into the Fields, till we stopt at a certain Vineyard, that I afterwards understood joined to the Gardens of Madam *Maintenon*'s Lodgings. Here the two Gentlemen alighted; Monsieur *Prior* calling to me, bid me search in the *Valise* for a small Box of Writings; after which the Coachman was ordered to attend in that Place; and we proceeded on some paces, till we stopt at a little Postern which opened into the Vineyard, whereof Monsieur *Bastide* had the Key. He opened it very readily, and shut it after them, desiring me to stay untill their return.

I WAITED with some Impatience for three Hours, the great Clock struck Two before they came out: The Coachman, who, I suppose, had his Instructions before, as soon as they were got into the Chariot, drove away to a small House at the end of the Town, where Monsieur *Bastide* left us, to our selves. I observed Monsieur *Prior* was very Thoughtful, and without entering into any Conversation, desired my Assistance to put him to Bed. Next Morning, *Thursday* the 22d, I had positive Orders not to stir abroad. About ten a Clock, Mons. *Bastide* came; the House being small, my Apartment was divided from Monsieur *Prior*'s by a thin Wainscot, so that I could easily hear what they said, when they raised their Voice, as they often did. After some time I could hear Monsieur *de la Bastide* say, with warmth, Bon Dieu!

&c. Good God! Were ever such Demands made to a great Monarch, unless you were at the Gates of his Metropolis? For the Love of God, Monsieur Prior *relax something, if your Instructions will permit you, else I shall despair of any good Success in our Negotiation? Is it not enough that our King will abandon his Grandson, but he must lend his own Arm to pull him out of the Throne? Why did you not open your self to me at* Bologn? *Why are you more inexorable here at* Versailles? *You have risen in your Demands, by seeing Madam* Maintenon'*s Desire for a Peace? As able as you are to continue the War, consider which is to be most preferred, the Good of your Country, or the particular Advantage of your* General; *for he will be the only Gainer among your Subjects?* Monsieur *Prior*, who has a low Voice, and had not that occasion for Passion, answered so softly, that I could not well understand him; but upon parting, I heard him say, *If you insist still on these Difficulties, my next Audience will be that of Leave.*

THREE Hours after Monsieur *de la Bastide* returned again, with a Countenance more composed: He asked Mr. *Prior* if he would give him leave to Dine with him? Having no Attendance, I readily offered my Service at * Table, which Monsieur *Prior* was pleased to accept with abundance of Apologies. I found they were come to a better Understanding. Mr. *Prior* has a great deal of Wit and Vivacity; he entertained Monsieur *de la Bastide* with much Pleasantry, notwithstanding their being upon the reserve before me. *That Monsieur, says Mr. Matthews, if he were* un¶ particulier, *would be the most agreeable Person in the World.* I imagined they spoke of the King, but going often in and out, I could not preserve the Connexion of their Discourse. *Did you mind how obligingly he enquired, whether our Famous Chevalier* Newton *was still living? He told me my good Friend poor* || Despreaux *was dead since I was in* France; *and asked me after Q.* Anne's *Health.* These are some of the Particulars I overheard, whilst at Dinner; which confirmed my Opinion, That Monsieur *Prior* last Night had an Audience of his Majesty.

ABOUT Ten that Evening Monsieur *de la Bastide* came to take

* By this and some other preceding Particulars, we may discover what sort of Secretary the Author was.

¶ A Private Man.

|| Monsieur *Boileau*, the famous French Poet.

Monsieur *Matthews*, to go to the same Place they were at before: I was permitted to enter the Vineyard, but not the Gardens, being left at the Gate to wait their return; which was in about two Hours time. The Moon shone bright, and by Monsieur *Matthews*'s manner, I thought he appeared somewhat dissatisfied. When he came into his Chamber, he threw off his Hat in some Passion, folded his Arms, and walked up and down the Room, for above an Hour, extreme pensive: At length he called to be put to Bed; and ordered me to set a Candle by his Bed-side, and to fetch him some Papers out of his *Valise* to read.

ON *Friday* the 23d in the Morning, Monsieur *Matthews* was so obliging to call me to him, with the assurance, that he was extremely pleased with my Discretion, and manner of Address; as a Proof of which Satisfaction, he would give me leave to satisfie my Curiosity with seeing so fine a Place as *Versailles*; telling me, he should return next day towards *Bologne*; and therefore advised me to go immediately to view the Palace, with this Caution (though he did not suppose I needed it) not to say any thing of the Occasion that brought me to *Versailles*.

MONSIEUR *de la Bastide* having staid the Afternoon with Monsieur *Matthews*, about Eight o' Clock they went to the Rendezvous: My Curiosity had led me in the Morning to take a stricter View of the Vineyard and Gardens. I remained at the Gate as before. In an Hour and half's time Monsieur *Matthews*, with Monsieur *de la Bastide*, another Gentleman, and a Lady, came into the Walk: *De la Bastide* opened the Gate, and held it some time in his Hand. Whilst Monsieur *Matthews* was taking his leave of those Persons, I heard the Lady say, at parting, *Monsieur, Songez vous*, &c. *Consider this Night on what we have said to you.* The Gentleman seconded her, saying, *Ouy*, *ouy*, *Monsieur*, *Songez vous en pour la dernier fois: Ay*, *ay*, *Sir*, *consider for the last time*. To which Monsieur *Matthews* answered briskly in going out, *Sire*, *tout ou rien*, &c. *Sir*, *All or none*, *as I have had the Honour to tell your Majesty before*. Which puts it beyond dispute what the Quality of those Persons were, by whom Monsieur *Matthews* had the Honour to be entertained.

ON *Saturday* the 24th, Mons. *Matthews* kept close as before; telling me, a Post-Chaise was ordered to carry him to *Calais*, and he would do me the grace to take me with him, to keep him

Company in the Journey, for he should leave Monsieur *de la Bastide* at *Versailles*. Whilst we were discoursing, that Gentleman came in with an open Air, and a smiling Countenance; he embraced Monsieur *Matthews*, and seemed to feel so much Joy, that he could not easily conceal it. I left the Chamber, and retired to my own; whence I could hear him say, *Courage, Monsieur, no Travelling to day, Madam* Maintenon *will have me once more conduct you to her*. After which I was called, and received Orders about Dinner, *&c*. Monsieur *de la Bastide* told me, we should set out about Midnight. He staid the rest of the day with Monsieur *Matthews*. About Ten a Clock they went forth, but dispensed with my Attendance; it was One in the Morning before they returned, though the Chaise was at the Gate soon after Eleven. Monsieur *Matthews* took a Morsel of Bread, and a large Glass of *Hermitage* Wine; after which they embraced with much Kindness, and so parted.

Our Journey to *Calais* passed without any Accident worth informing you: Mr. *Prior*, who is of a Constitution somewhat tender, was troubled with a Rheum, which made speaking uneasie to him; but it was not so at all to me, and therefore I entertained him as well as I could, chiefly with the Praises of our Great Monarch, the Magnificence of his Court, the Number of his Attendants, the Awe and Veneration paid him by his Generals and Ministers, and the Immense Riches of the Kingdom. One Afternoon, in a small Village between *Chaumont* and *Beauvais*, as I was discoursing on this Subject, several poor People followed the Chaise to beg our Charity; one louder than the rest, a comely Person, about Fifty, all in Rags, but with a Mien that shewed him to be of a good House, cryed out, *Monsieur, pour l'amour de Dieu*, &c. *Sir, for the Love of God, give something to the Marquis* de Sourdis: Mr. *Prior*, half asleep, roused himself up at the Name of *Marquis*, called the poor Gentleman to him, and observing something in his Behaviour like a Man of Quality, very generously threw him a *Pistole*. As the Coach went on, Monsieur *Prior* asked me, with much surprize, Whether I thought it possible that unhappy Creature could be * *un veritable Marquis?* For if it were so, surely the Miseries of our Country must be much

* A real Marquis.

greater than even our very Enemies could hope or believe. I made bold to tell him, That I thought we could not well judge from Particulars to Generals, and that I was sure there were great numbers of Marquises in *France* who had ten thousand Livres a Year. I tell you this Passage, to let you see, that the wisest Men have some Prejudices of their Country about them! We got to *Calais* on *Wednesday* the 28th in the Evening, and the next Morning (the 29th) I took my leave of Monsieur *Prior*, who thanking me in the civilest manner in the World, for the Service I had done him, very nobly made me a Present of Twenty Pistoles, and so we parted. He put to Sea with a fair Wind, and I suppose, in a few Hours landed in *England*.

THIS, Sir, is the utmost I am able to inform you about Monsieur *Prior*'s Journey and Negociation: Time alone will let us know the Events of it, which are yet in the Dark.

I am,
Sir,
Your most obedient and most
humble Servant,
Du Baudrier.

Postscript by the Translator.

THE Author of this Tract having left his Master on Shipboard at *Calais*, had, it seems, no further Intelligence when he Published it: Neither am I able to supply it, but by what passes in Common Report; which being in every Body's Mouth, but with no Certainty, I think it needless to repeat.

FINIS

APPENDIX A

A LETTER TO THE EXAMINER.

A
LETTER
TO THE
EXAMINER.

SIR,

WHEN I read the Introduction to your Paper, it was great Satisfaction to me to find, that some Body had undertaken to furnish Mankind, with a Weekly Antidote to that Weekly Poison, which by the President and Inferior Members of a *Factious Cabal*, is so profusely scatter'd thro' the Nation.

YOU have sufficiently expos'd the *Letter* which you chose to begin your *Examinations* with. How little of that Probability, which ought to be carried thro' the whole Thread of a well invented Fable, appears in it! How little Regard is paid to that Justness and Propriety of Character, without which, Compositions of this Kind are as Monstrous, as that Government must be, where Submission is made the Duty of the Prince, and Dominion the Prerogative of the Subject?

BUT such is the singular Modesty of that Faction, which the Ministers of the Crown have, with so much Advantage to Themselves, nurs'd up, in Opposition to the Crown; that you must expect to have the same Arguments still pursu'd. The *Observator*, the *Review*, the *Censor* of *Great Britain*, who resembles the Famous *Censor* of *Rome* in nothing, but espousing the Cause of the *Vanquish'd*, with the Crowd of Hireling Scriblers, will hope, by a few False Colours, and a great many Impudent Assertions, at last to perswade the People, that the General, the *quondam* Treasurer, and the Junto, are the only Objects of the Confidence of the Allies, and of the Fears of the Enemies: For the QUEEN, and the Whole Body of the *British* Nation—*Nos numerus sumus.*

SURELY therefore, the Argument which you have undertaken, should be carried further. Allow that the *French* have recover'd Heart, that they rise in their Demands, that the Conferences at *Gertruydenberg* were broke off by them, whilst our *Plenipotentiaries* did all that possibly could be done to obtain a Safe and Honourable Peace; Allow, I say, all this; not because it is True, for the contrary shall one Time or other be made out to the World, when the True State of our present Condition will be set in a clearer Light; yet that Odium which the *Ministers* and their Faction, endeavour to throw on the QUEEN, and on those who have appear'd at her Call, and in Her Defence, will with more Justice be laid at their own Door.

PAINT, Sir, with that Force which you are Master of, the present State of the War Abroad, and expose to Publick View, those Principles, upon which, of late, it has been carried on, so different from those, upon which it was Originally enter'd into. Collect some few of the Indignities which have been this Year offer'd to Her MAJESTY, and of those Unnatural Struggles, which have betray'd the Weakness of a shatter'd Constitution: And when this is done, *Dolben* shall blush in his Grave among the Dead, *Walpole* among the Living, and even *Volpone* shall feel some Remorse.

FORGIVE me, Sir, if in that Warmth which these Reflections occasion, I anticipate in some measure the Subject, and encroach on the Province, which belongs to you.

TO restore the *Spanish* Monarchy to the House of *Austria*, who by their own Supiness, and by the Perfidy of the *French*, had lost it; and to regain a Barrier for *Holland* which lay naked and open to the Insults of *France*; were the Wise and Generous Motives, which engag'd *Britain* in the present War. We engag'd as *Confederates*, but we have been made to proceed as *Principals*: *Principals* in expence of Blood and of Treasure, whilst hardly a *Second* Place in Respect and Dignity is allow'd to us.

IN the Year 1706, the last of these two Motives was effectually answer'd by the Reduction of the *Netherlands*; or might have been so, by the Concessions, which 'tis Notorious that the Enemy offer'd. But the first Motive remain'd still in its full Force; and we were told, That tho' the Barrier of *Holland* was Secur'd, the Trade of *Britain*, and the Ballance of Power in

Europe, would be still Precarious. *Spain* therefore was to be conquer'd, before we laid down our Arms, and we were made to expect, that the whole Attention of our *Ministers* would be apply'd to that Part of the War. Like Men of resign'd Understandings, we acquiesc'd, and flatter'd our selves, That since *Holland* had been secur'd in the First Place, *Britain* would be taken care of in the Second. But alas! these Expectations, like many others, have fail'd us.

FROM that Point of Time to this Hour, *France* has continu'd like a great Town Invested indeed on every Part, but Attack'd only in one. In *Spain*, in *Savoy*, on the *Rhine*, Enough and, but just Enough has been done, to serve as a Pretence for *Estimates*, and Demands of *Supplies*: But nothing Decisive, nothing which had the Appearance of Earnest, has been so much as Attempted; except that Wise Expedition to *Thoulon*, which we suffer'd to be Defeated, before it began. The whole Stress of the War has been wantonly laid, where *France* is best able to keep us at Bay; as if we Fought only to make Ostentation of our Valour, and of our Riches. Towns have been Taken, and Battles have been Won; the Mob has huzza'd round Bonfires; the *Stentor* of the Chappel has strain'd his Throat in the Gallery, and the *Stentor* of *Sarum* has deafen'd his Audience from the Pulpit. In the mean while, the *French* King has withdrawn his Troops from *Spain*, and has put it out of his Power to restore that Monarchy to us, was he reduced low enough really to desire to do it. The *Duke* of *Anjou* has had leisure to take off those whom he Suspected, to confirm his Friends, to regulate his Revenues, to encrease and form his Troops, and above all, to rouze that Spirit in the *Spanish* Nation, which a Succession of Lazy and Indolent Princes had lull'd asleep.

FROM hence it appears probable enough, That if the War continue much longer on the present Foot; instead of regaining *Spain*, we shall find the *Duke* of *Anjou* in a Condition to pay the Debt of Gratitude, and Support the *Grandfather* in his declining Years, by whose Arms, in the Days of his Infancy, he was upheld. The *Dutch* will have a larger and a better Country than their Own, at the Expence of *Britain*, conquer'd for them, by those *Ministers*, who Once thought it Impolitick to Consent, that even *Ostend* should be made a Part of their Barrier. The *Emperor* has already *Bavaria*, the *Dutchy* of *Mantua*, the State of *Milan*, and the Kingdom of *Naples*, *Sicily*, and some other Places dependent on these, may be added to his Portion; and by the little Care he now takes to Support King *Charles*, we may easily judge how Great his Concern will be, if that Prince should be deprived of all the rest.

Britain may expect to remain exhausted of Men and Money, to see her Trade divided amongst her Neighbours, her Revenues anticipated even to future Generations, and to have this only Glory left Her, that She has proved a Farm to the *Bank*, a Province to *Holland*, and a Jest to the whole World.

IF the Facts I have mentioned are true, and the Consequences I have drawn from them, are naturally deducible from such Causes, may not the King of *France* reasonably Hope, tho' *Holland* should be aggrandiz'd, that *Britain* will be in proportion weakened? May he not hope, in exchange for a few Towns, which he either Bought or Stole, in former Wars, to Secure the *Spanish* Monarchy to the House of *Bourbon* for ever, by happily concluding this?

LET us now survey the present State of our Domestick Affairs, and Examin whether from the Conduct of the Ministry, and of the Factious *Whigs*, the *French* King has not good Grounds to expect to see us in Confusion, and by consequence the great Band of the *Confederacy* dissolved.

DOMESTICK Occurrences, the more they are Examined, the greater Weight will they add to the same Argument.

YOU have, in your *Second* Paper, pointed out some few of those innumerable Obligations, which the *Whigs* have laid on the *French* King. Whenever you think fit to go to the bottom of the Subject, I make no doubt but it will evidently appear, that *Lewis* XIV. has Reason enough to hope for Success from the Measures taken by the *Ministers*, and their Faction at *Home*, as I have already shewn, that he has from the Conduct of the War *Abroad*.

NOTWITHSTANDING all the Pains which have been taken to lessen her Character in the World, by the Wits of the *Kit-Kat*, and the Sages of the *Cellar*; Mankind remains convinc'd, that a

QUEEN possess'd of all the Vertues requisite to bless a Nation, or to make a private Family Happy, sits on the Throne.

BY an excess of Goodness She delighted to raise some of Her Servants to the highest Degrees of Riches, of Power, and of Honour; and in this only Instance can be said to have Griev'd any of Her Subjects.

THE Rule which She had prescribed to these Persons, as the Measure of their Conduct, was soon departed from. But so unable were they, to associate with Men of Honester Principles than themselves, that the Sovereign Authority was Parcell'd out among a Faction, and made the Purchase of *Indemnity* for an Offending *Minister*. Instead of the Mild Influences of a Gracious QUEEN Governing by Law, we soon felt the Miserable Consequences of Subjection to the Will of an Arbitrary *Junto*, and to the Caprice of an Insolent Woman.

UNHAPPY Nation, which expecting to be Govern'd by the Best, fell under the Tyranny of the Worst of her Sex! But now, Thanks be to God, that Fury, who broke Loose to execute the Vengeance of Heaven on a Sinful People is restrain'd, and the Royal Hand is already reach'd out to Chain up the Plague.

Invisum numen terras cælumq; levabit.

ONE would expect, that on the First Appearance of the QUEEN's Displeasure, these little Tyrants should have had recourse to Submission, and to Resignation. But they believ'd the whole Nation as Debauch'd and Corrupted, as those Profligate Wretches, who were in their Confidence; they imagin'd, that under the Name of their Prince, they should be able to Govern against Her declar'd Intention; and having Usurp'd the Royal Seat, resolved to venture Overturning the Chariot of Government, rather than to lose their Place in it. They set their Mistress at open Defiance, neither the Ties of Gratitude, nor the Bands of Allegiance, were any Restraint to them.

THEIR First Attempt was to take that Privilege from Her, which the Meanest of Her Subjects enjoy, and Slavery was to pursue Her even into Her *Bed-Chamber*.

HERE the Nation in general took the Alarm; a Spirit of Loyalty began to rise, which the Faction foresaw would no longer bear to have the meanest Submission shewn to the *Ministers*, whilst Common Decency was hardly used towards the *Throne*. The Conspirators resolv'd therefore to precipitate their Measures, and a *Sermon* was made the Pretence of their Clamour. Those who prove themselves Friends to This Government by avowing Principles inconsistent with any, presum'd Daily to Try the *Title* of the QUEEN, and to *Limit* the *Allegiance* of the Subject. The Party-Agents of every Rank were employ'd to declaim in Publick Places, and we had the Mortification to see *Cabals* of Upstarts, Sit in Judgment on the Right and Authority of the Crown, who, had it not been for the Profusion of Royal Favour, could have had no Pretence to be Common Tryers in any Cause.

By long insipid Harangues and fulsome Panegyrick, the Merits of the *Ministers* were exalted: The whole Success of the *Administration*, both at Home and Abroad, was singly attributed to them; and lest the QUEEN should think fit to declare them *Dangerous*, she was by necessary Consequence from the Positions laid down, declared Her self to be *Useless*.

This Attempt had likewise an Effect, contrary to what the Projectors of it expected. The Ferment, instead of abating, encreased; the Bulk of the *Nobility*, *Gentry*, *Clergy*, and *Commonalty* of *Britain* declared themselves Loudly in the Cause of their Prince; and those Disorders which the Faction had rais'd for their Security, threaten'd their Destruction.

Not Daunted yet, they resolve to Try a new Expedient, and the Interest of *Europe* is to be represented as inseparable from that of the *Ministers*.

——*Haud dubitant equidem implorare quod usquam est*;
Flectere si nequeunt superos, *Acheronta movebunt*.

The Members of the *Bank*, the *Dutch*, and the Court of *Vienna*, are call'd in as Confederates to the *Ministry*, and such an Indignity is offer'd to the Crown, as no Man, who has the Honour of his Country at Heart, can with Patience hear.

What a Weakness in our Constitution, what a Sickness at Heart do these Symptoms, which appear too openly, discover?

THESE are Signs which shew a Government to be near its Dissolution; These are Things which justly give Encouragement to an Enemy. And if you would go to the Root of our Distemper, these are the Topicks you must insist upon, as the real Causes which have prolong'd the War, distracted the Nation, and given *France* Spirit enough at last to break off the *Peace*.

AND these are the Things, Sir, that deserve to pass under your Pen, that the Nation may be truly inform'd from what Springs our own Grievances, and the Hopes of our Enemies, have risen.

APPENDIX B

A Continuation of
A SHORT CHARACTER OF THOMAS EARL OF WHARTON

A Relation of several facts, exactly as they were transmitted to me from *Ireland*, about three Months ago, and at several Times from a Person of Quality and Employment there.

THE Earl of *Rochfort*'s Regiment of Dragoons was embarked for her Majesty's Service abroad, on the 27th of *August*, 1709, and left their Horses behind them, which were subsisted in Order to mount another Regiment to fill up their Room; as the Horses of Lieutenant-General *Hervey*'s Regiment had formerly mounted a Regiment raised, and still commanded by the Duke of *Ormond*; on which Occasion the Duke had her Majesty's Orders only for as much Money as would supply the Charge of the Horses 'till the Regiment was raised, which was soon after, and then it was put on the Establishment as other Regiments. But, that which was to supply the Earl of *Rochfort*'s had not a Commission granted until the 29th of *April*, 1710, and all the Pay from the 27th of *August* to that Time (being above 5,700 *l.*) was taken, under Pretence of keeping the Horses, buying new ones in the Room of such as should be wanting or unserviceable, and for provideing Accoutrements for the Men and Horses. As for the last Use, those are always produced out of the Funds for providing Cloathing, and the Duke of *Ormond* did so: As for Horses wanting, they are very few, and the Captains have Orders to provide them another Way; the keeping the Horses did not amount to 700 *l.* by the Accounts laid before the Committee of Parliament: So there was at least 5000 *l.* charged to the Nation, more than the real Charge could amount to.

Mrs. *Lloyd*, at first coming over, expected the Benefit of the Box-money; and accordingly talked of selling it for about 200 *l.* but at last was told she must expect but Part of it, and that the Grooms of the Chamber, and other Servants, would deserve a Consideration for their Attendance; accordingly his Excellency had it brought to him every Night; and, to make it worth his receiving, my Lady gave great Encouragement to Play; so that by a moderate Computation, it amounted to near 1,000*l.* of which a small Share was given to the Grooms of the Chamber, and the rest made a Perquisite to his Excellency. For Mrs. *Lloyd* having an Husband, and a Bishoprick promised her, the other Pretensions were cut off.

He met Lieutenant General *Langston* in the Court of Requests, and presented a Gentleman to him, saying, 'This is a particular 'Friend of mine; he tells me he is a Lieutenant in your Regiment; 'I must desire you will take the first Opportunity to give him a 'Troop, and you will oblige me mightily.' The Lieutenant-'General answered, he had served very well, and had very good 'Pretensions to a Troop, and that he would give him the first 'that fell.' With this the Gentleman was mighty well satisfied, returned Thanks and withdrew. Upon which his Excellency said immediately, 'I was forced to speak for him, as a great many 'of his Friends have Votes at Elections; but, d—n him, he is a 'Rogue, therefore take no Care for him.'

He brought one *May* to the Duke of *Ormond*, and recommended him as a very honest Gentleman, and desired his Grace would provide for him; which his Grace promised. So *May* withdrew. As soon as he was gone, his Lordship immediately said to the Duke; 'That Fellow is the greatest Rogue in Christen-'dom.'

Colonel *Coward* having received Pay, for some Time, in two or three Regiments, as Captain, but never done any other Service to the Crown than eating and drinking in the Expedition to *Cadiz* under the Duke of *Ormond*, finding he had not Pretensions enough to rise, after he had sold the last Employment he had, applied to his Excellency, who represented him in such a Light, that he got above 900 *l.* as an Arrear of Half-pay, which he had no Title to, and a Pension of 10 *s.* per Day; but he reckoning this as much too little for his Wants, as every Body else did too much for his Pretensions, gave in a second Petition to the Queen for a further Addition of 10 *s.* a Day; which being referred to his Excellency, he gave him a favourable Report, by Means whereof, it is hoped, his Merit will be still farther rewarded. He turned out the poor Gate-keeper of *Chapel-izod* Gate, although he and his Wife were each above sixty Years old, without assigning any Cause, and they are now starving.

As for the Business of the Arsenal, it was the Product of Chance, and never so much as thought of by the Persons who of late have given so many good Reasons for the building it; until upon enquiring into the Funds, they were found to hold out so well, that there was a Necessity of destroying sixty or seventy thousand Pounds, otherwise his Excellency, for that Time, could hardly have had the Credit of taxing the Kingdom: Upon this Occasion, many Projects were proposed, all which at last gave Way to the Proposal of a worthy Person who had often persuaded the Nation to do itself a great Deal of Harm, by attempting to do itself a little Good, which was, that forty thousand Arms should be provided for the Militia, and Ammunition in Proportion, to be kept in four Arsenals to be built for that Purpose: This was accordingly put into the Heads of a Bill, and then this worthy Patriot, with his usual Sincerity, declared he would not consent to the giving of Money for any other Use; as every Body thought by the Words he spoke, although after wards he shewed them, that his Meaning was not to [be] known by the vulgar Acceptation of Words; for he not only gave his Consent to the Bill, but used all the Art and Industry he was Master of to have it pass; although the Money was applied in it, to the building one Arsenal only, and Ammunition and other Stores proportionable, without one Word of the Militia. So the Arsenal was conceived, and afterwards formed in a proper Manner; but when it came to be brought forth, his Excellency took it out of the Hands that had formed it as far as he could, and contrary to all Precedents, put it out of the Care of the Ordnance-Board, who were properly to have taken Care of the Receipt and Payment of the Money, without any further Charge to the Public, and appointed his second Secretary, Mr. *Denton*, to be Paymaster, whose Salary was a Charge of above five hundred Pounds in the whole: Then, thinking this was too small a Charge to put the Public to for Nothing, he made an Establishment for that Work, consisting of one Superintendant at three Pounds *per* Week, eight Overseers at seven Pounds four Shillings a Week, and sixteen Assistants at seven Pounds four Shillings a Week, making in all seventeen Pounds eight Shillings a Week: And these were, for the greater Part, Persons who had no

Knowledge of such Business, and their Honesty was equal to their Knowledge, as it hath since appeared by the notorious Cheats and Neglects that have been made out against them; insomuch, that the Work that they have overseen, which, with their Salaries hath cost near three thousand Pounds, might have been done for less than eighteen hundred Pounds, if it had been agreed for by the Yard, which is the usual Method, and was so proposed in the Estimate. And, this is all a Certainty, because all that hath been done, is only removing Earth, which hath been exactly computed by the Yard, and might have been so agreed for.

Philip Savage, Esq; as Chancellor of the Exchequer, demanded Fees of the Commissioners of the Revenue for sealing Writs in the Queen's Business, and shewed them for it some Precedents; but they, not being well satisfied with them, wrote to Mr. *South*, one of the Commissioners, then in *London*, to enquire the Practice there. He sent them Word, upon Enquiry, that Fees were paid there upon the like Cases; so they adjudged it for him, and constantly paid him Fees. If therefore there was a Fault, it must lie at their Door, for he never offered to stop the Business; yet, his Excellency knew so well how to chuse an Attorney and Sollicitor-General, that when the Case was referred to them, they gave it against the Chancellor, and said, he had forfeited his Place by it, and ought to refund the Money, being about two hundred Pounds per Annum; but never found any Fault in the Commissioners, who adjudged the Case for him, and might have refused him the Money, if they had thought fit.

CAPTAIN *Robert Fitzgerald*, Father to the present Earl of *Kildare*, had a Grant from King *Charles* the Second, of the Office of Comptroller of the Musters, during the Lives of Captain *Charles Brabazon*, now Earl of *Meath*, and *George Fitzgerald*, elder Brother to the present Earl of *Kildare*; which the said *Robert Fitzgerald* enjoyed with a Salary of three hundred Pounds per Annum; and, after his Death, his Son *George* enjoyed it; until my Lord *Galway* did by Threats, compel him to surrender the said Patent for a Pension of two hundred Pounds per Annum, which he enjoyed during his Life. Some Time ago the present Earl of *Kildare*, as Heir to his Father and Brother, looked upon himself to be injured by the Surrender of the said Patent, which should have come to him, the Earl of *Meath* being still living: Therefore in Order to right himself, did petition her Majesty; which Petition, as usual, was referred to the Earl of *Wharton*, then Lord Lieutenant, who being at that Time, in *London*, referred it, according to the common Method on such Occasions, to the Lord Chancellor, and Lieutenant-General *Ingoldsby*, the then Lords Justices of this Kingdom; who, for their Information, ordered the Attorney General to enquire, whether the Earl of *Kildare* had any legal Title to the said Patent, which he in a full Report said he had: And, they referred it to the Deputy Vice-Treasurer to enquire into the Nature of the Office, and to give them his Opinion, whether he thought it was useful or necessary for her Majesty's Service? He gave in his Report, and said, he thought it both useful and necessary; and, with more Honesty than Wit, gave the following Reasons: First, that the Muster-Master-General computed the Pay of the whole military List, which is above 200,000 *l.* per Annum, so having no Check on him, might commit Mistakes, to the great Prejudice of the Crown: And, Secondly, because he had himself found out several of those Mistakes, which a Comptroller might prevent. The Lords Justices approved of these Reasons, and so sent over their Report to my Lord Lieutenant, that they thought the Office useful and necessary: But Colonel *P—r*, the Muster-Master-General, being then in *London*, and having given my Lord Lieutenant, One thousand Pounds for his Consent to enjoy that Office, after he had got her Majesty's Orders for a Patent, thought a Check upon his Office would be a troublesome Spy upon him; so he pleaded the Merit of his thousand Pounds, and desired, in Consideration thereof, that his Excellency would free him from an Office that would put it out of his Power to wrong the Crown; and, to strengthen his Pretensions, put my Lady in Mind of what Money he had lost to her at Play; who immediately, out of a grateful Sense of Benefits received, railed as much against the Lords Justices Report, as ever she had done against the Tories; and my Lord Lieutenant, prompted by the same Virtue, made his Report, that there needed no Comptroller to that Office, because he comptrolled it himself; which (now having given his Word for it) he will, beyond all doubt, effectually do for the future: Although since it hath been plainly made appear, that for Want of some Controul on that Office, her Majesty hath been wronged of many hundred Pounds by the Roguery of a Clerk; and that during the Time of his Excellency's Government, of which there hath been but a small Part refunded, and the rest hath not been enquired after, lest he should make it plainly appear, that a Comptroller in that Office is absolutely necessary.

His Excellency being desirous, for a private Reason, to provide for the worthless Son of a worthless Father, who had lately sold his Company, and, of Course, all Pretensions to Preferment in the Army, took this Opportunity: A Captain in the oldest Regiment in the Kingdom, being worn out with Service, desired Leave to sell, which was granted him: And, accordingly, for a Consideration agreed upon, he gave a Resignation of his Company to a Person approved of by the Commander of the Regiment, who, at the same Time, applied to his Excellency for Leave for another Captain of his Regiment, who is an Engineer in her Majesty's Service in *Spain*, and absent by her Majesty's Licence: His Excellency hearing that, said they might give him a Company in *Spain*, for he would dispose of this here; and so, notwithstanding all the Commander of the Regiment could urge, he gave the Company, which was regularly surrendered, to his worthy Favourite; and the other Company, which was a disputable Title, to the Gentleman who had paid his Money for that which was surrendered. Talking one Morning as he was dressing (at least a dozen People present) of the Debates in Council, about the Affairs of *Trim*, he said, the Lord Chief Justice *Dolben* had laid down as Law, a Thing, for which a Man ought to have his Gown stripped off, and be whipped at the Cart's A—e; and, in less than a Quarter of an Hour, repeated the Expression again: Yet, some Days after, sent Dr. *Lloyd* to assure his Lordship he said no such Thing. Some Time after, while he was in *England*, he used his utmost Efforts with the Queen to turn him out, but could not: And when he came once again, he took an Opportunity (when the Judges were to wait on him) to say to them, particularly to Lord Chief Justice *Dolben*, that perhaps some officious Persons might spread Stories, that he had endeavoured to do some of them a Prejudice in *England*, which he assured them he never had; but, on the contrary, would always, without Distinction, shew his Regard according to Merit; which the Lord Chief Justice *Dolben* was pleased to approve of, by saying, that was very honourable, that he was very gracious, although he knew the contrary himself.

IN *England* he bid Mr. *Deering* assure all his Friends and Acquaintance here, that they and every body might depend on his Favour, as they behaved themselves; with which Mr. *Deering* was much pleased, and wrote over to his Friends accordingly; and, as soon as his Back was turned, he jeeringly said, 'D–mn 'me, how easily he is bit.' When the Duke of *Ormond* was in the Government, he gave to Mr. *Anderson Saunders* the Government of *Wicklow* Castle, which has no Salary, but a Perquisite of some Land worth about 12 *l*. per Annum, which Mr. *Saunders* gave to the Free-School of the Town; but, his Excellency, not liking either the Person or the Use, without any Ceremony, or Reason given, superseded him, by giving a Commission for it to *Jennings* the Horse-courser, who lieth under several odious and scandalous Reflections, particularly of very narrowly escaping the Gallows for Coining. Some Time after his Excellency's landing the second Time, he sent for Mr. *Saunders*, among others, desiring their good Offices in the ensuing Session, and that Mr. *Saunders* would not take amiss his giving that Place to *Jennings*, for he assured him he did not know it belonged to him, which is highly probable, because Men of his Knowledge usually give away Things, without enquiring how they are in their Disposal. Mr. *Saunders* answered him, 'He was very glad to find what was done 'was not out of any particular Displeasure to him; because Mr. '*Whitshed* had said at *Wicklow*, by Way of Apology for what his 'Excellency had done, that it was occasioned by Mr. *Saunders* 'having it; and seeing his Excellency had no ill Intention against 'him, was glad he could tell his Excellency it was not legally given 'away, for he had a Custodium for the Land out of the Court of 'Exchequer; so his Excellency's Commission could do him no 'Prejudice.'

LIEUTENANT General *Echlin* had Pay on this Establishment

as Brigadier, until the Middle of *October*, 1708, when he was removed from it by his Excellency, because his Regiment went away at that Time, and Lieutenant General *Gorges* was put in his Room. Some Time after, Major General *Rooke*, considering the Reason why *Echlin* was removed, concluded, that *Gorges* could not come on, until some Time in *February* after, because his Regiment was also out of the Kingdom, until that Time, and therefore, he being the eldest General Officer, that had no Pay as such, was entitled to the Brigadier's Pay, from the Time *Echlin* was removed until *Gorges* was qualified to receive it; he having done the Duty. His Excellency, upon hearing the Reason, owned it to be a very good one, and told him, if the Money were not paid to *Gorges* he should have it, so bid him go see; which he did, and found it was: Then his Excellency told him he would refer his Case to a Court of General Officers to give their Opinion in it, which he said must needs be in his Favour; and, upon that Ground, he would find a Way to do him Right; yet when the General Officers sat, he sent for several of them, and made them give the Case against *Rooke*.

WHEN the Prosecution against the Dissenting Ministers in *Drogheda* was depending, one *Stevens*, a Lawyer in this Town of *Dublin*, sent his Excellency, then in *London*, a Petition, in the Name of the said Dissenting Minister, in Behalf of himself and others, who lay under any such Prosecution; and in about a Fortnight's Time, his Excellency sent over a Letter, to the then Lords Justices, to give the Attorney and Sollicitor General, Orders, to enter a *Noli prosequi* to all such Suits; which was done accordingly, although he never so much as enquired into the Merit of the Cause, or referred the Petition to any Body, which is a Justice done to all Men, let the Case be never so light. He said, he had her Majesty's Orders for it, but they did not appear under her Hand; and it is generally affirmed he never had any.

THAT his Excellency can descend to small Gains, take this Instance: There were 850 *l.* ordered by her Majesty to buy new Liveries for the State Trumpets, Messengers, *&c.* but with great Industry he got them made cheaper by 200 *l.* which he saved out of that Sum; and, it is reported, that his Steward got a handsome Consideration beside, from the Undertaker.

The Agent to his Regiment, being so also to others, bought a Lieutenant's Commission in a Regiment of Foot, for which he never was to do any Duty, which Service pleased his Excellency so well, that he gave him Leave to buy a Company, and would have had him keep both; but before his Pleasure was known, the former was disposed of.

The Lord Lieutenant hath no Power to remove or put in a Solicitor General without the Queen's Letter, it being one of those Employments excepted out of his Commission; yet, because Sir *Richard Levinge* disobliged him, by voting according to his Opinion, he removed him, and put in Mr. *Forster**, although he had no Queen's Letter for so doing, only a Letter from Mr. Secretary *Boyle* that her Majesty designed to remove him.

The Privy-Council in *Ireland* have a great Share of the Administration, all Things being carried by the Consent of the Majority, and they sign all Orders and Proclamations there, as well as the Chief Governor. But, his Excellency disliked so great Share of Power in any but himself: And when Matters were debated in Council, otherwise than he approved, he would stop them, and say, 'Come, my Lords, I see how your Opinions are, 'and therefore I will not take your Votes;' and so would put an End to the Dispute.

One of his chief Favourites was a scandalous Clergyman, a constant Companion of his Pleasures, who appeared publickly with his Excellency, but never in his Habit, and who was a Hearer and Sharer of all the lewd and blasphemous Discourses of his Excellency and his Cabal. His Excellency presented this worthy Divine to one of the Bishops, with the following Recommendation: 'My Lord, M— is a very honest Fellow, and 'hath no Fault but that he is a little too immoral.' He made this Man Chaplain to his Regiment, although he had been so infamous, that a Bishop in *England* refused to admit him to a Living he had been presented to, until the Patron forced him to it by Law.

His Excellency recommended the Earl of *Inchiquin* to be one

* *Afterwards Recorder of the City of* Dublin, *and Lord Chief Justice of the Common Pleas.*

of the Lords Justices in his Absence, and was much mortified, when he found Lieutenant General *Ingoldsby* appointed, without any Regard to his Recommendation; particularly, because the usual Salary of a Lord Justice, in the Lord Lieutenant's Absence, is 100 *l.* per Month, and he had bargained with the Earl for 40 *l.*

I WILL send you, in a Pacquet or two, some Particulars of his Excellency's Usage of the Convocation, of his infamous Intrigues with Mrs. *Coningsby*, an Account of his arbitrary Proceedings about the Election of a Magistrate in *Trim*, his barbarous Injustice to Dean *Jephson* and poor *Will Crow*; his deciding a Case at Hazard to get my Lady twenty Guineas, but in so scandalous and unfair a Manner, that the arrantest Sharper would be ashamed of; the common Custom of playing on *Sunday* in my Lady's Closet; the *Partie Quarree* between her Ladyship and Mrs. *Lloyd* and two young Fellows dining privately and frequently at *Clontarf*, where they used to go in a Hackney Coach; and his Excellency's making no Scruple of dining in a Hedge Tavern whenever he was invited; with some other Passages, which, I hope you will put into some Method, and correct the Style, and publish as speedy as you can.

NOTE, Mr. * *Savage*, besides the Persecution about his Fees, was turned out of the Council for giving his Vote in Parliament in a Case where his Excellency's own Friends were of the same Opinion, until they were wheedled out of it by his Excellency. The Particulars before mentioned I have not yet received; whenever they come, I shall publish them in a second Part.

---

* *The Rt. Hon.* Philip Savage, *Esq;*

APPENDIX C

A

LETTER

To the Seven Lords of the COMMITTEE *appointed to Examine* GREGG

A LETTER TO THE SEVEN LORDS OF THE COMMITTEE, Appointed to Examine *GREGG*.

LONDON
Printed, for J. BAKER at the *Black-Boy* in *Pater-Noster-Row*, 1711.
(Price 3 *d.*)

A

LETTER

To the Seven Lords of the COMMITTEE *appointed to Examine* GREGG.

YOUR Lordships have, for these Fifteen or Sixteen Months last past, been treated by the *Publick Writers*, such as say they are allowed, approved, and encouraged, by our Great Folks, as *Rogues*, and *Rascalls*, *Cheats*, and *Villains*, *Enemies of the Nation*, *Affronters of the Queen*, *Subverters of the Constitution*, and such as have been long endeavouring to destroy both *Church and State*. Thus you have been treated in common with the present *General*, the late Lord *Chancellor*, the late Lord *Treasurer*, the late *Secretaries of State*, and almost all that had any thing to do in what is call'd the *late Ministry*. But it is but since the 8th. of *March* last past, that your Lordships in particular, have been compared to *Murtherers* and *Assassines*; and exposed to all the Kingdom, as Men that would, by your *Menaces*, and *Promises*, and *Bribes*, have *Suborned* the Criminal *Gregg, to confess Mr.* H. (now E. *of* O.) *guilty of Corresponding with Her Majesty's Enemies, in order to the taking away his Life.*

The *Examiner*, who would have us believe he is employ'd to Write for the Government, and only against such as are Enemies to the Q. and State, this same *Examiner*, in *Paper* 33, speaking of *Guiscard*'s Villainous attempt upon Mr. *H.* makes the following Reflections on it, 'Had such an Accident happen'd under the '*late Ministry*, and to so considerable a Member of it, as Mr. *H.* '*Commissioners* would have been sent, to promise the Criminal 'his Life, provided they might have liberty to *direct and dictate his* '*Confession.* And a *Black List* would have been Printed of all 'those who had been ever seen in the Murtherers Company. But 'the present Men in Power hate and despise all such detestable 'Arts, which they might now turn upon their Adversaries, with 'much more Plausibility, than ever *These* (*i.e.* your Seven

'Lordships) did their Honourable *Negotiations* with *Gregg*.

'And here it may be worth observing, how unanimous a Con-'currence there is betwixt *some Persons* once in great Power and 'a *French Papist*, both agreeing in the great end of taking away 'Mr. *H.*'s Life, tho' differing in their *Methods*. The *First* (*i.e.* your 'Lordships) proceeding by *Subornation*; the *other* (*i.e. Guiscard*) by '*Violence*: Wherein *Guiscard* seems to have the advantage, as 'aiming no further than his *Life*; while the others (*i.e.* your 'Lordships) design'd to destroy at once, both *that* and his *Repu-'tation*. The Malice of *Both* (*i.e.* of *Guiscard* and your Lordships) 'against this Gentleman, seems to have risen from the same 'Cause, *i.e.* His discovering Designs against the Government. 'It was Mr. *H.* who detected the Treasonable Correspondence of '*Gregg*, and secured him betimes, when *a certain Great Man who 'shall be nameless*, had, out of the Depth of his Politicks, sent him 'a caution to make his escape; which would certainly have fix'd 'the appearance of Guilt upon Mr. *H.* But when that was pre-'vented, they (*i.e.* your Lordships the *Commissioners*) would have 'enticed the Condemned Criminal, with the promise of a Pardon, 'to *Write* and *Sign* an Accusation against the *Secretary*, *i.e.* Mr. *H.*

What do your Lordships think of this Passage? does not this *State Writer* charge you with intending to take away the *Secretaries* Life, by the basest of *Subornations?* It may be, your Lordships think he intended no such Charge, because, when he has said that your Lordships did *equally* concur with *Guiscard* to take away Mr. *H*'s Life, he afterwards proves, beyond all contradiction, from *Guiscard's own Confession*, 'That his chief design was 'not against Mr. *H.* but against Mr. *Secretary St. John*; and that 'Mr. *H.* was only Stabbed because he had changed Chairs with 'the *Secretary*, for more convenience of examining the Criminal.

Now, if your Lordships did no more design to take away Mr. *H.*'s Life, than *Guiscard* did, your Lordships may think the *Examiner* has acquitted you, because he has acquitted *Guiscard* of any such *Design*, tho' not of the *Fact*. But 'tis plain, my Lords, this great Defender of the Government intended seriously to charge you all, with *Subornation*, in order to proceed to *Murther*; and if he has acquitted you, it was by mere Mistake and Blunder: It was not in his Heart, to do you any such Service, by his account of *Guiscard:* It was what he thought not of: He has Repented of that Passage: He cannot blot it out, but denies the Consequence: And your Lordships shall see he does, for in the next *Paper* 34, he says, *He means not to be answerable for what* Guiscard *said: i.e.* He will not be tied to believe what is the natural and unavoidable Consequence of *Guiscard's Confession*: It is not, belike, to his purpose: *Guiscard* had told, what should not have been told again, at least so soon: But the *Examiner* thought it was then a fine Story, and out it came, and in my Opinion had like to have spoil'd all, for Wise Men immediately drew Inferences from it, that, one would have thought, should have quite prevented the use that was afterwards made of that *sore blow* ; but, as it happened, those Inferences did no great harm; and the World went on, just as if no such *Confession* had been made. But because it had, for Two or Three Days, some *seeming* Consequence, the *Examiner* deserts it quite, and will not be answerable for it, but sticks to somewhat he is sure of, and which no Body will presume to meddle with; and boldly begins again: 'They 'take, says he, abundance of Pains to clear *Guiscard* from a 'design against Mr. *H*'s Life, (but the *Examiner* did it *easily*) but 'offer not one Argument to clear their *other* Friends (your Lord-'ships certainly) who in the Business of *Gregg*, were equally 'guilty of the same design, against the same Person.

Your Lordships are now again, as very *Murtherers* by *Subornation* as you were in his first Paper 33. He has, he thinks, Authority now, to deal more freely with you, than before; and your Lordships shall find it. Because the *Parliament* has told the *Queen*, that '*They had reason to believe that Mr.* H.'*s. Fidelity to 'Her Ma. and Zeal for Her Service, had drawn upon Him, the Hatred 'of all the Abettors of Popery and Faction.* Therefore the *Examiner* is now sure, that your Lordships did as certainly intend to take away Mr. *H*'s. Life, by *Subornation*, as the *French Papist* did by a *Penknife*. The *Examiner* knows *You* are as much intended by Faction, as *Guiscard* was by *Popery*. But this is a consequence of the *Examiner*'s own making; the *Parliament* made it not. The *P*—— indeed says, this Stabb was an Instance of inveterate Malice. *Monsieur de Guiscard* said *it was an effect of sudden Despair*, and that his Design was to have kill'd Mr. *St. John*. But whose word shall be taken in such a matter as this? Shall we believe a *Villain* (and in his own Case too) against the P—— who certainly knew what he intended, and knew moreover that he had *long* intended it (let him say what he would) because it was an *Instance of Inveterate Malice?* Is it so new a thing, for *Frenchmen*, and for *Papists*, to dye with *Lies* in their Mouths, even when it serves no manner of Purpose, that they can have in View? But cannot these things be said by those who certainly ought to know what 'tis they say, without concluding, that *therefore* your Lordships did endeavour to suborn *another Wretch* to take away that important Life? If, press'd by such unanswerable Authority, we must at length, believe that *Guiscard*'s malice was inveterate, and that He made that Villainous Attempt to reach the *Heart* of a *Privy Councellor*, only because *it* was so full of *Fidelity* to the *Q*. and of *Zeal* against *Popery* and *Faction.* Yet how should we be made to believe, *from thence*, that *Seven great Lords* intended, heretofore, to Murther the same great Person, but by ways much more detestable and villainous? And yet this is the *Examiners* Consequence; this is the Conclusion of a Man, that, every day, tells us he Writes in Defence of the Government, and would make us believe he is set on Work by great People. He says in Paper 34. *Your Tongues were very Swords, and your Penknives Axes.* This, he thinks, is a very elegant Expression; but the *English* of it is, that your Lordships would by *Subornation* have taken away the Life of Mr. *H.* And least his Reader should (for want of knowing him) imagine it impossible for any Man that had any Sense of Justice, or Honour, to charge *Seven Peers*, with an attempt of such a horrid nature, He says it openly and in so many Words, in Paper 35. only with this Difference, that He now joyns *others* with your Lordships, of whose Company you have not been heretofore asham'd. '*I said, They had formerly a Design against Mr.* H.'s. *Life:* '*If They were now in Power, would they not immediately cut off his Head,* '*and thank Me, for justifying the Sincerity of their Intentions?* What sort of Consequence is this? I should *now* be extreamly glad to have the *Examiner* severely punish'd, for abusing the greatest Men of the Kingdom; and I should thank the *Justice* of the *Nation*, for doing what so well became them: And yet I never had one evil thought against the *Examiner*, *before*, much less design'd him any Mischief. And yet the *Examiner* affirms, as much as if he knew it true, that, because your Lordships would, if you were now in Power, *immediately* cut off Mr. *H.*'s Head, therefore you had *heretofore* a Design to destroy him, by *Subornation*. How the *Examiner* should know your Lordships Hearts, I, who hardly know my own, cannot imagine. 'Tis very well that Peoples Heads are to stand upon their Shoulders as long as the *Law* will let them; if it depended upon any thing *besides*, it may be, your Lordships seven Heads might be as soon cut off, as that one Gentlemans, were you in Power. *May the Head, that has done the Kingdom the greatest Mischief, fall first, let it be whose it will!*

After this abandon'd Wretch has screen'd himself under the Protection of the Address of P——, and made that *Great Body* say what he was pleased they should, that he might say it after them, 'tis wonderful to find him seeking for farther Security, in the Example of a great Man indeed, but yet a single Man, who had said, that *Mr.* H. *had been wonderfully Preserv'd from some unparrallel'd Attempts*. Now this great Critick of an *Examiner*, finding that *Some* was of the Plural Number, and that *Guiscard*'s attempt was but *One*, immediately concludes from the *Correct Style* of the foresaid *Orator*, that this Plural Number must, in all probability, take in the business of *Gregg*: And thereupon He falls to compliment that *eminent Person*, upon the matter of *Style*, and *Superiority of Spirit*; but tells him, that, let him express himself, as loftily and finely as he would, yet he meant to say in plain *English*, *that there was a Committee of Seven Lords, sent to a Condemn'd Criminal in* Newgate, *to bribe Him with a Pardon, on Condition he would swear High Treason, against His Master*. 41. And there, your Lordships have the matter out, in his own Words. He says —*He knows but of two unparallel'd Attempts against Mr.* H. *which are those of* Gregg, *and* Guiscard: That of *Guiscard*, he bestows (and yet as little as he can) on *Guiscard*: That of *Gregg*, he Fathers upon *Three Dukes, One Earl, One Viscount, and Two Barons*. Is not that *eminent Person* much indebted to the *Examiner*, who, because he will not let him speak (as he thinks) improperly, will make him call your Lordships, *Murtherers* and *Villains*? I should have thought, a Gentleman of Honour and of Virtue, would have been better pleas'd, to have made a *Solecism* in Speech (had it indeed been such) than rais'd a Calumny; and to have written somewhat less *correctly*, than to mean *Maliciously*. But thus it is, the *Examiner* had said these things himself before, That your Lordships were Guilty of intended *Murther*, by *Subornation*, and fearing his Authority and Credit were not great enough to support this dreadful weight, He does, with his own Impudence, and with the Malice of a *Devil*, bring in *Both Houses* of P—— to say and mean the same thing, and afterwards (upon another Occasion) this very Honourable *Gentleman*, to strengthen his security. Let the *Examiner* answer for his Usage of those *Great Names*, as well as he can, he seems, to me, to be distrustful of his Credit and his Safety, at the bottom: He who runs here, and there, and every where, for shelter, is far from thinking himself secure. This, *My Lords*, is the matter of Fact; thus are you handled by the *Examiner*, the *Favourite-Writer of the Times*, the *Tory-Ladies Politician*, the *Guide* and *Oracle* of the *Inferiour-Clergy*, and great Defender of the *New World*.

But I am bound to do Him Right, bad as he is; There was an Author of equal *Face*, and equal *Fame*, and almost equal *Esteem*, with the Children of the *New-Church*, that started this great Slander, four Days at least, before the *Examiner* could get it into Print; I dare not say before it came into his *Heart*, but before his *Periodical* Day of Slandering came, to *utter it*. The *Post-boy*, *March* the 10th, after he had given an Account of *Guiscard*'s villainous attempt upon Mr. *H.* adds—*It is said that Seven Great and Excellent Men, are to meet at a House near* Charing-Cross; *and that they will find Witnesses to prove, that, notwithstanding Mr.* H. *discover'd this Treason, as He did likewise that of Mr.* Gregg, *yet that He was an Accomplice of the Man, who would have Murder'd him.*

And March *the 17th, He says, His Intentions, in the foregoing Passage, were to expose the most Dishonourable and Scandalous Practices of Seven Men, in the business of* Gregg, And a little lower, in the same Paper—*to expose the blackest Conspiracy, that ever was form'd by Seven Men, or perhaps by any One Man in the whole World, against the Life of that Honourable and Innocent Gentleman.*

The *Examiner* alone can tell us, if he will, whether he truly borrowed his *Accusation* from that Rascally Paper, or whether (by a natural Concurrence of the Mind in Villainy) he also *in-*

vented it, as well as His Good Brother. But be that as it will, 'tis manifest, that the *Examiner* has improv'd it to the height, and only wants the Honesty of the other to set his *Name* to it, and at what *Sign* he Lodges; for I believe it is not his Modesty that hinders us from knowing who he is.

There is now also, *My Lords*, another Book, fresh in my Hands, whose Title is—*Secret Transactions*, &c. Printed in a better Letter, and on better Paper than is usual, and the whole Sheet is sold for a *Penny*, which, I am told, no *Bookseller* can well afford, at such a Rate, without the Assistance of some that bear *Good Will* to your Lordships, in order to spread the same *Charge* and *Accusation*. In this Book, your Lordships are gotten into the Hands of the *Ordinary of Newgate*, and of one *Francis Hoffman*, who may, for any thing I know, be *Another Officer* belonging to that House. And your Lordships shall see, how you are treated, by these two great Authors. *Francis Hoffman* tells the World, that the *Ordinary did in a most solemn and ready Manner, tell him of so many endeavours to corrupt* Gregg'*s Conscience not only with repeated Offers of Life, but of great Preferments and Advantages, that He felt as much uneasyness, least* Gregg *should betray his Master, as if it had been his own Case*. And Page 6. the next words—That *'tis apparent from hence, that* Some Persons (your Lordships certainly) *Stabbed, as directly andvillainously, at Mr.* H.*'s Life then, as* Guiscard *did since*. This is the Language that *Master Examiner* hath taught *Francis Hoffman*, (whoever he is) to speak. But I would take leave to observe upon this Passage, that a *Servant* is said to *betray* his Master, tho' what he confesses of him should *be true*. How comes *Hoffman*, therefore, to be under such an uneasyness, least *Gregg*, should *betray his Master*, when he might, for ought he knew, confess what was exactly *True* of that his Master? Could any one alive, but *Gregg*, tell whether what he would say of his Master, should be true or false, till he knew what was said? An indifferent Person might as well have been uneasy, for fear *Gregg* should discover something of his Master, that would touch his Life, and yet might have been *True*. 'Tis certain he neither did, nor would confess any thing, but what did manifestly clear his Master; and his Master was accordingly untainted. This uneasyness therefore of *Francis Hoffman*, or of the *Ordinary*, seems to me, to be ill-timed, and has rather appear'd since the Advancement of *Gregg*'s Master, than whilst he was under Examination, and his Master's Conduct only *inquired into*. These Poor Creatures would compliment the *Great Man*, with their Solicitous concern for his Safety, (but they tell him so now he is safe and great) and since that cannot be done thoroughly, without doing your Lordships the greatest Injury in your Honour and Good Name, that, it seems, is now to be ventured.

The *Ordinary* himself says, P. 8, *that when* Gregg *had clear'd Mr*. H. *of knowing any thing of his Corresponding with* France, *He* (i.e. the *Ordinary*) *grew jealous of those People that frequently came to Him*. And he says moreover, *that to some of Mr*. H.'s *Friends*, *who came to* Gregg, *He* (i.e. the *Ordinary*) *express'd some dislike of* Gregg'*s being so much disturb'd by Persons that resorted to him*, *at unseasonable Hours*, *when he should have been at Prayers*; *But he knew not* Who those Persons *were*, *that thus came to him*. And again—*As* Gregg *also told me*, *he was proffered his Life*, *and a great Reward if he would accuse his Master*; *so I must own to you*, *I was uneasy at his frequent Visiters*, *when I consider'd how they disturb'd his Mind*, *and how much they took up of his precious Moments*.

The *Ordinary*, my Lords, leaves room for *other People* to tempt *Gregg* (if he indeed was tempted) to betray his Master, and does not lay it on your Lordships wholly, if at all. He talks of *many Persons*, and of *frequent Visiters*, that resorted to the Prisoner, and says *He knew not who they were*. Now, I believe, that tho' your Lordships may not know the *Ordinary of Newgate*, yet *He* may very probably know *your Lordships*, after a sight or two, at least; and it is not likely that you came in a *Disguise*, or *Singly*, or in the *Dark*. 'Tis likely enough that a *Committee* of *Seven Great Peers* would be as quickly known as any other People. He knew *the Friends of Mr*. H. it seems, because he made his complaints to them, of the frequent Resort of *Visiters* to *Gregg*. Now it is not very probable, that the *Ordinary* should complain of the *frequent Visits* made by *the Lords of the Committee*. One might therefore imagine, that if there were any *Subornation* in the Case, it should not necessarily follow, that your Lordships were the *Suborners*. And therefore if I had been the *Examiner*, I would not (for the mere sake of Reason and Justice) have charg'd your

Lordships *only*, with *Subornation* and intended *Murther*, when *other* People might, as easily, be guilty of it. But nothing below the *Greatest Quality* can be abus'd by him. He has (because he is so great a Man with the new Governors) led *Francis Hoffman* to make the very same conclusion, notwithstanding all his good Correspondent the *Ordinary* has said. *Who those Persons were* (says *Francis*) *that offer'd* GREGG *his Life, with great Preferments and Advantages* (*if he would but accuse his Master*) *may not uneasily be guessed at; for, most of the time he was lock'd up,* NONE BUT PEOPLE OF NOTE *were permitted to come near him, who made him strange Promises, and often repeated them.* Here, I think, the matter is brought within a little compass. The *Ordinary* left the *Subornation* to abundance of People, who might share the Guilt, and *whom*, he says, *he knew not*. But *Hoffman* pins us down to *Persons of Note only*; and for fear we should not, after all this, know whom he means by *People of Note*, he has caused *your Lordships Names* to be Printed *at length*, at the Conclusion of the Libel; only (to screen himself from the Vengeance of the Law) he has put over those your Names, the Title, I have presum'd to Address you by, *viz. The Committee of Lords appointed to Examine* Gregg—were the Duke of *&c.*

And now I Challenge all the Books in the *New Lord*'s Library (because I hear it is the largest) to furnish us with an instance like this—Where *Seven Great Peers*, distinguish'd by their *Birth*, *Estates*, *Honours*, *Offices*, and great *Abilities*, as much as any Seven besides in all the Kingdom, have been, day after day, expos'd to the Rage of an irritated People, in *Penny-Papers*, as the most Villainous *Suborners*, *Murtherers*, and *Assassines*, because they were appointed by the *House of Lords*, to Examine *Gregg* and see if they could bring him to discover, who (if any one) was privy to his Corresponding with the Queen's Enemies: And promised him, it may be, to obtain his *Pardon*, if he would make a full Discovery. I do not know that such a promise was made of Pardon, but I suppose it was, because no other Offer could, 'tis probable, prevail to the making a Discovery of that kind; and it is what is every Day done, by the Ministers of State, and must be done, if they will gain the Secrets they want to know:

And it is no more than was very lately done (and rightly done) to the *Sieur de Guiscard* himself; The D. of *O*——, and the *Secretaries of State*, and several *Privy Councellors*, went to him in the *Prison*, and Examin'd him, put several Questions to him, and tried, if it were possible, to bring him to confess who were his Accomplices, and promised him the *Queen's Pardon*, if he would make a full Discovery. Would any but an *Examiner*, a *Post-boy*, or such Licentious Writers, charge these Honourable Councellors with *Suborning Guiscard*, by Promises of Pardon, and Life, and Pension, to accuse the Innocent, and betray his Friends? Is this the turn that any one, but a Villain, would give to such an Inquiry, and Examination? Supposing *Guiscard* had been intimate with some *Great Officer* of State, and had been suspected to Communicate his most Secret Affairs to this *Great Officer*, had it been *Subornation?* had it been *seeking the Life and Blood* of this *Great Officer*, in these *Great Lords* of the *Council*, if they had narrowly examin'd this Affair, inquired with all Exactness, what he knew of this *Great Officer*, what Secrets he had imparted to him, and whether he were Privy to his Corresponding with the Banker *Moreau*, or any thing more Dangerous? The Injury (if any) had not been, in pressing *Guiscard* to say what he knew of this *Great Officer*, and in promising to obtain his Pardon, if he would discover all he knew; but it had been in *Suspecting* him if Innocent: And how far that may be done without any manner of Ill-will, Malice, or Mischievous Design, I leave to all the World to judge: But of this I am certain, that when once a *Great Officer* is suspected, there is no coming at him (ordinarily speaking) but by such Ways and Promises as these, of *Pardon* and *Life*, to such as are thought to be in his Interests and Secrets, and will, for such a Recompence, discover them. And therefore the *Patience* (I must say no more) of our New Governors, is hardly less to be wondered at, than the Insolence and Wickedness of these Audacious Wretches, in suffering the *Peerage* of *England*, and *Seven such Noble Lords*, to be treated like the most Flagitious Villains, for doing what Courts, and Ministers of State have always done, and always must do, if they will preserve the Crown and secure the People. But this, it seems, is the thing that is so much in Fashion! to Run down *a Set of Men*, for taking such Courses in their Ministration, as those who succeed them *must* take, or ten times worse! to make the Common People believe they have been beggar'd and undone, by such a management of Affairs, for some years past; when it is very well known, that those Affairs are still under the *like* Management, and must be so, because there is no better! This way of *Representing* Things and Persons, and rend'ring them Odious both to Prince and People, may serve a present turn, but it is certainly (as all things Wicked are) the falsest Policy that can be, not only because the Cheat is soon detected, but because it will as soon destroy those who use it, when the humour of Change comes on, as those against whom it is used. When a King, thro' the Multitudes of Complaints, Secret Teazings, and Importunate Clamors of a Rout of People (led by their *Priests*, and Spirited underhand by Crafty *Emissaries*) hath been brought to discard his old Officers, who had, till then, been accounted Able, Faithful, Diligent, and Dutiful, and by whose Service he had lived, Glorious Abroad, and Easie and Beloved at Home; but who have of late been *Represented* to Him, as Weak, False, Careless, and Insolent, such as have engag'd Him in Desperate Measures Abroad, and run Him at Home into Immense Debts, and caused Him to be ill thought of by his overburthened and abused Subjects: When this Prince comes, in time, to consider his Affairs, and finds things go much as they used to go, that his New Servants (tho' every day finding fault with the Old Ones) take the same Courses, go on in the Old Methods, and give him the same Counsel and Advice, on like Occasions, and when they find themselves in Straits, and under any new Exigencies (as such will be, in spight of all the Care and Caution in the World) they are forced to go out of the Common way, and do as well as they can, just as their Predecessors did: When the King finds this (as he will, in a year or two, if he make any Observations at all) He will consider, who they were that made those Complaints, that rais'd those Cries, that Cheated those poor Priests, that Spirited those Multitudes, that taught them what to say, what to Petition from Him, what to promise for themselves, and who they were that encouraged them to come, and *hawked* to introduce them; and that after all, He has only chang'd Hands, got new Faces about him, and is serv'd (it may be) with more obsequious Words, more humble Adorations, and a more seeming Resignation to his Will and Pleasure, than he was before; but that his Affairs Abroad are in no better Posture, that his Influence is no greater on his Neighbouring Princes and States, nor his People at Home eased of one Penny-Tax, or Publick Credit in better Health, or Trade increas'd, or his Subjects in better Humour. The Prince I say, will consider this, and tho' he will not think of calling for his Old Servants again, because He will not be thought to be Inconstant, or to have been misled, or over-reach'd, or because He will not bear the uneasiness which even the Looks of Wrongfully suspected Servants, tho' restor'd to Favour, give; and tho' He will much less think of discarding his new Choice, upon the finding his Mistakes, yet every Body will agree, that He is in the readiest Disposition to such a Change, that can be; and that he wants no handle or pretence to do it, on whatever Day of the Week he pleases to begin. The Example is set, The People are ever ready to be moved; the Priests are seldom wanting to become the Tools of Cunning Managers; and let but the Inclination of the *Great Superiour* once be made to appear, the *Revolution* of *Ministry* follows naturally and easily.

I say therefore, that it is matter of Wonder to many People, to see such *Representations* of the late Management of Publick Affairs, so little Discountenanc'd by those who Manage them, at present. To see the *Greatest Ministers of State* we ever had (*till now*) treated by a Poor *Paper-Pedlar*, every *Thursday*, like the veriest *Rascals* in the Kingdom; and as oft besides, as any of his *Scribling Brethren* please. This great Indignity, and Insolence, if common Honesty could Suffer, yet common Prudence and good Policy should not. I could, if it were needful, bring a great many Instances, of this Licentious way of the *Scum of Mankind*'s treating the *greatest Peers* in the Nation, but I have chosen to do it but in One, which tho' I have offered to those Lords that are more particularly concern'd, yet it will I hope be seriously considered by all others of that Quality, and by those especially who have it in their hands to repress such daring Insolence and Wickedness; least People should come, in time, to think they like it, and incourage it; than which a worser thing can scarcely be said of them. And yet it is so observable, that no body can easily overlook it, that these *Hedge-Writers* seldom speak a word against these *Seven* or any other *Lords* of the *late Ministry*, but they presently fall to Complimenting the *New L. F——ite*, and others in great Places, as tho' they wanted it; or shone more bright by the Comparison; or could receive additional esteem from the Applauses of such base Breath. Cannot the Successors be Excellent Men, unless the Predecessors be Villains? Cannot they who are in great Offices, be very Worthy of them, unless those who lately left them, be Represented the most Odious and Abominable of Mankind? Cannot the Q. change Ministers, but they must presently be *such as neither God nor Man can endure*? Do Noble Men fall from all Honour, Virtue, and Religion, because they are so unhappy as to fall from their Prince's Favour? These were not used to be the Consequences of such Placings and Displacings. But this it is, for poor unskilful Sycophants, to think of pleasing Great Men in Offices. They heap up all the vile, dishonourable, reproachful, wicked things, that they alone can think on, and then throw them on the Predecessors Heads of their New *Patrons*; least, otherwise, it should be wondred at how they should come to loose their Places, and their *Patrons* get into them. But neither are their Patrons Heads so weak, nor their Hearts so vain, as to receive with any satisfaction such Accounts, either of others or of themselves; they know them both, much better. When Men have long supported their Characters with Honour and Reputation, and the whole Kingdom has approved and applauded their good Services, and Providence has Crown'd them with astonishing Success, Years after Years, it is not the sudden turn of a giddy Multitude, made to believe and call them *Villains and betrayers of their Country*, that will make them truly such, with serious People: They may, for the present be abused, and treated as if they were truly such; but Men will recover their Senses; the Witchcraft will wear off; these publick Cheats will be every Day more and more detected: In a word, as fast as the People of *England* return to their understanding and Sobriety of Mind, so fast will these *Great Men* recover their Esteem and Credit; and tho' they may never enjoy (as I hope they will never want) their *Places* again, Yet 'tis great odds but some of their Places may come to want them, which is much worse for the Kingdom. And because I will do the fairest thing in the World, I will appeal to the King of *France* and all his *Councellors*, to the *Pretender* and all his Favourers and Abettors, to the King's of *Spain*, *Denmark*, and *Sweden*, the *Electors*, *Princes* of *Germany* and *Italy*, and to the *States*, as *Wise* as *High* and *Mighty*, i.e. I will appeal to all the *Enemies* and *Friends* we have in *Europe*, to give their Judgment, whether they think the *Late Ministry* were wanting in *Faithfulness*, *Ability*, or Diligence, to serve their Prince and Country.

FINIS.

A Learned Comment ON Dr. HARE'S SERMON

A Learned Comment UPON Dr. HARE's Excellent Sermon Preach'd before the D. *of* Marlborough, On the Surrender of BOUCHAIN.

By an Enemy to PEACE.

Et multis utile Bellum.

LONDON,
Printed for *John Morphew*, near *Stationers-Hall*, 1711. (Price 2 *d.*)

A Learned Comment
ON
Dr. HARE'S SERMON

I HAVE been so well Entertain'd by reading Dr. *Hare*'s Sermon, Preach'd before the Duke of *Marlborough* and the Army, in way of Thanksgiving for passing the Lines and taking *Bouchain*, that I can't forbear giving part of my Thoughts thereupon to the Publick. If a Colonel had been to preach at the Head of his Regiment, I believe he would have made just such a Sermon; which, before I begin with, I must beg leave to consider the Preface, and that stale Topick in the Publisher, of Printing a *Discourse without the Author's leave, by a Copy got from a Friend; being himself so modest, that he would by no means hear of Printing what was drawn up in so much haste*. If the thing be not worth Publishing, either the Author is a Fool, or his Friend a Knave. Besides, the Apology seems very needless for one that has so often been complimented upon his Productions; of which we have seen several without either *Art or Care*, tho' Publish'd with this famous Doctor's Consent. A good Argument, indeed, is not the worse for being *without Art or Care*, but an ill one is nothing without both. If Plainess and Honesty made amends for every hasty foolish Composition, we should never have an end, and every Dunce that blotted Paper would have the same Plea. But the good Doctor's Zeal for the continuation of the War, must attone for the rest of his Defects: His Politicks and his Divinity seem to be much of a size; there is no more of the last in his Sermon, than what is to be found in the Text; he is so great an Enemy to a *Partition*, that he scorns to divide even *That*.

He begins, *Pag*. 5. *I can't but think, that one of the properest Acknowledgments to God for the manifest Tokens we receive of his good Providence, is to consider their natural Tendency, and what is the true use which he has put into our Power to make of them*. May we not very well Query whether this be Sense or Truth? The properest

Acknowledgments to God for the manifest Tokens, *&c.* is to offer him Thanks and Praise, and obey his Laws. Pag. 6. *Persevere bravely in the just and necessary War we are ingag'd, till we can obtain such a Peace, as the many Successes he has given us naturally lead to, and by the continuance of the Divine Favour must end in, if we be content to wait his leisure, and are not by our Impatience and misgiving Fears, wanting to our selves.* At this rate when must we expect a Peace? May we not justly enquire, Whether it be God's, or the D. of *M*—'s Leisure, he would have us wait? He is there in an Army well paid, sees nothing but Plenty, nay Profuseness in the Great Officers, and Riches in the General. Profuseness, when they every day in their Turns receive the Honour of his G's Company to Dinner with them: At that sumptuous Table which his G. once a Week provides for himself and them, the good Doctor never considers what we suffer at Home, or how long we shall be able to find them Mony to support their Magnificence. I should think the Queen and Ministry, next under God, the best Judges what hence we ought to make. If by our *Impatience* be meant the Army, it was needless and absurd; if he meant our *Impatience* here at home, being so far remov'd from the Scene, and in quite another View, he can be no judge of that.

Pag. 7. *One would think a People, who by such a Train of wonderful Successes were now brought to the very Banks of* Jordan, *could not be so fearful as to stop there, or doubt with themselves, whether or no they should try to pass the River,* [Quere *Senset* or *Scheld*] *and get Possession of the Land which God had promis'd them; that they could, with their own Eyes, take a view of it* [apply'd to *Picardy*] *and behold it was exceeding good, &c.* Our Case and the *Israelites* is very different: What they Conquer'd they got for themselves; we take a view of the Land, as they did, and, *behold it to be exceeding good*, but good for others: If *Joshua* had spent many Years in Conquering the *Amorites* (with the loss of infinite Blood and Treasure) and then deliver'd the Land over to the *Gibeonites*, the *Israelites* might have had good reason to murmur; and that has been our Case. *Pag.* 7. *It seems incredible, that Men should for many Years together struggle with the greatest Difficulties, and successfully go through innumerable Dangers, in pursuit of a Noble End, an End worthy of all the Pains and Trouble they are at, and yet lose their Courage as they gain*

Ground, &c. Tho' this be a Falsity, yet to lose Courage as we gain Ground, may very probably happen, if we squander our Courage by the Yard, and gain Ground by the Inch.

Pag. 7. *Of all the Virtues Human Nature wou'd aspire to, Constancy seems to be that 'tis least made for: A steady pursuit of the same End for any long time together, has something in it that looks like Immortality* [hath not this Flight something in it that looks like Nonsense?] *and seems to be above the reach of Mortal Man.* How does a steady pursuit look like *Immortality?* If it looks like *Immortality*, it certainly *seems to be above the reach of Mortal Men. The Earth we live on, the Air we breath, the Nourishment we take, every thing about us is by Nature subject to continual Change; our Bodies themselves are in a perpetual Flux, and not a Moment together the same they were. What Place then can there be for a constant steady Principle of Action amidst so much Inconstancy?* If these Reasons were true, it would be impossible not to be Inconstant: With this old beaten Trash of a Flux, he might go on a hundred Pages on the same Subject, without producing any thing new: It is a wonder we had not the grave Observation, That nothing is Constant but Inconstancy. What does all this end in? his *first Heat* and *Edge* shows us indeed a Flux of what we did not expect.

Pag. 9. *And tho' the end we aim at be the same it was, and certainly nearer.* This puts me in mind of a Divine, who Preaching on the Day of Judgment, said, There was one thing he would be bold to affirm, That the Day of Judgment was nearer now, than ever it was since the beginning of the World: So the War is certainly nearer an end to Day than it was Yesterday, tho' it does not end these twenty Years.

Such fickle, inconstant, irresolute Creatures are we in the midst of our bravest Resolutions, when we set out we seem to look at what we are aiming at, thro' that end of the Perspective that magnifies the Object, and it brings it nearer to us; but when we are got some way, before we are aware we turn the Glass, and looking thro' the little end, what we are pursuing seems to be at a vast distance, and dwindl'd almost into nothing. This is strange Reasoning, where does his Instrument-maker live? We may have the same *Constancy*, the same Desire to pursue a thing, and yet not the same Abilities: For Example, In Hunting many Accidents happen; you grow weary, your Horse falls lame, or in leaping a Hedge throws you; you have the same Reason to pursue the Game, but not the same Ability.

P. 10. *Their Zeal perhaps flames at first, but 'tis the flame of Straw, it has not strength to last. When the Multitude once begin to be weary and indifferent, how easily are they then seduc'd into false Measures? How readily do they give into Suspicions against those who would incourage them to Persevere, while they are fond of others, who to serve themselves, fall in with their Complaints, but at the bottom mean nothing but their own Interest.* How base and false soever this Reproach be, I have set it almost at length, that I may not be charg'd with unfair Quotation. By the Company the Doctor keeps, and the *Patrons* he has chosen, I should think him an undoubted Judge when People mean their *own Interest*; but that I know, Conversing only on one side, generally gives our Thoughts the same turn; just as the Jaundice make those that have it, think all things yellow. This Writer is prejudic'd, and looks upon the rest of the World to be as Self-Interested, as those Persons from whom he has taken his Observation. But if he means the Present Ministry, it is certain they could find their own Interest in continuing the War as well as other People; their Capacities are not less, nor their Fortunes so great, neither need they be at a loss how to follow in a Path so well beaten. Were they thus inclin'd, the way is open before them, the means that enrich'd their Predecessors, gave them a pretence to continue in Power, and made them almost necessary Evils to the State, are now no longer a Secret. Did their Successors study their own Interest with the same Zeal, as they do that of the Publick, we should not have the Doctor in these Agonies for fear of a Peace, things would be then as he would have them; it would be no longer a *flame of Straw*, but a solid Fire, likely to last as long as his poor Country-men had any Materials to feed it: But I wonder he would talk of those who mean their own *Interest*, in such an Audience, especially before those *who fall in with their Complaints*, unless he had given it quite another turn, and bestow'd some of his Eloquence in showing what he really thinks, that nothing in *Nature*, is *so Eligible* as Self-Interest, tho' purchased at the Price of a lasting War, the Blood and Treasure of his Fellow-Subjects, and the Weal of his Native Country.

P. 11. *This is a Misfortune, which free Assemblies, and popular or mixt Governments, are almost unavoidably expos'd to; and 'tis for this Reason, so few Nations have ever steadily pursued, for any long time, the Measures at first resolv'd on, were they never so right and just; and 'tis for the same Reason, that a single Power seldom fails at long run to be too hard for a Confederacy.* A very good Argument for this War, a good Overture and Warning, to make a General for Life: It is an excellent Panegyrick upon Arbitrary Power; at this rate the *French* King is sure to get the better at last. This Preacher must certainly be an admirable Judge of *popular Assemblies*, by living in an Army. Such poor Writers get a Rote and common place of talking, by reading Pamphlets, and from thence presume to make general Observations upon Government, and set up for Statesmen. If the *D.* of *M*— be *Moses*, what *promised Land* is he bringing us to, unless this Sermon be preach'd only to the *Dutch*? He may have *promised* them *Land*, and they Him something else, and both been as good as their Words. In his Allegory of the People brought out of *Egypt*, does the Doctor mean our Army? The Parallel must then be drawn to make the War last Forty Year, or else it can be no Parallel: We may easily see how near the Comparison grows. *Moses* was accused by certain *Israelites*; *Is it a small thing*, say they, *that thou hast brought us out of a Land that floweth with Milk and Honey, to kill us in the Wilderness, except thou make thy self altogether a Prince over us?* Hath the D. of *M*— been suspected of any such Design? *Moses was wroth*, and said unto *the Lord*, *Respect not their Offerings, I have not taken one Ass from them, neither have I hurt one of them. Whose Ox have I taken? Or whom have I defrauded? Whom have I oppressed? Or of whose Hand have I receiv'd any Bribe*, &c. Does the *British Moses* speak thus to the People? Is there any sort of Agreement between them? Nor are we sure of Gods Commands to go up against the *Amorites*, p. 13, as the *Israelites* were, and we have fifty times more reason to murmur. They were carried from the Wilderness, *into a Land flowing with Milk and Honey*; we from such a Land into the Wilderness, that is Poverty and Misery, and are like to be kept in the Wilderness till this Generation and the next too are consum'd, by Mortgages, Anticipations, &c. *Ibid*, Where the Doctor says, the Country it self, was much too narrow for them, he must certainly mean the *Dutch*, who never think their Frontiers can be too much extended.

The Doctor tells us, p. 15. *The Justice and Necessity of our Cause, is little short of the Force of a Command:* Does God command to Fight, because the Chaplain-General will have no Peace? He asks, *what is bidding us go on, if our Successes are not*? At this rate, whenever any new Success is gain'd, or a Town taken, no Peace must be made. The whole Exhortation against Peace, which follows, is very proper for the Chaplain of an Army, it looks like an other Essay of the *Management of the War. These Successes have generally been so much wanted and so little expected.* If we have been ten Years at this vast expence getting Successes that we could not expect, we were mad to begin this War, which hath ruin'd us with all this Success. But why this Acclamation? Is taking one small Town such great Success, as points out to us the *Finger of God?* Who is his God! I believe the General has no little share in his Thoughts, as well as the present Ministry, tho' upon a quite different Consideration. *The Clouds have never this War thickned more, or look'd blacker than this Year: Things look'd so black on every side, as not to leave us the faintest glimpse of Light, we apprehended nothing less than the dissolution of the Alliance.* Whatever the Doctor may be for a Preacher, he has prov'd but an indifferent Prophet. The General and Army may be oblig'd to him for the dissipation of these Clouds, tho' the Ministry are not: Were they the Cause that such Clouds gather'd, *as made him fear an universal Storm, which could no way be fenced against?* To hear him run on in praise of the Wonders of this Campaign, one would scarce believe he were speaking to those very Persons who had formerly gain'd such memorable Victories, and taken Towns of so much greater Importance than *Bouchain*. Had the *French* no Lines before? I thought *Mons, Lisle,* &c. had been once esteem'd considerable Places; but this is his youngest Child, he does like most Mothers, when they are past the Hopes of more, they doat upon the youngest, tho' not so Healthy, nor Praise-worthy, as the rest of the Brethren. Is it our Fault, that *three of the Princes in Aliance with us resolve to recall their Troops?* we brought our *Quota*'s, if our Allies did not, by whose Indulgence was it, that some of them have not been press'd more closely upon that

Head, or rather have been left to do as they please? It is no matter how hard a Bargain People pretend to make, if they are not ty'd to the Performance.

P. 18. *If the Enemy are stronger than they were*, how are we so near our great Hopes, the *Promised Land?* The affectation of Eloquence, which carries the Doctor away by a Tide of Words, makes him contradict himself, and betray his own Argument. Yet by all those Expressions, p. 19, we can only find, that whatever Success we have, must be *miraculous*; he says, *we must trust to Miracles for our Success*, which as I take it is to tempt God: Tho' p. 20. he thinks, *the most Fearful cannot doubt of God's continuance.* We have had *miraculous Success* this nine Years by his own Account, and this Year, he owns, we *should have been all undone without a new Miracle, black Clouds*, &c. *hanging over our Heads*; and why may not our Sins provoke God to forsake us, and bring the *black Clouds* again? Greater Sins than our *Inconstancy!* Avarice, Ambition, Disloyalty, Corruption, Pride, Drunkenness, Gaming, Profaneness, Blasphemy, Ignorance, and all other Immoralities and Irreligion! These are certainly much greater Sins, and whether found in a Court, or in a Camp, much likelier to provoke God's Anger, than *Inconstancy.* If we have *not Patience to wait 'till he has finish'd by gradual Steps this great Work, in such a manner as he in his infinite Wisdom shall think fit.* I desire the Doctor would explain himself upon the Business of *gradual Steps*, whether three and twenty Years longer will do, or what time he thinks the General and himself may live; I suppose he does not desire his *gradual Steps* should exceed *Their* date, as fond as he seems of Miracles; I believe he is willing enough they should be confin'd to his Grace's Life, and his own.

What does he mean, P. 21. by *the natural and moral Consequences that must lead us?* If those moral Consequences are Consequences upon our Morals, they are very small. *Whatever Reason if so can be for putting an End to the War but a good one, was a stronger Reason against beginning it.* Right! so far we allow: *And yet those very Reasons that make us in so much haste to end it, shew the Necessity there was for entring into it.* I am in mighty hope to get out of a Squabble, and therefore I had Reason to get into it; generally the contrary is true. *What Condition should we have now been in, had we tamely let that prodigious Power settle and confirm it self without Dispute?* It could never settle and confirm it self but by a War. P. 22. *Did we not go into the War in hopes of Success? The greatest Argument for going on with the War, is that we may have more Success.* According to the Doctrine laid down by our Author, we must never be inclined to Peace till we lose a Battle; every Victory ought to be a Motive to continue the War. Upon this Principle, I suppose a Peace was refus'd after the Battle of *Ramillies. How can we doubt that we shall not still succeed, or that an Enemy that grows every day weaker and weaker?* &c. The Doctor's Zeal overbears his Memory: Just now the Enemy was stronger than ever. P. 23. *If we consider that our Strength is from God*, &c. Tho' all Men ought to trust in God, yet our Saviour tells us, we ought to regard Human Means: And in the Point before us, we are told, St. *Luke* xiv. 31, 32. *That a King going forth to war against another King, sitteth down first, and consulteth whether he be able with ten thousand to meet him that cometh against him with twenty thousand; or else while the other is yet a great way off, he sendeth an Embassage, and desireth Conditions of Peace.* Our Saviour was a Preacher of Peace; St. *John* xiv. 27. *Peace I leave with you; my Peace I give unto you*, &c. But the Doctor chuseth rather to drive on furiously with *Jehu*; he answers to the Question, *Is it Peace?* as that King did to the Horsemen, *What hast thou to do with Peace? get thee behind me.* He saith, *Our Ingratitude and Impenitence may defeat the surest prospects we have.* May we not ask him, whose *Ingratitude?* As to *Impenitence*, I think this Paragraph is the only one wherein he vouchsafes, and that but very slightly, in his whole Sermon, to remind the People of *Repentance* and *Amendment*; but leaves *a Subject so little suted to a Day of Joy*, to encourage them to *go on to obtain the End towards which they have made so many happy Steps.* We differ about that End; some desire Peace, others War, that so they may get Mony and Power: It is the Interest of some to be in Action, others to be at Rest: Some People clap their Finger upon one Point, and say *That* alone can be a good Peace; We say there may be many sorts of good Peace, of all which we esteem the Queen and Ministry to be the best Judges. The Doctor tells us, *Our Sins may force us to put an ill End to the War*; he should explain what he calls an ill End; I am apt to think he will think nothing good that puts an

End to it, since he saith, *Vengeance may affect not only us, but Generations yet unborn:* That they have taken care of already; We have pretty well mortgag'd Posterity by the Expences of this Devouring War, and must we never see an End to it till there is not an Enemy left to contend with, for so our Author would intimate? In what a Condition must we expect to be, long before that? It is very happy for the Nation, that we do not lie at the Mercy of this Gentleman; that his Voice is not necessary towards the great End we pant after, the unloading of our Burthen, and the Mitigation of our Taxes. A just and necessary War is an ostentatious Theam, and may bear being declaim'd on. Let us have War, what have we to do with Peace? we have beaten our Enemy, let us beat him again: God has given us Success, he encourages us to go on. Have we not won Battles, and Towns, pass'd the Lines, and taken the great *Bouchain?* What avails our Miseries at home? A little paultry Wealth, the Decay of Trade, Increase of Taxes, Dearness of Necessaries, Expence of Blood, and Lives of our Country-men. Are there not Foreigners to supply their Places? Have not the Loss of so many brave Soldiers been offer'd to the Legislature as a Reason for Calling in such Numbers of poor *Palatines*, as it were to fill up the Chasm of War, and attone for the Desolation amongst our Subjects? If we continue thus prodigal of our Blood and Treasure, in a few Years we shall have as little of the one as the other left; and our Women, if they intend to multiply, must be reduc'd, like the *Amazons*, to go out of the Land, or take them Husbands at home of those wretched Strangers, whom our Piety and Charity relieved. Of the Natives there will be scarce a Remnant preserved; and thus the *British* Name may be endanger'd once more to be lost in the *German*.

Were it not for fear of offending the worthy Doctor, I should be tempted to compare his Sermon with one that some time since made so much Noise in the World; but I am with-held by the Consideration of its being so universally Condemned, nay Prosecuted on one side: Perhaps the Chaplain General will not like the Parallel: There may be found the same Heat, the same *Inuendo*'s, upon different Subjects, tho' the Occasion be not so pressing. What Necessity was there of Preaching up War to an

Army, who daily enrich themselves by the Continuation of it? Does he not think, Loyalty and Obedience would have been a properer Subject? To have exhorted them to a Perseverance in their Duty to the Queen, to prepare and soften their Minds, that they may receive with Resignation, if not Applause, whatever Her Majesty shall think fit to Transact. The Doctor, without suspicion of Flattery, might very well have extoll'd their great Actions, and Congratulated with them upon the Peace we are likely to enjoy, by which they will be at leisure to reap the Harvest of their Blood and Toil, take their Rest at Home, and be relieved from the Burthen and Danger of a Cruel War. And as our Gratitude will be ever due to them for delivering us from our distant Enemy the *French*, so shall we have Reason to bless whoever are the Authors of Peace to these distressed Nations, by which we may be freed from those nearer and much more formidable Enemies, Discontent and Poverty at Home.

TEXTUAL NOTES

THE EXAMINER

Printed weekly from August 3, 1710; half-sheet folio. 2 pages. *LONDON: Printed for John Morphew, near Stationer's Hall*, 1710.

Reprinted in Dublin, weekly from August 14, 1710; 4to. 4 pages. *DUBLIN: Printed by C. Carter at the Old Post-Office in Fishamble-Street.*

First collected edition of *The Examiners for the Year* 1711 published by Morphew and Dodd in 16mo, in 1712. See facsimile of the title-page, p. 1.

Swift's *Works*, Dublin, 1738, Vol. V, p. 75.

The present text is printed from Faulkner's edition of the *Works*, 1738, which has been collated with the original Examiners, printed in London and Dublin and with the collected edition of 1712. As already pointed out in the Introduction to this volume, p. xxviii, there is some reason to believe that Swift may have glanced over the proofs, and made one or two significant changes. He cannot have taken much interest in the volume, or he would not have allowed Faulkner to include the last Examiners from June 14 to July 28, 1711, which in the prefatory note to the volume are distinctly stated not to have been written by Swift.

Page	Line	Present Text	Variants
3	11	although	though 10, 12; altho' 35
4	2	already	lately 10, 12
	31	Civil	Peaceable 10, 12
	32	who otherwise would	who would otherwise 10, 12
5	7	as we call ourselves	as we take ourselves to be 10, 12
	22	continue	continues 10, 12
6	5*f.b.*	the Nation	a Nation 35
7	11	prudent	Prudence 10, 12
	16	last	lasts 10, 12
	20	if our Fathers had left	had our Fathers left 10, 12
9	23	*Rabble*	*Mob* 10, 12
10	16	*Moderation*	and *Moderation* 10, 12
	21	*Ways*	*way* 10, 12
	28	*Exchange-Alley* 12	*Popes-head Ally* 10
12	3*f.b.*	undeceive or discover	undeceive 10, 12
17	*b.*	such a Doctrine	that Doctrine 10, 12
19	21	the People who	the People that 10, 12
	26	If a	Should a 10, 12
	4*f.b.*	Rabble	Mob 10, 12
22	8–9	Comparison of	comparison with 10, 12
23	7*f.b.*	and all	also all 10, 11
	b.	Consequences	Consequence 10, 12
24	9	Debtor	Creditor 10, 12
	18	her own Allowance	her Allowance 10, 12
	22	Pounds	Pound 10, 12
	23	Pounds	Pound 10, 12
25	16	were	was 10, 12

Page	Line	PRESENT TEXT	VARIANTS
	17–18	all my Income	half my Income 10, 12
	5*f.b.*	Rascal who	Rascal that 10, 12
27	19–20	brought here a Man before you	brought a Man here before you 10, 12
	8*f.b.*	objected, the Criminal	objected that the Criminal 10, 12
	2*f.b.*	so High or Holy	so High or so Holy 10, 12
28	24	In *Sicily* he sold	he sold all Employments in *Sicily* of Judicature 10, 12
30	11	peaceably	peaceable 10, 12
31	12	fourscore of	fourscore others of 10, 12
	27–28	alledge, that a good and wise Prince may be allowed to change his Ministers	alledge, what no Body doubts, that a Prince may chuse his own Servants 10, 12
	29–30	probable, that he will not make such a Change	certain that a wise and good Prince will not change his Ministers 10, 12
32	23	be Men	are Men 10, 12
33	29	spirit up	Spirit 10, 12
34	12	*Debts on* 10, 12	*Debts of* 35
35	8	or	nor 10, 12
	15	*Shrewdness*	*Smartness* 10, 12
37	18	by taking off	for taking off 10, 12
40	4*f.b.*	must allow	will allow 10, 12
41	1–2	yet in Winter	however in Winter 10, 12
	6	in *England*	here in *England* 10, 12
42	2	at a Distance	at distance 10, 12
43	22	Contempt on	Contempt of 10, 12
45	8*f.b.*	they were	it were 10, 12
46	17	of some	of those 10, 12
	21	or more	nor more 10, 12
47	4*f.b.*	the Convocations	their Convocations 10, 12
48	23	every	any 10, 12
50	10	was thus	is thus 10, 12
52	8	EXAMINER 10	Examiners 12, 35
53	24	Junta	J - - - - to 10, 12 [regular]
56	29	the Clergy	their Clergy 10, 12
57	23–24	a *late Examiner*	the *late Examiner* 10, 12
60	3	*What? Shall*	*What shall* 10, 12
	17	concerning	relating to 10, 12
63	12–13	if the former Danger had been	had the . . . been 10, 12
64	3	know 10	have 12, 38
	4	several	some 10, 12
67	4	into 12	in 10
68	3*f.b.*	to confess	to acknowledge 10, 12
70	5*f.b.*	*he*	*they* 10, 12
	2*f.b.*	who durst	that durst 10, 12
71	5–6	spur on an	spur an 10, 12
	10	the proper Time	the Time 10, 12
	29	*Employment, Ecclesiastical, Civil, or Military.*	*Employment*, 10, 12

Page	Line	Present Text	Variants
72	7	James *Duke of* Ormonde;	C. *D. of* Sh., 10, 12 'i.e. Charles, Duke of Shrewsbury.'
	9	Henry St John	H.S. 10, 12; William Shippen 38
	10	Abigail Masham	A.M. *Spinster* 10, 12
	16	Contract	Compact 10, 12
	18	Junta.	Junto. Order'd, *That a Bill be brought in for further limiting the* Prerogative 10, 12
73	12	in Council 12	at Council 10
74	*b.*	my Paper	this Paper 10, 12
75	24	*Commiseration*	Besides, *Commiseration* 10, 12
	26	if your Friends	if your Party 10, 12
79	21	many amiable Qualities	all the amiable Qualities that can accomplish a great Man 10, 12
	25–26	who ventured	that ventured 10, 12
82	9	a hundred Times	ten times 10, 12
84	3	*Million* 10	*Millions* 12
	25	*ingenuously* 10	*ingeniously* 12
86	17	be	are 10, 12
	27	that the	the 10, 12
	30	also	likewise 10, 12
	3f.b.	who live	that live 10, 12
	2f.b.	besides	likewise 10, 12
88	*2f.b.*	Act for *Toleration*	Act of *Toleration* 10, 12
89	10	at an End 10, 12	at End 35
	2f.b.	and Stables 10	and the Stables 12, 38
90	26	his Mother	the Lady 10, 12
92	5	conceal his Opinions, . . . endeavour	conceals his Opinions . . . endeavours 10, 12
93	9	Monarch who	Monarch that 10, 12
	13	their *Minions*	*Minions* 10, 12
	17	and some others	the Earl of *Oxford* 10, 12
94	1	disobliging it	disobliging of it 10, 12
95	1	*the Faction* 12	a Faction 10
	6	Prince *George's* Death	the Prince's Death 10, 12
	19	if he still remain	remains 10, 12
	26	*administered* 10	*administer* 12
96	18	to be a Secretary	for a Secretary 10, 12
97	28–29	be rewarded	is rewarded 10, 12
98	13	upon most	on most 10, 12
99	3	in great	in all great 10, 12
	15	the false Merit	he 10, 12
100	30	Congregation, which	Congregation, who 10, 12
102	3	of the Fable	the Table 10; the Fable 12
	12	Brood	Crowd 10, 12
	6f.b.	dreamt	Dream'd 10, 12
103	11	*she fled*	*fled* 10, 12
	13	*being driven out*	*driven out* 10, 12
109	30	*belonged*	*belonging* 10, 12
113	12	as a Doctrine	as Doctrines 10, 12
114	7	interpose	interposes 10, 12

Page	Line	Present Text	Variants
	18–19	Prerogative.	Prerogative; when according to the Judgment of those who know our Constitution best, Things rather seem to lean to the other Extream, which is equally to be avoided. 10, 12
115	13	one of which 10, 12	one; to which 35
116	4*f.b.*	a Pension	a larger Pension 11, 12
119	19	allowed	allowed to be 11, allowed to 12
122	9*f.b.*	upon settling Points 11	upon Points 12
	7–6*f.b.*	the Duke of Venice	a Duke . . . 11, 12
123	21	against the next	against next 11, 12
124	17	lead them	tempt them 11, 12
	30	or why	nor why 11, 12
125	14	in this Case	in that Case 11, 12
129	1	being a *Party*	being of a *Party* 11, 12
130	20	hath felt	has had 11, 12
135	9–10	the present War	this present War 11, 12
136	13	their Lies, and for twice	their Scandal and Malice and . . . 11, 12
138	7–8	they can win	and win 11, 12
	3*f.b.*	in a Degree	in any Degree 11, 12
141	3	least Pretensions	least Pretensions to it 11, 12
142	20	Aversion against	Aversion for 11, 12
143	15	here:	among us: 11, 12
144	15	but	and 11, 12
145	15	at last	at least 11, 12
146	1	Power	Tyrant 11, 12
147	5	latter were 11, 12	latter was 35
149	19	the Sons	these Sons 11, 12
153	*b.*	intended to be of	thought was of 11, 12
154	6	this worthy	that worthy 11, 12
156	30	other Motives 11, 12	no other Motives 35
	b.	*Maitre de Langues*	*Maitres des Langues* 11, 12
165	29	by any other	under any other 11, 12
167	27	and Liberty	Liberty 11, 12
168	9	believe	think 11, 12
	13	It is pleasant	It was pleasant 11, 12
169	29	incapacitating all Men 11	incapacitating Men 12, 35
170	24–25	the first Fruits . . . known to have already done . . .	a Remission of the First Fruits . . . formerly known to have done . . . 11, 12
	29	ever	always 11, 12
172	25–26	their *Factors*	these their *Factors* 11, 12
173	23	dress it in 11	dress in 12

A SHORT CHARACTER OF HIS EXCELLENCY THOMAS, EARL OF WHARTON, LORD LIEUTENANT OF IRELAND

First printed in December, 1710, apparently without imprint. I have been able to find no copy of this. Swift refers to it in the *Journal to Stella*, Dec. 8: 'Here's a damned libellous pamphlet come out against lord Wharton. . . . It has been sent by dozens to several gentlemen's lodgings, and I have one or two of them, but nobody knows the author or printer.' Again he writes on Jan. 1: 'It was first printed privately here; and then some bold cur ventured to do it publickly, and sold two thousand in two days:' This is probably the edition printed for William Coryton, dated 1711. See facsimile of title-page, p. 175. I have examined a number of copies; and there appear to be three different issues with slight variations in the title and first sheet (ff. 1–16). (See Teerink, pp. 242–3.)

Possibly the copies without 'Price 4d' on the t.p. belong to the first issue.

Another edition in smaller type without a t.p. appeared with the same imprint in 1711.

Reprinted again after the death of Wharton in 1715, omitting the introductory paragraphs, and with other minor alterations and a different title: A Short Character Of the late M——S of *W——n.* &c. Extracted from an Irish Manuscript, By The Author of the *Tale of a Tub*. London: Printed, and Sold by A. Dodd without Temple-bar, and E. Smith at the Royal Exchange, and most Booksellers of London and Westminster. Price 4d.

Swift's *Works*, Dublin, 1762, Vol. X, p. 283.

Swift's *Works*, London, 1764, 4to, Vol. VII, Part i, p. 188.

The present text is printed from the Faulkner reprint, 1762, not because that has any authority, but because it provides conveniently some uniformity in matters of spelling, punctuation and capitalization with the rest of this volume. In any case the Coryton editions were also booksellers' reprints, without any authority; and all important variants are given below.

Page	Line	Present Text	Variants
177	11	Events in 11	Events of 62
	15	had by 11	had of 62
	18	Degree, however 11	Degree; however, 62
	24	in which	wherein 11
	25	such as under	such as 11
	32	by which	whereby 11
178	4	next: and because this Account may be judged	next. [new par.] And because the Relation I am going to make, may be judged 11
	6	to his Person	of his Person 11
	11	Consciousness of Innocence	Consciousness of his Innocence 11
	15	these	those 11
	16	Whoever, for the Sake of others,	Whoever were . . . to do it for the sake of others 11
	29	to which his Excellency hath arrived, which	which his Excellency has arrived to, which 11
	33	Government,	Government in Ir-d, 11
	35	Administration in *Ireland*,	Administration in that kingdom 11
179	2	hath some Years passed his Grand Climacteric,	hath, some Years past his past grand Climaterick, 11

Page	Line	PRESENT TEXT	VARIANTS
179	28	to impose on	Imposing on 11
	36	Friendship	Friendliness 11
	37	Familiarity,	familiarity in the World 11
180	2	the very	that very 11
	6	on a sudden	upon a sudden 11
	16	maketh use . . ., whose Talents reach	he makes choice . . ., whose Talent reaches 11
	22	a Gallantry 11	Gallantry 62
	28	most common	commonest 11
181	3	Ireland	that Kingdom 11
	8 ff.	Promise; as I remember he told a Lady, but with an Exception to the Promise he then made (which was to get her a Pension) yet he broke even that, and I confess, deceived us both. 11	Promise. But . . . 62
	23	just as he recollected them;	as they came into his Memory: 11
	24	will, I hope, pardon me	I hope will pardon me 11
	27	Chirurgeon-General	Surgeon-General 11
	30	the Phoenix Park	the Park 11
182	10	to me	me 11
	12	here	here in Town 11
183	6	Provost 11	the Provost 62
	24	here when	here, where 11
	31	introduced himself	produc'd himself 11
	35	never before seen nor thought of him	never seen nor thought on him in his Life 11
	38	fully	circumstancially 11
184	2	to stop Dr. *Pratt*'s Promotion	to hinder Dr. *Prat* from the Provostship; 11
	6	especially that of	especially the last, of 11
	13	the Doctor and his Excellency	his Ex-y and the Doctor 11
	23	owned he did not oppose him directly, but confessed he did it collaterally.	confess'd that he did not *directly* oppose him, but *collaterally* he did: 11

SOME REMARKS ON A PAMPHLET, ETC.

First printed in August 1711. See facsimile of title-page, p. 185.

Reprinted in Dublin by E. Waters in 1711. I have not seen the copy of this edition in the Marsh Library. (See Teerink, No. 535.)

Reprinted in Dublin by Cogan in 1752, and first included among Swift's collected *Works* in 1801 by John Nichols. See *Works*, London, 1808, III, 369 ff.

The present text is printed from a photostat of one of the Bodleian copies (8vo. L. 2. Linc.). Names have been printed in full, and elisions removed in accordance with Swift's later practice.

A NEW JOURNEY TO PARIS

First printed in September, 1711. See facsimile of title-page, p. 206.

The Second Edition Corrected, 1711. This was not reset throughout, but a few corrections were made.

The Third Edition, 1711.

First included among Swift's collected *Works* in 1801 by John Nichols. See *Works*, London, 1808, III, 370, & 401 ff.

The present text is printed from a photostat of the Bodleian copy of the second edition, collated with the first edition and the following variants noted. Names have been printed in full and elisions removed.

Page	Line	Present Text	Variants
210	12	*Hostelrie*	Hostellerie
213	4	before for his Reception	before his Reception
218	4	Marquises	Marquisses
	9	civilest	civillest
	10	Twenty	Fifty

APPENDIXES

A. A LETTER TO THE EXAMINER

The present text is printed from a copy of the 12mo reprint of the Examiners for the Year 1711, printed for John Morphew in 1712, to which it was prefixed, pp. v–xvi.

B. A RELATION OF SEVERAL FACTS ETC.

The present text is printed from Swift's *Works*, Dublin, 1762, X, 297 ff.

C. A LETTER TO THE SEVEN LORDS ETC.

The present text is printed from a photostat of one of the Bodleian copies (8vo. L. 2. Linc.), printed for J. Baker at the Black-Boy in Paternoster Row, 1711.

D. A LEARNED COMMENT ON DR. HARE'S SERMON

First included among Swift's collected *Works* by John Nichols in 1801. See Works, London, 1808, III, 421 ff. The present text is printed from a photostat of the copy in the British Museum (698.h.13) printed for John Morphew in 1711.

THE INDEX